THE GENESIS CODE
god has spoken

— BY —

ABRAHAM LOPIAN
JULIE A. SNYDER

Copyright © 2011 Abraham Lopian & Julie A. Snyder
All rights reserved.

ISBN: 1461159210
ISBN-13: 9781461159216

Table of Contents

Introduction — viii

Chapter 1 — 1

The Bible's Secret	1
The Torah: The Source Doctrine	7
A Paradox: The Torah and Religion	10
The Ever-Evolving Torah	14
Who Wrote the Torah and Is It True?	19
The Revelation of "The Genesis Code"	22

Chapter 2 — 28

The Game of God	28
We Are Creators of Our Own Illusions	33
What is God?	41
A Journey into the Hidden	47
All That IS: The Highest Level of God	52
Awareness within the Godliness	55

Chapter 3 — 61

The All Becoming	61
God Is More than You Ever Imagined	68
God's Many Aspects	72
The Elohim: A New Revelation	82
Man Meets an Aspect of God	85
The Unknown World of Mysticism	90

Chapter 4 — 96

In the Beginning	96
Hashomayim: The Heavens Above	101
HaAdam: A Realm in Heaven	103
The Heavens Decoded	106
The Earth Decoded	112

Chapter 5 — 119

Darkness Upon the Face of the Deep	119
The Secret of Water	124
Separation within the Elohim	130
Adam: A New Reality	133
"Let Us Make Man in Our Image"	140

Chapter 6 — 146

The Highest Level of Man: Moses	146
"From the Waters I Drew Him Forth"	149
The "Unnamed" Egyptian Princess	153
Entering No Man's Land	158
Moses and the Mountain of God	163
The Burning Bush	168

Chapter 7 — 176

The Secret Code in "Moshe"	176
The Return of the Cryptic Luchot	188
The Portal of Enlightenment Opens	192
The Secret of Sinai	196
The Luchot Enters Man's Reality	200
The Observer and Witness	204

Chapter 8 — 208

The Transformative Luchot	208
The Power of the Matrix	213
The Egyptian Matrix	220
Moses Descends the Mountain	223
The Mask of Egel Masecha	227
Breaking the Matrix	232

Chapter 9 — 237

The Paradox at Mount Sinai	237
The Rejection of the Luchot	242
The Portal of Enlightenment Closes	245
Adam: An Extraordinary Creator	249
Moses Ascends Sinai Once Again	252
"My Face Is Your Face"	255

Chapter 10 — 258

The Metaphorical Mountain	258
The Revelation of the High Priest	265
The Last Mountain Moses would Climb	271
The Giving of "The Genesis Code"	276

The Power within Belief Systems	281
DNA: The Program of You	285

Chapter 11   289

The Battle of Jacob and Esau	289
A Dark Night of the Soul	294
"Let Me Go, It Is Daybreak"	305
The Secret Code within "Israel"	313
The Blessing	320
God Has Spoken	324

About the Authors   330

Definitions   332

Deuteronomy 32:1-2

Listen, O heavens, and I will speak;

Hear, O earth, the words of my mouth.

Let my teaching fall like rain

and my words descend like dew,

like showers on new grass,

like abundant rain on tender plants.

Moses, the Prophet

1500 BCE

Giver of the Five Books of Moses

Introduction

Let us reveal a secret...
We have hidden from ourselves
since the beginning.
This is the untold story of creation.

Throughout the ages, mankind has set his eyes upon the stars and wondered, "What is it all about? Is there a God? Why am I here?" Our eyes have always been drawn to the starlight flickering in the vastness of space; and as we gaze towards the mysterious universe, the light seems to communicate with us in some unfathomable way.

Even though this awesome presence is somewhat hidden from our awareness, we can feel this unseen force of intelligence drawing our spirit closer to its powerful essence—enticing us to realize there is so much more beyond what our eyes can see and what we currently know. We are being summoned to awaken and journey into the unknown depths of ourselves.

In some strange way, that which once seemed afar, now feels peculiarly familiar and close to us. There is a reason we feel acquainted with this awesome force and presence—it is us, and we are a facet of it. We are realizing the ultimate truth: *Mankind is intrinsically interwoven within God's mesmerizing vastness of being.*

While God may appear to be hidden, know God is always present and communicates with us in various ways and forms. In fact, God is speaking to you right now, expressing its essence through the words of this book. As you turn each page, know your consciousness is awakening to new revelations that have risen from the depths of the Bible.

As we near the end of a creative cycle, we find something extraordinary has happened. A coded language embedded in the Bible's Five Books of Moses has been discovered, bringing vast enlightenment to the male and female of today.

What God's code of creation reveals will change your world. God wants you to awaken to its truth. God wants you to know what it truly is. God wants you to activate your creative power and manifest a new reality in this world. We have been given the message of life—wisdom that will guide humanity through the next era of experience.

The Genesis Code is the core of God's message to mankind. It is the most advanced level of enlightenment in our world today.

Humanity is playing an extraordinary game. We are playing the "Game of God." As seen through the eyes of the Godliness, man is a powerful creator. The time is now for mankind to deeply realize we manifest this dimension's reality. We are the creators of our world. We must know it. We must believe it. We must see it and create a new reality that expresses the Godliness that is us.

Each of us is a powerful facet of the Godliness being experienced in one of God's many dimensions of self. The Bible's Genesis Code reveals magnificent insight into creation: *Each male and female is the head of the Godliness witnessing and manifesting this creation.* Through mankind, God comes to know and experience new aspects of consciousness that have never before been realized. Through each of us, God becomes more than it was before.

Know, however, God's game is riddled with secrets. Although the Godliness is fully aware of man, the Godliness remains mostly hidden from our awareness. No longer pure energy consciousness in the unlimited higher realms, our consciousness has been seeded in a dimension of limitation and distanced from its source. Man's consciousness has become bound to a dimension of time and matter, activated as a self-aware living consciousness known as Adam.

As we experience our life, our awareness will continuously be challenged by the game, itself. Through our immense potential and keen sense of observation and awareness, we come to know we are truly the master of our own reality with the power to choose, the power to create, and the power to alter our destiny.

There are times in human history when mankind stands at a precipice. We will either take a quantum leap into the unknowing waters of enlightenment, or fall back into the shadows and darkness of self. This is one of those times.

The Game of God is much like a mind-boggling maze filled with hidden potential and fascinating stratagems. With the revelation of The Genesis Code, the Godliness has thrust new insight into our reality—enlightenment humanity has never known and, possibly, never even thought about. Yes, man has advanced on the playing field, but we must now ask ourselves an important question, "Are we ready to play the next level of the game?"

The time for transformation is upon us. The fact these extraordinary revelations have risen from the depths of the Bible is certainly no coincidence—nothing ever is. Everything happens for a reason. We are being called upon to implement a creation of a different kind. A portal has opened, and new enlightenment is streaming into man's awareness. The Genesis Code has been revealed for a purpose: *We are being summoned to find the truth and advance to the next level of human potential.*

This book is a work of passion and a love story about all that was, is, and will ever be. Together, we will venture into the world we know and into the unseen world which is difficult to know. Using the code's wisdom as a catalyst, we will travel on a path not travelled where wisdom falls on human consciousness like soft droplets of rain. And on this path, something remarkable will happen. You will discover the source of your existence, find out what you truly are, and come to know the truth of the Godliness.

The Genesis Code reveals extraordinary tales of the "Godliness becoming." Its message is brilliant, mind-bending, and fascinating. You are about to be shocked and emotionally moved as you take in the most captivating view of creation. Prepare yourself, for this coded wisdom is new to man's awareness and profoundly different from both past and current interpretations of the Bible. The Genesis Code's revelations reveal new insight into God, the formation of our universe, and the power and creativity within one of God's greatest creations—man.

It has taken thousands of years, but a new door has opened making it possible for the Creator's ancient message to find its way back to us. Through The Genesis Code, you will be showered with extraordinary enlightenment and learn why humanity's voyage to find and know the deeper aspect of God and creation has taken such a very, very long time.

You are about to tumble down the rabbit hole of advanced conceptions and be challenged to know and become your truth. This book is in your hands because you are ready to advance to a new level in God's magnificent game. Know you are a masterful player, and you are being summoned to manifest a new level of creation that will soon be experienced by all.

The Genesis Code will guide mankind.

CHAPTER 1

The Bible's Secret

The Bible holds a secret. It always has. Hidden within the ancient Hebrew letters and words of the "Five Books of Moses" (also known as the Hebraic Bible and Torah), a highly intelligent code exists at the Bible's core. Much like a heart that holds the secrets of the Godliness, this message of life is pulsating with anticipation.

The Torah's Genesis Code is the revelation of a 3,500-year-old message. It has emerged from the Bible's shadows to speak to the man of today. God wants to be heard, and this enlightenment has been given to resonate within the mind, heart, and soul of mankind. It has been given to be absorbed by today's generation of Adam.

The Bible is read more than any other book in the world—its stories and metaphorical characters coming to life through each passing generation. Whether you believe in a creative intelligence or not, the Bible is an astonishing work of divine art, and its hidden code is even that much more remarkable.

It is widely understood the Hebraic Bible contains various levels of enlightenment that satisfy unique levels of human consciousness. Since the beginning, the Bible's Five Books of Moses has held a secret code. Even more incredible, our world is learning of the code's revelations only now.

Why does a secret code exist within the Bible? Who was God hiding this message from?

Today's interpretations of the Bible reflect an understanding and point of view from the man of our past. Throughout the ages, these interpretations have, for the most part, satisfied human consciousness. Yet, there are elements of the Bible's stories that lack deep understanding and fail to deliver a logical interpretation.

Since the inception of the "Torah" (the Hebraic Bible), important questions have gone unanswered. We have always wanted to know more than what we currently understand. Mankind has searched, studied, and used computer technology—in essence, done everything humanly possible—in an attempt to decode the Bible and discover its secrets.

It is well known the Bible's current translations and interpretations fail to reveal the whole story. In fact, all translations derived from the authentic Hebrew language have missed the mark and left humanity with interpretations that lack crucial details. Our point is this: *The "source Hebrew doctrine" (the Five Books of Moses) holds an astonishing amount of coded enlightenment that has never been revealed to mankind.*

We realize much of humanity has become familiar with age-old interpretations of the Bible. It is what people have been taught, and these interpretations have become widely accepted. However, this certainly doesn't mean humanity has found all of the answers, or that mankind deeply understands God, God's creation, or how God's creation works to manifest infinite worlds and realities. Therefore, it would be more than unfortunate if modern-day man were to deny the primary message brilliantly embedded within the authentic Hebrew texts because they were raised to believe in a God of another kind.

It only takes a moment for new knowledge to stream into our awareness and change our next moment. Enlightenment works to challenge all we have ever believed to be possible, true, and even real. Man's perspective can change and does change. If man never evolved consciously, we would still believe the world was flat. There are always new levels of enlightenment waiting to transform man's perceptions of reality and change his belief in what is possible and true.

Moreover, man's interpretations of the Bible's stories, whether accurate or inaccurate, have manifest into powerful religions. It is important to point out The Genesis Code's message is vastly different from accepted religious ideology that has emanated from misunderstood translations and metaphors in the Bible.

Paradoxically, and quite remarkably, The Genesis Code is mostly embedded in the Torah's Five Books of Moses, the doctrine that is the foundation for major world religions. However, there is one powerful difference: *The Genesis Code's message is derived and interpreted from the source Hebrew doctrine; whereas most religions have risen through interpretations of misguided translations stemming from the source Hebrew texts.* This, in itself, changes everything.

The Torah's message is ever-evolving and its pages hold the secrets of transformative enlightenment. Also extraordinary, The Genesis Code's brilliant revelations will directly challenge many interpretations of the Bible's stories. The question is, "Which message and interpretation of the Bible will merge with and enlighten your consciousness?"

> *If we do not know
> from where we have come,
> we cannot know where to go.
> If we do not know our source,
> we can never know who we are.
> For what has come before us, defines us.
> What we are in the present
> shows us what we have become.
> And what have we become?*

The Torah's Genesis Code is not another "familiar" translation of the Bible. It is much more than that. Its wisdom takes us closer to the mind of God than ever before as it powerfully and skillfully challenges age-old interpretations and philosophies of God and creation.

But it also takes us somewhere else. It takes us into the depths of that which we are and teaches us an extremely important truth we have, thus far, failed to absorb: *We are extraordinary creative beings who actually manifest our realities.* The Genesis Code's insight into human reality transcends current conceptions and exists to elevate human consciousness. Its message of enlightenment has been given to change the minds of man and alter existing belief systems.

Opening one's mind and letting go of pre-conceived notions is the first step to enlightenment. What you believe in matters in the dimension of matter. Belief systems are extraordinarily powerful. In fact, they are the energy force that drives your creativity. What you "believe" (be alive) in—your unique perception of truth—becomes the foundation for the reality you face from moment to moment.

The outer world we experience will always be a reflection of our inner world. Therefore, we must ask ourselves a profoundly important question, "Have we formulated our perceptions of God through misunderstood metaphors and mistranslated stories of the Bible?" Know the outer world we are experiencing today is a reflection of our misguided understanding and perception of God and creation. There is no other way around it.

Man has created wars, chaos, famine, poverty, terrorism, and shown great disrespect toward the nourishing earth that gives us life. Our reality is the result of our belief systems, and it is time we face an undeniable truth: *If our belief systems are flawed, our outer world will reflect those flaws as it manifests the consequences of our most deeply felt beliefs.*

Furthermore, most wars are fought over humanity's diverse beliefs in what God is or what God says—one God being more correct, or right, than another man's God. In fact, mankind has needlessly been battling one another over God since the idea of a supreme entity rose within man's awareness. The time is now for mankind to realize the following: *War and separation amongst men is the direct result of distorted ideologies driven by a lack of awareness to creation, itself.*

While many have shown compassion and love in the name of God, others have killed, and continue to kill, in the name of righteousness and "their idea" of God. History has shown us that man will love for God, sacrifice for God, die for God, and even kill for God. In the end, know man has, does, and will forever create his world and reality through the Godliness he believes to be real. Now, when you hear others say, "My God is the only God there is!" you will know why they do so.

The Genesis Code reveals a phenomenal revelation: *What a person believes God to be is what that person believes himself to be.* How we imagine God to be, is truly how we imagine ourselves to be. The universe will always give us back to ourselves—even our level of Godliness.

As we look at the world around us, it becomes clear we have gotten it all wrong. Until we awaken to this truth, humanity will continue to wander, lost in the reflection of its own consciousness. Know we project the Godliness that we believe in—whether we live to love or live to destroy. We are not separate from God, and God is not separate from us. God becomes through man, and man becomes through his particular level of awareness.

The Torah: The Source Doctrine

The majority of humanity believes the Bible is the word of God, yet much of mankind knows little of the Torah's history. Also true, many fail to realize that the Torah is the source doctrine from which all translations of the Five Books of Moses originate. While everyone knows of the Holy Bible, it is startling as to how few people have heard of the Torah or are aware of its existence in our world.

So let's set it straight: *The Torah is that which came first.* It is the story of creation, a doctrine filled with metaphors, laws, and rituals. It has been kept intact—perfectly so—for thousands of years and is attributed with holding the memory of God and man's becoming. The Torah consists of the Five Books of Moses: "Genesis" (Bereshit), "Exodus" (Shemos), "Leviticus" (Vayikra), "Numbers" (Bamidbar), and "Deuteronomy" (Devarim). These five books were originally written in ancient Hebrew, but with the passing of time, they were subsequently translated from Hebrew into various languages through numerous interpretations.

These five books, written by the prophet, Moses, were the first revelations given to man by God. Of importance, the enlightenment within these five books continues to be the most astonishing insight into God, creation, and human emotions. Also fascinating, the Torah's Genesis Code is most prominent within these five books. It is our opinion no other works compare to their wisdom, and they are the most profound revelations of the Godliness to have ever entered man's reality.

Interestingly, the Five Books of Moses precede all other biblical writings. In fact, subsequent biblical writings, spiritual doctrines, and prophets—including Jesus, Muhammad, and Buddha—brought down enlightenment many centuries after Moses and his Torah.

The knowledge secreted from the Torah will always match the consciousness of those who study its sacred texts.

Also extraordinary, the Five Books of Moses are considered to be the supreme wisdom and source doctrine in our world today. Other outstanding works such as the Talmud and Kabbalistic Zohar encompass further interpretations of the Torah. These outstanding masterpieces have taken hundreds of years to compile and do not attempt to replace the Torah, but rather expound upon the Torah's wisdom.

The Torah is the most powerful and influential book in the world. Due to its vast wisdom, the Torah also has the reputation of being the most misunderstood doctrine to date. The challenge lies in translating, interpreting, and ultimately understanding its complicated texts, stories, and metaphors.

Also of importance, the all-encompassing Torah contains the only uninterrupted timeline in our world. It offers insight into our past and provides a chronological accounting of man's emotional and intellectual evolution. Its stories begin with the creation of this universe and end with the destruction of the second Temple in Jerusalem in 70 CE.

The Torah contains layer upon layer of enlightenment designed to fulfill various needs within human consciousness. Interestingly, the knowledge secreted from the Torah will always match the level of consciousness of those who work to interpret its sacred texts. The Talmud describes the Torah as "the living Torah" due to its ability to move in rhythm with the consciousness it serves. It is written with purpose, and as man evolves, so does the Torah's message.

You will soon discover the Torah is a sophisticated programmed language containing numerous levels of wisdom. In fact, the word, "Torah," means: *An ordered and complete doctrine; A program of creativity.* The Torah is a super highway of enlightenment, branching into many, many roads that lead to different levels of awareness and unique points of view.

Also fascinating, and even somewhat alarming, the Torah's consciousness is dual in nature. Once energized by man, an interpretation will give rise to new ideologies that will, ultimately, create realities in both negative and positive ways. Because of the Torah's overwhelming influence in our world, how man interprets its message can either empower life or take it away—it will always depend on the consciousness that is interpreting, absorbing, and activating the Torah's message in man's reality.

A Paradox: The Torah and Religion

The Torah has greatly impacted human reality. With its introduction into man's world, a portal opened in the minds of men that resulted in a reality of religious scenarios and philosophy. Religion, and its aftermath, is an inescapable outcome of the Torah's presence in our world. As humanity delved into this doctrine, various interpretations rose from its texts. While not the intent, the Torah became the foundation for Judaism, Christianity, and Islam—three powerful religions that greatly influence human reality.

Due to its very nature, the Torah is the motivating force that alters man's idea of God and creation. We must reiterate an extremely important fact: *The Genesis Code was embedded in the Torah, hidden from man's awareness, long before religion entered human reality.* Even though the Torah's coded language is being revealed in the twenty-first century, don't lose sight that The Genesis Code came first. Our point is this, the religions of today lack the understanding of God's most extraordinary revelations of enlightenment. This changes everything.

For thousands of years, our world has experienced the power of religion and all it encompasses—both its beauty and vengeance. Yet, while many believe the Torah is about religion, we want to emphasize it is not. Understand the Torah was given to elevate the individual—not the organization—to his or her highest potential. The Torah is a legacy of God and man coming into being, and we must remain aware of the fact that man created religion—not God.

In fact, the Torah is the Creator incarnate streaming into our consciousness through a programmed language. Through its teachings and wisdom, we discover and experience the extraordinary that exists within the seemingly ordinary.

The majority of humanity believes the Bible is God's way of communicating to mankind. The Bible's Genesis Code has risen to be revealed and communicated to the man of today.

We will now go back to our past. The Torah was given to Moses by God in approximately 1,500 BCE. However, the ancient texts remained amongst the Israelites and were mostly unknown until 300 BCE when the Hebraic texts were translated into the Greek language. This would be the first of subsequent translations, and the world would soon know of a book called the "Holy Bible."

The Five Books of Moses, together with the remaining books of the Torah, circulated throughout humanity—altering man's perception of God and creation. Humanity's belief systems were transforming, and it wouldn't be long before the man of our past saw himself through a new set of eyes. When our consciousness transforms, moving from one level of awareness to another, so does our reality.

Man's old consciousness had died, replaced with an altered perception of creation through a higher level of awareness. Mankind began to live through a new idea of God, and what people believe in, they project and become. Again, how we see God is truly how we see and imagine ourselves to be.

When new consciousness rises, it extinguishes old perceptions. Past belief systems soon fade into the shadows of one's self. As man distanced himself from his old consciousness, he gave birth to a new reality through which he would experience the demise of paganism, slavery, human sacrifice, and witchcraft.

Interestingly, the societies that led our world into the modern era of advanced technology, nuclear power, psychology, mass production, quantum physics, the emancipation of women, and the abolishment of slavery are the very same societies that formulated their philosophies of life through the Bible.

There is no doubt the Torah has changed our world in monumental ways. In fact, the Torah became the foundation for the teachings of Jesus and Muhammad and shed light on a transforming idea: *The perception of a single Creator, or God, that reigns over our world.* With humanity's acceptance of a singular God, a new philosophy of freedom was born. The sensitivity towards a singular God, the right to be free, and the idea of equality amongst men began to spread throughout Greek and Roman societies.

A new era of man was coming to life and transforming through a new belief system: *The belief in a God that created this universe; a God that rules over nature; a God to be worshipped; a God to be feared; a God that exists "outside" of man; and a God that rules "over and above" all others.* While humanity has advanced, we must point out the idea of a singular and male-like God continues to be the dominant perception in our world today.

Regardless of your belief or non-belief in the Bible, it is an inescapable fact we live in a world shaped, fundamentally, through the interpretations of its stories and metaphors. Humanity believes in this doctrine, so much so, that most of the world's population considers the interpretations of the Torah's Five Books of Moses to be true and correct. This fact is astounding. The interpretation of the Torah, and what mankind understands of this profound doctrine, affects the lives of every human being in one way or another—whether they believe in God or not.

The Ever-Evolving Torah

Today, the Torah remains an enigmatic and highly complex metaphysical doctrine that is extremely difficult to decipher and interpret. There is no doubt its deeper and primary level of understanding is enormously complicated and its coded language is most challenging to find.

Important to realize, today's man is able to study the pages of the Torah and discover its secret message because the Torah was kept intact since its inception. The original Torah, written by Moses, was copied with exact precision—word-for-word, letter-for-letter, line-for-line, and dot-for-dot.

This tremendous effort put forth by the Children of Israel guaranteed exact replicas of the original Hebrew Torah would circulate throughout the land. As our eyes peer over today's Torah, we can know we are looking at the same letters and words written by Moses.

While it was necessary for Moses' writings to be copied with exact accuracy, know it was considered unacceptable for any interpretation of Moses' writings to be written down or documented. There was a reason for this: *An impending danger exists when an interpretation of the Torah is written as a finality of God's word.*

Once an interpretation is accepted within a group or society, the written interpretation can become fixed within the minds of men—humanity believing the "interpretation" is the final truth. Nothing could be more perilous or threatening to man's continued evolution of self. When a person or group believes they have found all of the answers, they unknowingly limit themselves from discovering new revelations hidden at the Bible's core.

Most people are other people. Their thoughts are someone else's opinion, their lives a mimicry, their passions a quotation.
~ Oscar Wilde

To the rabbis of long ago, a written interpretation of the Torah was a means through which humanity could know God's revelations to man. While their intentions were good, they unknowingly created fixed ideologies surrounding God and creation. Obviously, written interpretations of the Torah didn't end with the Jewish people; it also became the pattern for the Christians, Muslims, and many other groups attempting to form religious structure.

It cannot be denied, each religious philosophy—and there are many of them—supports one specific idea of God and God's creation. Therefore, any opposing ideas—even profound enlightenment that streams into man's awareness—will never be accepted by the religious establishment if the idea or enlightenment challenges or opposes the religion's core foundation and belief system.

Not to be overlooked, most establishments will attempt to suppress enlightenment that truly empowers the individual. Quite frankly, if every man and woman had a deep and personal relationship with the Creator, there would be no need for the religious establishment. Know the goal of the Torah was, and continues to be, for new insight and enlightenment to surface from the source Hebrew doctrine—not its translation. Furthermore, realize the Torah was given so that every male and female could establish a deep and personal relationship to the Creator.

Danger rises through fixed perceptions of the Godliness. Stagnation threatens man's personal growth and, ultimately, limits the Creator and the Creator's creation.

Another profound example of the Torah's written interpretations is the Talmud, a famous doctrine that has taken centuries to evolve into a masterpiece of philosophy and thought. Its pages embellish various interpretations of the Torah, and the Talmud attempts to explain the Torah's infinite depths. Today, thousands of written interpretations of the Torah are circulating our world, paving the way for various perceptions of the Godliness.

Paradoxically, the Talmud—the very doctrine that serves to interpret the Torah's ancient texts—implies the Torah's message should be an ever-evolving consciousness and never become fixed in nature. The message has been given: *One generation's interpretation is not intended to be another's.* Regardless of how profound these written interpretations may be—or may not be depending on one's point of view—a particular perception of God has been established through the mind of someone else.

With the passing of time, the written interpretations of the Torah—the Talmud, the Midrash, and Kabbalistic Zohar—became the primary teachings for much of the world. Since their inception, these primary doctrines have been accepted by the masses, studied by the scholars, and come to be known as the final interpretation for God and the universe. As predicted, that which was written became the established truth for most of humanity.

Also important to know, most no longer search for enlightenment in the source Hebrew doctrine, but choose to accept the interpretations of the translated Bible, Talmud, Midrash, and Kabbalistic Zohar. One final point, even the Talmud states there are three levels of enlightenment within the Torah: *A simple explanation, a detailed explanation, and the Torah's secret revelations.*

Our point is this, while the Talmud, Midrash, and Kabbalistic Zohar contain a wealth of insight and perspective, it is our belief that if one is seeking to find and know the secrets of the Godliness, there is only one place to look: *The source doctrine that is the ancient Hebrew Torah—the original writings of Moses that is the Five Books of Moses.* This is where the secrets to the Godliness live and wait to be found.

Each and every one of us must find our inner truth. One man's truth is never another's.

Know today's Torah is exactly the same as the original Torah brought down the mountain by Moses. As each generation attempts to find new revelations within its ancient pages, they can be assured the texts are exactly the same as that which Moses wrote.

As The Genesis Code is revealed to you, know it is our intention for you to formulate your own opinion and perception of what God is and what God is not. Understand we deeply believe in, support, and wish to empower the fluid nature of the Torah's ancient Hebrew texts and its ever-evolving consciousness. This is the way it was meant to be.

Listen to your heart, your mind, and your soul. Connect with the Godliness that reflects the true you, and never be persuaded by another, or become what someone else wants you to be. You are a unique level of Godliness here to express your light that is you.

Who Wrote the Torah and Is It True?

There is no doubt the Torah is an inspired doctrine of revelation, and the question is always asked, "Who wrote the Torah?" Whether one holds the belief that God dictated the text to Moses, or those who wrote its stories were merely inspired by an idea or concept of God, it is apparent the Torah was created through pure levels of genius.

The Torah is nothing short of an unbelievably brilliant, sophisticated, and metaphysical window into the unseen and immensely creative self-aware universe. We unequivocally believe the Torah is an absolute consciousness left for mankind, through mankind, from the Divine. Quite frankly, the Torah was not created by man, alone.

One inevitable question, "Is the Torah true?" Whether its stories happened or not becomes irrelevant. You may be asking, "Why wouldn't this be important? If these people aren't real, or the stories didn't happen, wouldn't the message lose credibility and purpose?" First and foremost, the Torah was absolutely a gift from the Godliness to mankind. Therefore, hidden within the stories, characters, metaphors, and laws of the Torah are the secrets of creation. These stories were given to lead mankind closer to the source and enlighten human consciousness to a higher reality.

Humanity, as a whole, greatly underestimates the vibratory force pulsating from within these stories into man's reality. Humanity's belief in these stories, characters, metaphors, and laws was, and continues to be, the driving force that creates realities. Whether an event happened or didn't happen, whether an interpretation of the Torah is right or wrong, true or untrue, real or unreal becomes insignificant. Let us explain why.

It all comes down to man's personal beliefs. What we believe to be possible becomes real to our consciousness. Our consciousness doesn't recognize one truth over another truth, or one illusion over another illusion. What our consciousness recognizes is: *Our belief in what we perceive to be true and possible.*

The core of the Torah is a parallel universe waiting to be unleashed in man's world.

Whether an event is real or unreal, right or wrong, happened or didn't happen, carries no weight within our consciousness and makes no difference to our mind. Our mind cannot distinguish the virtual world from the physical world—it is all the same to the mind.

As unbelievable as this may sound, our consciousness is powered by the following: *What we believe in and our perception of the potential possibility within any given circumstance, choice, and reality.* What we believe in—what our minds and hearts perceive as real or possible—manifests our realities.

Although you may be realizing this for the first time, know this has always been the way of creation and how realities manifest. Our belief systems have continuously paved the way for the realities we experience. This is one truth that will never change. Whether our age-old idea of God is accurate or inaccurate, or true or untrue, our reality is what it is because of our belief—or non-belief—in a God we perceive to be real or unreal.

The Torah was given by God and created through man—for man. The intelligence it holds is far too vast, and The Genesis Code is far too intrinsic, to be created by man, alone.

The Torah was given to open our minds to creative possibilities and to imagine that which is possible. In truth, the Torah's stories were given by God to bring mankind closer to the Godliness than ever before. The Torah is much more than man has realized, for it offers the promise of a new reality that will reflect a new level of man. Much like a portal, the Torah is a gateway that opens to the wisdom of the Godliness through which man can enter and find his other side of self.

The Revelation of "The Genesis Code"

The Torah's Five Books of Moses are the home of The Genesis Code and where its revelations shine most bright. As this code is unveiled, its numerous revelations expose a brilliant message for mankind. As the code enters our awareness, questions immediately surface, "Why did God hide this profound enlightenment from man's awareness? Even more perplexing, from whom, or what, was God hiding this code from?" There is no doubt this phenomenal source of enlightenment was hidden in the ancient Hebrew texts and purposefully concealed from the eyes of humanity. The quintessential question is, "Why?"

Before these questions can be answered, we must ask ourselves the following, "Do we walk in the same level of awareness as those who lived 3,500 years ago? Do we believe the ancients saw and understood their reality the same way we see and understand ours? If we came face-to-face with a man from the distant and far off future, could we possibly grasp and understand his super-advanced consciousness?" The answer to all of the above is, "No." As we reflect on these questions, it is obvious the man of our past, compared to the man of today, experienced his life through a drastically different level of awareness.

One generation's consciousness is no better or worse than another's, only different. The rabbis and scholars have always known a precious code was embedded in the ancient Hebrew texts. However, the code could not be unraveled because mankind required more time to experience his many levels of self—both emotionally and intellectually. Man's consciousness had not evolved—enough. Everything has its place in time. It is abundantly clear, the man of our past was unable to see or realize the Torah's Genesis Code because his heart was beating to a different pace.

We are no longer who we were before. We are different. We have grown. Humanity has come to understand the magnificent intelligence and program within DNA, the fascinating world of quantum mechanics, sub-atomic realities, and the existence of black holes throughout our universe. We have voyaged to space, made great achievements in science and technology, and have come to understand the effect of man's nature on nature, itself. We have changed and now possess the necessary elements to appreciate and understand the code's sophisticated enlightenment.

Knowledge streams into our reality when we are ready and able to absorb new wisdom. Have you ever wondered why scientific and highly advanced patents are filed within minutes, even seconds, of one another? If man was void of a genius idea for thousands of years, it seems remarkable that a few sophisticated minds experience a particular type of enlightenment almost simultaneously.

The moment human consciousness elevates to a particular level of potential, new levels of knowledge stream into man's three-dimensional reality that match his new level of awareness. When our consciousness elevates, new enlightenment is always given. Our experiences are always the outcome of our energy consciousness activated through a space/time continuum.

It is the same with the Torah. The Torah will always relate to the man of the time, whether the man of long ago or the man of a future world. Its message evolves as man evolves. Another truth must also be brought to light: *The revelations of the Torah's Genesis Code may begin here, but today's revelations certainly won't be the last.*

The Genesis Code has lain dormant for thousands of years. There is a reason for this: *Humanity had to grow before this seed of enlightenment could be nourished by human consciousness and flower into a beautiful creation—God's beautiful creation.* Deeply realize the enlightenment within this book has come into being with a purpose. The time is now for mankind to face, nourish, and empower his next level of self. The time is now for humankind to know a new reality is being offered.

When a message rises through a divine doctrine such as the Torah, accurately interpreting and understanding its enlightenment is of the highest priority. All language is a projection of the Godliness. The Torah's expression is a vibratory energy field which calls for our upmost respect. When God speaks, we would be wise to listen.

Language is a projection of consciousness
expressing its vibratory force
through a given reality.

Interestingly, the Torah's Hebrew language differs from all other languages. One word can contain many meanings through which various thoughts, ideas, concepts, and philosophies are projected into light. This, of course, is always dependent on the consciousness of those who read and interpret the message they seek to understand.

To give you an example of the coded Hebrew language, we will explain The Genesis Code's deeper insight into the word, "dalet," which means "doorway." What is fascinating, when you invert the word, "dalet," you have a new word, "telad," which means "birth." From the seemingly straight-forward word, "dalet," new insight enters our awareness through the words, "doorway" and "birth."

First, we will examine the irony within the word, "doorway." A doorway is that which we enter or exit through when we desire to reach the other side of where we are. Through a doorway, we leave one realm and enter another. On a metaphysical level, the "doorway" represents a "portal" between two perspectives and points of view. As consciousness seeks to experience a new perspective, it moves through the portal to perceive a reality that exists on the other side.

Now that we understand the deeper meaning within the once simple word, "doorway," it is time to understand its metaphysical relationship to the word, "birth." As the Godliness brought forth a new universe, a magnificent portal took form—a portal through which consciousness would be seeded in a new dimension. Through the portal, consciousness takes form and gives "life" (birth) to its essence. New aspects of potential consciousness pass through the "portal" (doorway), leaving one dimension and reality only to enter another.

The Genesis Code's revelations are unique and found in no other work or doctrine.

As consciousness moves through the portal and reaches the other side, its essence is seeded in a new reality. Through this act, God is able to witness and observe consciousness as it transforms from potential into a self-aware entity. What is fascinating is that this new reality is an alternate dimension that slows energy consciuosness down—what we know as "time."

This dimension is unlike the dimension the consciousness has exited. It is a slower vibrational field and an environment through which the transformed consciousness can express its individuality—what we know as "space." In this new dimension within the Godliness, the new aspect of consciousness can now become—what we know as an "experience."

The transformed "singularity of consciousness" (man) is now a living entity that perceives himself as being "born" (telad). Man's consciousness has travelled far. His potential has been seeded in a new reality. He has achieved awareness, together with a new perception of "existence" (exit-stance)—man's time on earth from which he will eventually exit and return to the source.

Interestingly, as each of us open our eyes to this dimension, our awareness to the formless realms of creation diminishes significantly. This is so because our consciousness has moved from its original starting point—the place from which we came. Once human consciousness seeds itself in this dimension, the portal closes making it difficult for us to remember the place on the other side—the place we came from.

Now, in a three-dimensional world, we experience our consciousness through a space/time continuum. Now, from where we stand, on one side of the portal, we look to the Heavens and ask, "What could possibly exist out there—on the other side? Is there a God? What is this vast universe that I exist in?"

Using The Genesis Code, extraordinary insight is brought to light through the once ordinary word, "dalet." This is one example of the beauty and depth within God's revelations to mankind through the coded Hebrew language within the Five Books of Moses.

The code is real.
It will elevate man's perceptions of
God, creation, and reality.

The Genesis Code was intended to be difficult to find and challenging to decipher. Therefore, much is demanded from the seeker before the code reveals its face to the one seeking out its carefully hidden secrets. Many methods become profound factors in finding and understanding The Genesis Code's enlightenment. These include metaphysical insight, a deep understanding of theology, an intimate relationship with the Hebrew language, and an in-depth knowledge of the Torah's laws, characters, and stories. Most importantly, The Genesis Code has revealed its essence through a like-minded relationship between man and the Godliness.

Language is how one soul communicates with another. Language is an expression of an entity's consciousness—a consciousness projected to express ideas, motives, desires, and emotions to other facets of consciousness. Language works to attract and communicate with other like-minded human beings; and this includes the language within the Torah's Genesis Code.

No other Biblical translation—whether Greek, Latin, or English—contains the fascinating language of The Genesis Code. Through this highly sophisticated coded language, the Godliness is expressing its highest truth for an advanced level of human consciousness. Once absorbed, this enlightenment will give birth to a new reality within the space/time continuum and man will never be the same again.

CHAPTER 2

The Game of God

The Creator has a phenomenal imagination. Everything we know, including that which we will never know, began in the mind of the Godliness. Much like a game, our universe is full of choices and contains an infinite number of possible scenarios and players.

Consciousness thrives in and through various dimensions. What we are far exceeds our human body, and where we come from reaches far beyond our three-dimensional reality. Through our relationships—our loves, losses, failures, success, and experience—we begin to understand the essence of our soul and our unlimited potential to become more than we were before.

So how can one envision the Game of God? Our universe, and all it encompasses, is the background and playing board through which this particular game is experienced. It is a reality through which our consciousness can express its nature to realize its nature.

Yet, who are the players that shape this game and fill it with experiences? They are us. We are the players that create our world. It is vital you know that you are an active and powerful participant in the magnificent Game of God—a game that is not simple, nor a program of pre-determination. You may be asking, "What are the rules in this game we are playing? Is there a winner and a loser? Who is the conqueror and who is the defeated? Who are we playing against?"

First and foremost, God's game is not about winning or losing, but founded on the ability to increase one's awareness, strengthen one's belief in self, and project the Godliness that is us—the Godliness hidden behind our inner doors. This game is about "becoming."

While there are no rules, illusions are inherent within the game—God and man being separate from one another the greatest illusion of all. Although you may think you are playing against others, know you are truly playing with, and against, yourself. A secret within the game: *You will always face yourself.* Everything that enters your personal universe, regardless of the situation, will always be "you" experiencing "your projection and reflection" of your creative power in action. What you face, each and every moment, is your inner Godliness expressing itself in a dimension of matter.

Your level of Godliness is reflected back to you in many circumstances and scenarios. What you currently perceive as other participants, allies, and opponents are merely "projections" of your consciousness being expressed into reality. Life is consciousness expressing itself—revealing its essence—through form in a dimension of time. As you observe your outer world and face your many experiences and scenarios, know all that you face is your inner world being reflected back to you through your outer world.

One comes to realize creation's rabbit hole runs deep. A truly astonishing revelation rises: *The outer world we face is truly a manifestation that projects the "depths of our unknown self" (our hidden and suppressed emotions), together with "the self we are aware of" (our conscious mind).* What must be realized, our outer world reflects our "total consciousness"— the "you" that you know (your conscious mind), and the "you" that you have, quite successfully, hidden from your awareness (your subconscious self).

Every participant and scenario you face has manifest in order for you to experience and understand the unfolding story of your consciousness. The key is to be aware of your own story. Your awareness to your life's scenarios, together with how you react to the experiences you face, is the way you come to know your truth and advance to higher levels of consciousness.

Your life's ups and downs, together with your perceived accomplishments and failures, are manifestations of your active, creative, and self-aware energy consciousness. There is no winning or losing—there is one's level of "knowingness." You can never defeat yourself in God's game, but you will absolutely choose your life path of experience. It is always "you manifesting you."

Also true, as you walk your life path and strive to create your destiny, know it will be you who subconsciously creates any and all obstacles you face. In your metaphysical realms of self, you subconsciously manifest earthly obstacles that reflect challenges within your consciousness. Deep within, each of us has hidden agendas which percolate as scenarios and implement themselves in our reality.

*So much had to happen before the
Creator could experience you.
You are a masterpiece.*

Always remember, what happens "outside of you" is a reflection of what is happening "inside of you." As your awareness elevates, you will come to know the total you—your "conscious and subconscious" self. A revelation rises: *Through your outer world, you are able to see and know the "you" that is "hidden and suppressed" in your subconscious self.* This is a phenomenal realization.

Everything you are, including the beautiful and not so beautiful aspects of you, manifests as an experience and takes form in your reality. Your outer world reveals your "total" truth, including the pain and anger you have held on to and suppressed in your subconscious self. What you face each day reflects what you truly are.

Your life, together with every experience you partake in, reveals a unique and fantastic story that was previously hidden within God's immense potential. Again, you are never separate from the Godliness in both the physical world and unseen world. A secret is revealed: *Everything is you.* What you face is a projection of your fears, insecurities, anger, compassion, love, and understanding—all taking form through matter to express your vibratory energy consciousness.

Your life is an unfolding "mystery" (my + story), and when all is said and done, your life will become God's "history" (his + story). The mystery within the history—it is all one—and an unfolding experience of the unknowing waters within the Godliness. The universe will always give you back to you. You can never run from yourself. You will always face yourself—through your experiences and reality—allowing you to become aware of that which you are continuously projecting to the universe.

A phenomenal revelation rises through The Genesis Code: *You are God's unrealized and never-before experienced self that has been projected into play.* Your essence has been realized, and your potential is being experienced within the vast unlimited consciousness of God. You have been felt and will forever be felt. Nothing could be more spectacular. Through the doorway of your own consciousness, you will give birth to your next level of self in God's mysterious game of life.

We Are Creators of Our Own Illusions

We all live and die according to our unique and individual perceptions. We come from a perception; we are born into a perception; and ultimately, we die into a perception. All creative beings become through their unique perception of reality.

The Godliness perceived humanity, and a new creation was born. Furthermore, your parents—two powerful creators in their own right—perceived you and your consciousness came alive in their reality. As your life ends in this dimension, you will close your eyes for the final time, and your consciousness will enter another reality and dimension it perceives and anticipates.

There is great power in perception. Every human being lives and exists through their individual and unique perceptions of reality. Realize that our perceptions are a powerful creative force and greatly affect how we identify and interact within two worlds—the three-dimensional world and the formless world. Our perceptions are an outcome of our awareness, overall consciousness, intentions, thoughts, emotions, and belief systems.

In truth, your perceptions define and empower your illusions; and both the perception and the illusion are the result of what you believe to be real and true. Your illusions are your creation. It is extremely important to realize when you validate the energy within an illusion, the illusion becomes alive within your consciousness. You are a phenomenal creator that breathes life into your most powerful illusions, and your illusions become real to your consciousness.

*Shatter your illusions of limitation.
You are pure potential that has
transformed into a powerful
creator in a world of matter.*

So what does all of this mean to you? In order for your creativity to evolve, it is vital you become acutely aware of two powerful creative forces: *Your "perceptions" that create your "illusions."* From this moment on, catapult your perceptions to the forefront of your awareness and peer into the illusions you validate as real.

Your illusions reflect the way you see, feel, and believe yourself to be, and your beliefs are the engines that power your manifestations and life experiences. Your illusions are what you believe to be truth. Deeply absorb the following statement: *Whether your illusions are true or not, real or unreal, they are your illusions and become your truth.* Through your belief in your illusion, your illusion becomes real.

Interestingly, it doesn't matter if your illusions are right or wrong, acceptable or unacceptable, real or delusional—an illusion's credibility is insignificant within the creative process. What does matter is your belief in your own illusion, and your knowingness that, one day, your illusion will manifest your reality. It may not be today. It may not be tomorrow. However, when the time is right, your truth will project as an energy consciousness in your world. Know you will, without a doubt, face your truth.

Furthermore, you must also remain aware that your perception of truth is just one of an infinite number of possible truths. Paradoxically, just because you have your own viewpoint and perception of truth, this certainly doesn't validate your viewpoint and perception. Be aware. Be objective. Be compassionate. Be understanding. Move through life with a calm hand knowing your truth is not necessarily another's.

One's illusions are truly one's realized self.

We will now journey into the power within the perceptions and illusions that face you each day. You have peered into a mirror your entire life. As you gaze into the image that peers back at you, what is it you see? While you may believe your mirror's portrayal is an accurate reflection of you, know the image peering back at you is nothing more than a reflection of "vibratory light."

What is fascinating is that everything the image portrays as you is everything you are not. While this may be hard to believe, it is the way of creation. You may be asking, "If I am not what I see in the mirror, what am I looking at?" What you are observing is an outward reflection of light bouncing off of "matter consciousness" (the human body). Know you can never "see" another's inner essence—that is something you "feel."

We will now introduce the world of physics and quantum reality. Every moment your body absorbs light. What you see—the color of your hair, eyes, and skin—is a reflection of light your body has not absorbed. If your eyes appear to be brown, know your eyes are reflecting the vibratory light and the color your eye has rejected. What you see is what is not. What you see is a reflection of light bouncing off of the matter which has rejected it.

For example, what do you perceive as real when you observe a red rose? Know even the vermilion rose you gaze at with admiration is reflecting an illusion your eyes perceive as real. Like all other matter consciousness, the rose absorbs every color except for the vermilion red that is reflected from its vibrant pedals. Our point is this: *Your perceptions do not always reflect the true reality of any situation you may think you understand.*

A red rose is every color "except" red.
Everything is not what it appears to be.
You must look deeper to find
another level of truth that is
waiting to be realized.

Not to be forgotten, we live our lives and make choices based on perceptions formulated through what our eyes, mind, and senses perceive as reality. Our perceptions are not always accurate. Moreover, our mind is always working to make sense of, and put form to, reflective light and vibratory energy reflecting off of the matter we face. Remain aware of a hidden truth: *What you see is nothing more than reflective light and, quite astonishingly, a reflection of what the matter is not.*

You, together with all that surrounds you, are much more than what your mind can process through its natural boundary of limitation. For example, you are an immensely powerful energy body that appears to be solid. This, however, is a perfect example of yet another influential perception within a mind caught up in its own illusion. While it appears your physical form is an unyielding solid entity of matter, you are actually vibratory light folded up on itself, continuously unfolding in this dimension.

In the unseen world—at the subatomic level of reality—you are re-creating yourself every moment. While the human body appears solid, it is not.

Most people are unaware that particles enter and exit the human body at extremely high vibratory rates of speed. This transmutation of energy takes place at such phenomenal rapidity, it is virtually impossible for our mind to observe what is actually transpiring. In fact, the reality before us is far different than what our eye can see or our mind can process.

You may be asking a question, "If life is full of illusions, how can I know what is real and true?" We must use the code's wisdom, together with scientific data and theory of the subatomic universe, to deeply realize the truth of our existence. What is absolutely remarkable, on the outset the human body appears to be a solid form of tissue and mass. This, however, isn't exactly so. The human body is truly an energy machine that eludes our senses.

Let us explain. You are energy. Moreover, you are a self-aware embodiment of consciousness that is forever searching to experience your essence and truth. Every moment, your sub-atomic level of self vibrates at enormous speeds. The energy that is "you" leaves this dimension and enters another. Know, however, your subatomic self isn't absent for long. The particles that make up "you," instantaneously return. This is an extraordinary revelation. Your energy consciousness leaves this dimension, then returns to this dimension, over and over again, repeating the same process every moment of your life.

Our greatest scientists are fully aware of this energy exchange, yet they are unable to identify the place, or dimension, these sub-atomic particles exit to. If our energy consciousness is continuously exiting this dimension, only to re-enter, what is the purpose? Could our essence and core vibration be transforming through an alternate dimension within the Godliness? Through its connection to a higher realm, does human consciousness refresh its essence much like a computer program updates its software? Once man's consciousness manifests as an experience in the physical world, does the outcome of this vibratory experience travel throughout creation's many dimensions to be observed and deeply felt by the Godliness?

Much like a computer program, your consciousness uploads to reflect the most up-to-date version of you. This is a never-ending and constant process that allows for transformation to take place each moment of your existence. We are continuously being re-created. Yet, what does this truly mean? As man is re-created each and every moment, so is man's reality. Both man and reality are re-created from moment to moment. This knowledge is truly astounding and offers new insight into how human consciousness evolves through each new moment.

You form new perceptions from moment to moment through a myriad of illusions; and within every moment, you manifest realities—whether you realize it or not. Much like a game, our illusions become our experience. They manifest for us to realize who we are and who we are not. Through higher awareness, we learn to maneuver within the Game of God that contains trickery and truth, love and hate—objective and subjective consciousness.

Unfortunately, when most human beings look at themselves and one another, they tend to limit their perceptions to what their eyes see and what their mind can understand. In essence, you are an energy field projected into matter and, astoundingly, you contain more energy than a nuclear bomb. Never underestimate the power of you or the power of another human being. Know man has the power to create.

Another extraordinary fact is that the brain only sees what the person believes is possible. Moreover, the brain does not know the difference from what we see versus what we imagine. And if our imagination is real to our brain, what does our consciousness perceive to be reality? To the brain, an imagined reality, as well as the recollection of a memory, is real. In fact, from the brain's perspective, the virtual world is just as real to the mind as man's outer world. Your brain does not differentiate the information you see from the information you imagine. This is truly extraordinary.

There is nothing "out there" independent of what is going on inside of us.
~ Fred Allen Wolfe, Physicist

What you believe you are seeing, even if a virtual reality imagined by your mind, is very real to your consciousness. Why is this important? Through this revelation you will come to understand all that you believe to be real—whether a philosophy, idea, emotion, or thought, including your idea of the Godliness—become powerful perceptions that work to manifest your reality.

Know and believe God gave you the power to create reality. This is truly an amazing realization. Yet, we are also constrained by what we believe is possible and impossible. The following statement is so important to catapult to the forefront of your awareness: *You create based on what you believe is possible.*

You are the observer of your own reality. It is no secret it can be difficult to accurately perceive what is objectively real and possible. Therefore, be keenly aware of your perceptions. Know your perceptions can entangle your consciousness in a delusional trap. Never lose sight of your enormous creative power and the infinite possibilities creation offers you. A secret is revealed: *You are an extraordinarily magnificent creator in this vast universe.* But the real question is, "Do you know you are?"

What is God?

The English version of the Bible references the God of this universe. However, you are about to learn God is much more than the English translation reveals. So what is the God that creates the many universes, together with the galaxies, stars, suns, planets, and multitudes of life that inhabit the many dimensions within the Godliness? Billions of people have come to envision God through their religious teachings. They are told of a singular being, usually male in nature, which resides over creation. However, a truth of the highest importance has eluded man's awareness.

Before we can move forward and understand the Godliness that has escaped our understanding, mankind must first look back to know how and where we went off track. So, let's begin with the most common name used in the Western world when referring to the Creator—the name, "God." This name is used to describe an all-knowing male entity that created our universe and rules over everything within it.

The name, "God," is used every day by millions of people. But where did this name come from? More importantly, is the name, "God," ever referenced in the Bible's ancient Hebrew texts? Astonishingly, the name, "God," is nowhere to be found in the Torah. And while this may be surprising, it is true. The name, "God," appears only in subsequent Biblical translations.

While accepted for ages, the time has come for mankind to deeply realize the name, "God," is a man-given name for the Creator and, thereby, fails to reflect the authentic Hebrew names given for the Godliness—by the Godliness. Also of extreme importance, the name, "God," is absent of code and lacks additional insight into that which it attempts to define.

The name, "God," is a metaphor and is not the authentic name given for the Godliness...by the Godliness.

We understand many of you are learning this for the first time and, more than likely, you are saying, "What? 'God' is not God's name? This can't be true!" While the Creator is most always referred to as "God," it is time the authentic Hebrew names for the Creator are brought to light.

Before we can have a close relationship with the Godliness, we must revisit and bring to light the names the Divine chose to call itself. Furthermore, if the Creator has defined its reality through these names, mankind must know enlightenment prevails within the names the Creator specifically chose to name itself.

For this reason alone, we revisit the original and authentic Hebrew names given for the Creator within the Torah. These names are where the code lives and where deep insight into the Godliness is found. There is much to be said for a name and the secrets they hold.

The name, "God," is a metaphor and, quite frankly, a general and all-inclusive reference that exists to override and replace the original names referenced in the Torah. You may be asking, "If 'God' is not the real name for the Creator, what is the name the Creator gave itself?" First and foremost, the Creator did not give itself one name, but many. One name would be far too simple and fail to accurately reveal the essence, evolution, and depth of the Godliness.

The Torah reveals the Creator defines itself through many different names, each name embedded with numerous codes revealing insight and wisdom into the Godliness that IS. Therefore, know the following names have been given for the Creator in the Torah: *The "Elohim," the "Jehovah Elohim," and "Jehovah," to name only a few.*

If we truly want to understand that which created us, we must not ignore the names the Creator uses to describe its essence through its various relationships to man and its creation. We cannot overlook an undeniable fact: *Through the Torah's subsequent translations, the Creator's name became victim to interpretation, as did other metaphorical characters in the Bible.*

One can only surmise the people of our past chose the name, "God," as a replacement for the original Hebrew names in an attempt to simplify the complexity of the ancient Hebrew texts—even when it came to the name of the Creator. The priests and clerics of long ago worked diligently to satisfy an unsophisticated mindset and, possibly, this man-given name was a close fit to their viewpoint of a Creator that was "good" (g-o-o-d = G-o-d).

One man arbitrarily changing another man's name is an issue in itself. Yet, for man to capriciously alter the name of the Godliness is detrimental beyond one's imagination. This drastic revision to the Creator's identity denies humanity specific enlightenment and inhibits the truth from being known.

You may be asking, "Why are the authentic and original names of the Creator so vital?" The authentic names are significant because they contain immense insight and understanding into the Creator. They hold a code which leads man closer to the Godliness than ever before. Also of relevance, "God," a translation, has no code whatsoever. Understand, "no code" can only mean "no additional insight." Without code, the fictitious name becomes empty of meaning and only reflects man's simplified understanding of what the Creator is not.

Understanding this fact, you can see why the authentic Hebrew texts become vital for man to achieve further enlightenment, and why subsequent translations of the authentic texts are misleading in many ways. Ironically, the ancient Hebrew names for the Godliness—"Elohim," "Jehovah Elohim," and "Jehovah"—contain abundant amounts of coded wisdom and provide invaluable insight into the vast nature of the Godliness as it works to manifest, express, and experience its various aspects of self. A brief overview of the coded insight into the Divine's various names will be revealed in a future chapter.

There is no denying this man-given name for the Creator has become deeply embedded in human consciousness and interwoven in human cultures. Because of this, the name, "God," is sometimes used throughout this book as a generalization, as this term is familiar to our readers.

Know, however, the revelations within the Creator's true and authentic names should not be underestimated and great effort should be made to familiarize your consciousness to their higher meaning and deeper truth. The original Hebrew names for the Godliness are important, for they hold a coded truth and deeper reality of the Godliness.

Most people are unaware the Torah, written in ancient Hebrew, is both extremely subtle and highly refined. The Hebraic Bible is much more sophisticated than all subsequent translations that would follow—whether Greek, Latin, Arabic, English, or any other language. Due to language barriers, detailed nuances escape the message and important insight is lost in translation.

A perfect example follows. Amongst humanity, man envisions a singular, male, and human-like God that governs over man and man's world. This illusion masks the more complicated truth of the Godliness. It is calming for some to visualize a male God—a King that sits on a throne in Heaven looking down on man. It is far easier for the human mind to comprehend a male-like figure that is dominant and powerful—an image our minds are familiar with. However, just because it is easier for our minds to imagine a human-like reflection, it certainly doesn't justify past perceptions or their validation of the Creator's true form and nature.

Various aspects of the Godliness exist to be realized. The Godliness is not a "fixed" entity or image. The Creator is much more than that.

Simplicity comes with a price. We cannot escape the fact that critical details vanish and deep understanding is lost through simplistic translations. The Torah's Genesis Code reveals extraordinary revelations about the Godliness. First and foremost, God is not a male-like figure that rests on his throne. Yet, powerful religions have persuaded the masses to believe this is so, influencing and programming the minds of men.

Through religious persuasion, powerful belief systems were formed empowering the idea of a male-like humanistic God that lived in the Heavens above. This ideology changed man's world and societies were built and realities created through this particular level of God consciousness.

When the Torah references the Creator through various names, a message is being revealed to the man of today. The Creator has many names because various aspects of God prevail in not only man's dimension, but throughout creation. In other words, there is not "one" extraordinary God, but various aspects of an extraordinary Godliness that partake in various relationships in its creation.

If God were a fixed aspect—an all-inclusive entity devoid of any variables of self—then one name would absolutely be suitable to define the Creator of our universe. However, this is not the case, and why the Creator has purposefully identified its transformative nature through its given names.

As we delve into the depths of The Genesis Code, a once simple translation—God—is suddenly engulfed in convolution, complexity, and fervor making it necessary to better define that which has been inaccurately referred to. As mankind strayed further from the Torah's authentic path, the Creator's true nature, essence, and purpose—even the authentic names for the Godliness—became distanced from man's consciousness. Because of this, you may have conceptualized the Creator as something it is not and failed to realize the depths of the Godliness that IS.

We are about to introduce something new to your awareness: *The Godliness works in mysterious ways, has different purposes, and morphs on many levels and through countless means and formats—always dependent on the dimension of self it is projecting, activating, and integrating into reality.* Know the Godliness is not a fixed being that is static within itself. The Godliness takes on many forms and operates through various energies and dimensions.

It is time to change your perception of God. We are a new generation and different level of man. Know the Godliness retracts, expands, transmutes, inverts, and evolves within its own self. The Creator is much more than you ever imagined, and so are you.

A Journey into the Hidden

Our original home, our starting point in creation, has been distanced from our awareness. For this reason, we will now remember our original home—the place from which we came and will one day return.

While you may not know it, your consciousness moves in and out of dimensions between the heavens and the earth. This hidden aspect of you continuously travels between the formless and physical worlds, and back again, every moment of your existence. As it moves, your consciousness transforms, morphing within the dimension it is activated within.

Clear your mind, for your life, as well as that which you currently perceive to be death, is far more mysterious than you ever imagined. Realize, however, death is only an illusion. While many people believe their existence forever ends as they draw in their last breath of air, this is not so. Your consciousness will never cease to exist.

Your energy never dies, it only transforms. Energy can never be destroyed. Once energy consciousness exists, it will transition into various forms of matter consciousness. This is a scientific fact. Your consciousness will continue to experience its essence long after your eyes close for the last time in this dimension.

You, a phenomenal energy consciousness, are on a fantastic journey. While you may not have realized it, you have already travelled far—exiting one dimension only to arrive in another. Here on earth, where you currently stand, you feel quite comfortable; however, know this is a temporary location for your consciousness. Your eternal home, and the source of your existence, is on the other side of the portal in another dimension hidden from your awareness.

Your life on earth began when you drew in your first breath of air. This was the moment your consciousness awakened to a new reality and your eyes took in a three-dimensional world. For you, this was a new experience and transformation of consciousness. Your life, on earth, was to be a new beginning.

From the other side, you had chosen a new and specific life path that would be a journey of self-realization on earth. Now, through a three-dimensional reality, you will experience that which you desired to know from your other side of self. Know the life you experience today was your choice. Your earth-bound destination and starting point for your soul's adventures was chosen by you—to be experienced by you. And here you will stay until it is time to go back to the place from which you came—your eternal home on the other side of the portal.

Before you ever arrived,
you chose this destination.

As you experience your life, your soul will take in new sights, experience amazing things, and feel both joy and tremendous sorrow. This is an inescapable fact. All that you live through, the good together with the bad, will elevate your consciousness bringing forth wisdom, strength, and understanding. Hopefully, when all is said and done, you will have loved and been loved like never before.

Man stands firmly on the earth and looks back, attempting to perceive the unlimited through a reality of limitation.

For a moment, allow your spirit to travel to that place which is eternal—a realm of existence that has been distanced from your awareness. From where you stand now, you will travel to the other side of the portal into that distant and mostly forgotten realm of Oneness.

As you transcend the physical world of time and matter, you find yourself drawn to a doorway—a portal that leads to a formless reality far different than the earthly world you are accustomed to. On earth, you never truly understood the unseen realms of creation; but now, in this timeless dimension, a deep sense of understanding "everything" engulfs you. Whereas before you understood limited aspects of creation, you now seem to have meshed with creation, itself, through a heightened sense of knowingness.

You are now much lighter and free, and the flesh that once confined you is no more. You are no longer a physical body of matter, but a magnificent body of energy consciousness. This is when you know you have transformed. Not only has your position within creation changed, but so has your awareness to all things. Your consciousness has expanded.

You are now pure energy consciousness, and your energy has fully merged with the Godliness. You are now part of everything and nothing. You are eternal in nature in a timeless realm. Instinctively, you somehow know this is your true home—the place where everything and anything begins. You have entered the garden of the Godliness. You have returned to the source and totality of "Oneness."

This was your first trip into one of the many dimensions of the Godliness, and through these pages there are many more journeys to come. These voyages will challenge your current level of awareness and motivate you to reach your next potential of self. From your human stance of limitation, you will delve into the many dimensions and realms that exist in creation—and within you. Together, we are going back—all the way back—to the source of everything. We are going to that which is the source of our universe—the starting point for anything and everything that was, is, or will ever be.

Currently, you are bound to a three-dimensional world that is limited in nature. In other words, your consciousness has become limited in this dimension. From where you stand, you attempt to imagine "what God is" from your current position in creation. However, before you encounter that which lies beyond the boundaries of your world, you must open your mind to new understanding. This requires a quantum leap of consciousness—something only you can make happen for yourself.

So where does one begin? First, you must attempt to view creation through a new perspective and push your limited consciousness to the limits of itself. You must enter uncharted territory. Every human perceives the Godliness through a limited level of awareness. Quite simply, humans don't know everything, aren't everything, and their consciousness is bound within a three-dimensional reality.

Your consciousness is programmed to function through limitation, in a dual environment, through a dimension of time and matter. Your consciousness cannot transcend various dimensions unless it becomes aware—consciously—of the hidden dimensions it desires to reach and know. One of our goals is to awaken your consciousness to what it already knows but has forgotten. While it may be difficult for you to fully perceive that which has been distanced from your awareness, it certainly is possible once you set your spirit to it.

All That IS:
The Highest Level of God

A question is always asked, "Where did God come from? Who created God?" The Godliness—what it is, how it operates, and its relationship to mankind—is greatly misunderstood. A phenomenal opportunity faces us as we journey into one of the many levels of the Godliness—the highest level and prime cause for any and all creations. The time has come to increase your awareness to the unknowable. The time has come for humanity to reach the next level of human consciousness.

We will now go back as far as one can go—to that which precedes the beginning of our universe where the unfathomable source of everything IS. This is no ordinary journey, and together we will fall into the most abstract rabbit hole within creation—a mind-bending complexity that is the reality of the Godliness.

First and foremost, the source of any and all creations—the point from which everything begins—is, what we term, "All That IS" (the All). The All is a description that most closely reflects an unfathomable and immeasurable realm that is everything and nothing simultaneously—a reality that is timeless and void of form. The Genesis Code reveals the source of the Godliness is: *The Prime Cause and Motivator for anything and everything that will ever be.*

Individual creations, universes, planets, suns, duality, human beings, together with their powerful emotions that manifest realities, cannot be experienced or realized at the source level of the Godliness—the All. Anything that is "something" cannot take form as a "separate energy consciousness" at the core of All That IS. This is a realm of "Oneness" where individuality is impossible and non-existent. In other words, nothing can "be."

To emphasize the abstract nature of the All, imagine the finality, as well as the starting point, within a realm that is truly timeless. It is daunting for human consciousness to understand a totality that is nothing and everything simultaneously. This is truly an unfathomable level of Godliness that was, is, and will forever be.

Know nothing—absolutely nothing—exists outside of All That IS. Furthermore, if a new creation cannot exist at the "core" of the All, where do individual creations exist? Everything that has ever been, or will ever be, has been projected from the immeasurable source Godliness and can only exist "within the All" within and through new dimensions of creativity.

To help you better imagine the All, think of an onion and the many layers it contains. The onion, as a whole, is All That IS. Moreover, the onion contains many "layers of creative programs of consciousness" (dimensions)—each layer different from the other and each dimension containing a unique aspect of creative consciousness.

While the upper realms of the Godliness are extremely difficult to comprehend, let alone explain, we will describe why this highly advanced and complex level of Godliness is a realm that is impossible for human consciousness to tap into or enter. Any attempt to travel within this eternal, formless, and timeless realm is impossible for human consciousness. No man ever has, or ever will, travel there.

The core of the Godliness is a realm of total awareness. Within its totality, an unknown number of immeasurable dimensions of limitation prevail—each dimension bound to its own space within the unlimited All That IS. In other words, each layer of the onion is independent and separate from the layer of consciousness that resides next to it, because each independent layer of creative consciousness is bound to the layer it exists in. Again, the new dimension is not All That IS, but a limited level of creativity that operates through its own dimension and reality of self-awareness within All That IS.

Every creation within the All does not operate at the "core of the totality," but through its own "dimension of awareness" within the All. Each creation is an extraordinary entity of consciousness, and it perceives itself as just that—a magnificent creation and active level of Godliness. What is extraordinary, through its self-awareness, each creation transmutes to create the reality that reflects its essence and core desires.

Within the unlimited All That IS, numerous dimensions and alternative levels of awareness prevail. Everything that exists within the All is a "facet" of the All. Therefore, the Godliness morphs and transforms as it gives life to new dimensions of limitation that work to express limited aspects of the All's creative consciousness.

All creations manifest through limitation and become realities far different than the unlimited core of the All. The All's separate dimensions of self vibrate unique and limited realities that give birth to new life, individuality, and possibility. Within each dimension, the All's creative consciousness is realized as a distinct individuality within the totality.

Everything is the Godliness. Knowing this, different levels of awareness prevail within and throughout the unlimited All. All of it—every particle, every atom, every world, every living consciousness, every galaxy, every universe, and every new creation—is the Godliness experiencing its many potentials of self, through various dimensions of limitation.

Awareness within the Godliness

If we had to exist in total awareness—at the core of All That IS—we would never exist at all. All life forms, including human beings, exist through limited awareness. Through unique levels of awareness, potential forms of energy consciousness evolve.

Therefore, before new potential becomes possible within the All, the Godliness must formulate an environment—distanced from its core—through which potential energy consciousness can transform into a self-aware living consciousness in a new dimension in the All.

Before "Adam" (mankind) could be realized, the All had to manifest a new reality within its totality that would allow the potential of Adam to transform into matter consciousness. Whether an "atom" (Adam), insect, tree, planet, star, galaxy, universe, or energy consciousness of a new creation, everything is an aspect of the All playing itself out in its immense reality. From the smallest particle to the most magnificent universe, it is all the Godliness experiencing its essence in light through limitation.

From the All's point of view and all-knowing awareness, there is no separation between God and man. The perception of man being "separate from the All is a powerful illusion" supported through a three-dimensional reality. In his world, Adam would perceive himself as being separate from God.

Man will do whatever is needed to survive. He fears death—another illusion—and sees himself as the great "I Am" of his reality. However, the "perception of separation" is necessary in God's game. The illusion of separation was created so man could become an independent, self-aware consciousness that perceives himself as an independent and powerful creator of "his" reality.

The Godliness experiences itself through a state of total and complete awareness, but also through infinite dimensions of limited awareness.

To the Godliness, it is all God. Yet, Adam would see himself as a living, independent, self-aware being that "is something." Adam would perceive himself as "I am this, or I am that" in a world full of choices. Adam wasn't programmed to exist through the consciousness and realm he was "projected from," but programmed for his consciousness to thrive in the dimension he was "projected into."

In God's game, Adam would be projected from a timeless realm of potential within the All and, unknowingly, be distanced "in perception" as his consciousness became self-aware through a new dimension of time and matter. Adam is a powerful life force with great will, drive, and passion. Through his perception of self, Adam would experience deeply felt emotions only possible in a three-dimensional reality.

New creations exist through limitation. The question is, "Why?" Wouldn't the Creator want its new creation to be all knowing? Why are the secrets of the universe hidden from human awareness? If the All were to manifest a new creation in total awareness—matching the total awareness of All That IS—it would basically be creating a clone and exact replica of itself. If this were to happen, the All could only experience "what it already is."

If two "everythings" were to suddenly exist—a scenario which is impossible, impractical, and would accomplish nothing new through a lack of creativity—this act would serve no purpose for the All. Basically, if the All were to clone its totality, its projection would take up the same space, contain the same creative force, know everything there is to know, be everything and nothing simultaneously, and, quite simply, the cloned level of All That IS would gravitate and merge instantaneously with its exact replica of self.

In truth, the core of the All would only be experiencing itself. But even this isn't exactly accurate. Within total awareness, at the core of the All, duality is non-existent and the act of "experiencing anything is impossible." This is an inescapable challenge at the highest level of creation—creating something that can exist and thrive in the midst of "total awareness that is everything and unlimited."

So what does the All do? It projects potential energy consciousness into a separate dimension and space of limitation. The All creates something new and something different than what it is. New dimensions are a necessity before self-aware potentials of limited consciousness can flourish. Therefore, the All must create a new dimension within its totality that will harbor the potential creativity it desires to experience through a new creation.

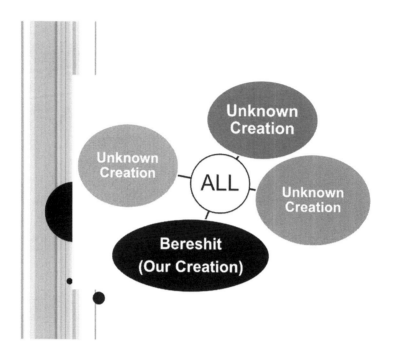

Through an infinite number of creative programs, the All experiences itself through its new dimensions of awareness. As consciousness evolves within a particular dimension, its essence and truth transmutes into a vibratory force. This vibratory signal expresses the particular level of awareness through which the dimension thrives. Through vibrations, the All comes to feel and know its various aspects of self as the dimension's consciousness is expressed, transformed, revealed, and realized through light.

Know our creation operates through a particular vibration—a vibration that continuously transforms to match its momentary truth realized through its creation's collective consciousness. Through each dimension's vibratory consciousness, the All comes to know its creation and becomes unfathomably more than it was before. Regardless of the positive or negative nature of the creation's vibratory signal, the All comes to know the truth of this dimension and the collective energy consciousness that is actively manifesting the signal's force.

As our creation evolves, it is in constant communication with the All through its awesome vibratory force and signal. The collective consciousness of our creation is felt by the All from moment to moment. This creation's truth flows into the All, gathering as a cosmic reflection of this creation's realizations and evolution of self.

Imagine independent rivers flowing into a valley, gathering, and forming an immense sea of water. Now, replace the flowing rivers of water with potent vibratory rivers of energy consciousness. Much like a sea that forms and grows through the gathering of waters flowing into it, the All becomes more than it was before as it absorbs the vibrations of its many creations within its totality. Our creation's vibratory energy flows into All That IS, and through this transference of energy consciousness, the All comes to know itself.

All creations—including ours—exist in a state of limited awareness. The question rises, "Which level of awareness and vibratory force does our creation project?" Know the answer to this question is exactly what the Godliness feels and experiences. The All will forever experience the outcome of its creations—be it a positive or negative experience.

Know the collective consciousness of our creation, including its Adamic Universe, the earth, and mankind, is deeply felt, experienced, and realized by the All. Levels of awareness are profoundly important to the Godliness; so much so, a creation's level of awareness actually defines the outcome of the dimension to which it is bound. The space or dimension doesn't define the creation. Just the opposite is true. The evolving self-aware consciousness within the dimension moves to define the creation's reality of limitation.

Long ago, in the timelessness of the Godliness, our creative universe was imagined, together with a creative being known as

Adam. Man's consciousness is an ever-evolving transformative experience pulsating within All That IS. Adam is the heart of the Godliness. Everything was created for us.

Every dimension begins with total possibility, as does every aspect of self-aware consciousness that thrives within the dimension it is bound to. Ultimately, it is up to us to manifest the level of awareness we choose to experience, knowing our experience becomes a profound emotional experience within the Godliness. We are not separate from one another.

CHAPTER 3

The All Becoming

The first sentence in the Torah has been translated as, "In the beginning, God created the heavens and the earth." Know, however, the very first word of the Hebraic Torah is "Bereshit," a deeply coded word that reveals the beginning of a new creation—our new creation. Bereshit, like any other creation, must exist through its own dimension—distanced from the core of the All and its overpowering essence.

Bereshit is not fully aware of all things, nor can it participate with a consciousness outside of its space and dimension. Every creation is independent of one another, each dimension containing separate entities of consciousness and unique matrixes of self-awareness.

Many questions surround the intricate code within Bereshit. We all want to know how our creation was born. How did Bereshit happen? How did it come to be? How did Bereshit, a reality of limitation, come to be within the unlimited All? How does "something" become out of "nothingness?" We will now venture into Bereshit and reveal how our creation "became" within a timeless realm that is "non-existence and everything" simultaneously.

Anything that will ever be begins within the imagination of the Godliness. Following is an example. For a moment, imagine you are the All, a magnificent sculptor. Within your totality, anything you can imagine becomes possible. You have made the choice to create and experience that which you most desire.

You have imagined your greatest masterpiece, and now you will bring this hidden potential out of a beautiful block of black marble. You, as the sculptor, feel your greatest work rising within you, and you know it is time to express your creativity—a glorious statue that will be a "black horse and rider."

The "black horse and rider" has always existed within the totality of the stone and within the totality of you. However, it has lain forever dormant in a state of non-existence, unknown, as unrealized potential. It is a facet of the Godliness, and an expression of you, yet to be experienced in a dimension of time and matter.

As the sculptor, you deeply desire to experience your imagination. You also know that your desire to express that which has been forever unknown will change your reality and environment forever. Now, a space must be created for your "black horse and rider." You must free the statue from the marble that conceals its individuality within your totality.

You, the sculptor, begin to chip away at the marble to reveal the potential and essence of the "black horse and rider" hidden within its depths. The "black horse and rider" must become through its unique dimension of self. It must become a magnificent statue within your reality.

What was once potential, will now become an extraordinary creation of independent expression that has risen out of non-existence within the totality of the stone. The limited has risen from the unlimited, and a new relationship within the Godliness is born. The idea, desire, and potential "within" the sculptor has been brought forth from within the "totality" (the potential for anything within the block of marble) and becomes manifest in a new dimension—the sculptor's "outer world."

The following diagram shows a box that contains all colors and all potential which you perceive as "white." For now, the "white" will serve as an example of the All—the totality that is "everything and nothing" simultaneously. The diagram to your right shows the "black horse and rider," and this will serve as an example of what the All imagines and desires to express and know.

Submersed and hidden within the "All's totality" (the white) is the "potential the All imagines and desires to experience" (the black horse and rider). The "black horse and rider" cannot be seen in the "white" because it has never been expressed or experienced in light. It is consumed by the All's awareness and, for now, remains an unrealized aspect of self.

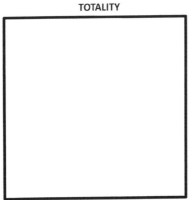

TOTALITY   IDEA PROJECTED

EVERYTHING AND NOTHING   DESIRED CREATION

In order for the All to manifest the "black horse and rider," the All uses its creativity to reveal the unrealized potential of the "black horse and rider" hidden within the block of marble. To do so, the All "retracts" its "all-knowing and overpowering awareness" from the potential that is the "black horse and rider."

Much like the sculptor that removes the marble to reveal the statue that has always existed within the stone, the All retracts its all-knowing awareness from the expression of the "black horse and rider." Through retraction, a space of limited awareness that is also a limited facet of the All has been separated out within the totality.

What is fascinating is that this new space and dimension is not any random shape or size, but a mirror image that "is" a new reality reflecting the "black horse and rider." The new space is the exact dimension of all that can be experienced from within the All's imagination.

A new creation has been realized in a new dimension of the All. The "black horse and rider" has been imagined to life—exposed as "something" separated out within the All's "totality." The new dimension has become through the All's expression of self. The sculptor has revealed its masterpiece.

As you come to better understand how the All manifests new dimensions of self, you realize it is impossible for life—the expression of the All's idea—to survive in total awareness at the core of the All. An individual creation, such as Bereshit, must exist through a space and dimension of limited awareness.

Deep within the core of the All, infinite creations are imagined and projected within the totality. Furthermore, each expression is only one of an infinite number of expressions that is possible within the All's totality. With each new expression, a new creation is born through an individual dimension within All That IS.

Understand the core of the All is the totality of all experiences and the culmination of any and all creations within the All. At the All's core, the vibrations of the infinite creations come together, meld, and beat as "one moment." To imagine this reality, envision all of the orchestras in the world, together with their many instruments, coming together and forming one vibrational note. At the All's core, its many facets of self are realized as a realm of "Oneness"—everything and nothingness and everything in between.

It is vital you understand a new creation is a reality far different than the core of All That IS—a realm that is the "many orchestras" (individual creations) coming together to form "one vibratory note" (Oneness). We will now explain why. The new creation is a dimension of limited awareness. It is not "everything and nothing" like its source, but "something" within the "totality." It is an independent, self-aware, "limited aspect of the All" created to express a particular "idea and imagination" the All desires to experience.

Until retraction occurs within All That IS, any potential hidden within its totality remains undefined, unmanifest, and unrealized. Just like the "black horse and rider," our creation was also a "state of pure potential" within All That IS. In the case of our creation, the All first imagined, and then deeply desired to know, a never-before-realized potential within its totality. All That IS imagined Bereshit, and in this new creation, was the "idea" of "Adam" (mankind) that would become the extraordinary potential the All desired to experience and know.

An idea had been born, and this was the beginning of a new creation. What is fascinating, Adam came first and everything else that would support Adam, such as Bereshit and the Adamic Universe, would follow. In a fraction of a second, everything changed within the Godliness.

At this stage of the creative process, Bereshit was in its infancy. It had become a dimension of limited awareness, yet it was still an expression of possibility. As Bereshit became its own dimension within the Godliness, the space became a "dimension of percolating possibility and pure energy consciousness." In other words, time and matter were non-existent and all had not yet formed. Much, however, had happened, and the All had become more than it was before. It had manifested a "limited dimension of differential" making future life and experience possible.

Bereshit now contained the necessary elements and potential for a self-aware creative consciousness to evolve independently—as something—through its unique and limited level of self. It was a "dimension of possibility that contained its own unique creative consciousness." A new level of experience was becoming and would one day, in a realm of time and space, be realized.

Furthermore, "something" can only be realized through a "dimension that contains duality." Through duality, "experience becomes possible" and the "idea" is realized through a space/time continuum. A fascinating revelation rises: *Through a dimension of time and matter, vibrations slow down making it possible for emotions to be deeply felt and experienced.*

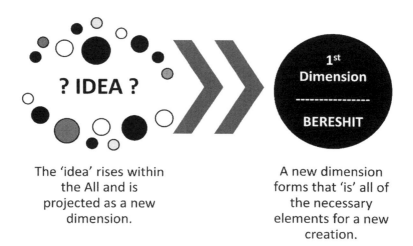

The 'idea' rises within the All and is projected as a new dimension.

A new dimension forms that 'is' all of the necessary elements for a new creation.

Time is "creation in motion." As time becomes a reality within a dimension of the All, it becomes possible for an experience to be played out—much like a vibration in the mode of "slow motion." From one idea, an instantaneous chain of events was thrust into a dimension that operated through a slower vibration. This gave way to an extraordinary space that contained all of the elements necessary for an abundant universe to become and give life to new experience.

Understand All That IS does not create a new dimension that "is what it is," the All creates an "expression of what it passionately desires to know." Every creation exists in limitation and is differentiated from all other creations—including the source that projected it—the All.

Also fascinating, just as the All cannot place its total awareness on the potential of its new creation, the new creation cannot be fully aware of the All that created it. If it did, our creation would be overcome and no longer remain as a state of limited awareness. The new creation knows it is a creation, but it does not view itself as the totality and All That IS. It is a limited aspect of the All and "it is what it is."

God is More than You Ever Imagined

The Torah's Genesis Code takes us down a shocking path of enlightenment. The God of The Genesis Code is far different than what mankind has perceived God to be. A profound revelation rises: *When new dimensions are activated, these independent spaces of creativity are governed by a new facet of the All.* This, in itself, changes everything we have ever imagined God and creation to be.

A new creation was forming, a creation called Bereshit. As the All projected and retracted to allow for a new space/dimension, Bereshit formed and became an extraordinary creative program that was a new and limited aspect of the All. Bereshit was a new dimension that contained "all of the elements and potential" for a new creation to manifest.

Bereshit was a vibrating duality with massive amounts of transformative energy consciousness. Bereshit was not only a new dimension within the All, but a self-aware creative program that vibrated a new level of Creator to govern the new creation. A phenomenal revelation and secret is revealed: *Bereshit was a new creation and creative program that transformed into a new level of Godliness.* As Bereshit was transforming within itself, an extraordinary happening took place within the All. Bereshit morphed into a God that would be called the "Elohim."

The Genesis Code reveals the deeper meaning of "the Elohim" is the "many energies that create." The Elohim is an awesome self-aware creative entity that is a level of Godliness never before realized within All That IS. The Elohim is not all things, nor is it the source level of creativity. The Elohim is not All That IS, but an aspect of All That IS.

The Elohim was given tremendous power. Furthermore, its creative program was of the highest possible intelligence. This new aspect of Godliness was created by the All. The Elohim was now a magnificent Creator of an immense and independent universe.

The Elohim is an independent and alternate vibratory level of the All that IS a massive creative force, sentient consciousness, and the God of the Adamic Universe. Realize, however, as Bereshit transitioned into the Elohim, the Adamic Universe had yet to form. Much was still unknown.

An Idea = A New dimension
= A New Creative Program
= A New Level of Godliness
= A New Creation

Bereshit had energized into a creative program that is the Elohim. This extraordinary revelation is not only new, but ground-breaking. Therefore, we must attempt to perceive the Godliness through the eyes of the Godliness. Everything is within the All. Nothing, absolutely nothing, exists outside of All That IS.

Through the Torah's Genesis Code, we learn how the Elohim, a new level of Godliness, came to be within the All's creation. The Elohim is the God that created the Adamic Universe that supports the idea of Adam. Bereshit had transmuted into the "Elohim" (God), and within the Elohim was "Hashomayim" (the Heavens) and "Aretz" (God's spirit). Within the Elohim, infinite possibilities now percolated with anticipation. At this point in the creative process, the Elohim was to become the God of Adam—a creative being that was desired and would one day be realized through a future dimension within the Elohim in a reality of time and matter.

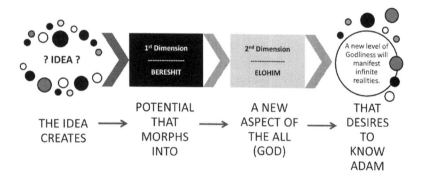

The Genesis Code reveals that different levels of the All exist, interact, and create unique realities through various levels of God consciousness. The All works in different ways and moves to create various realities to fulfill multiple desires and purposes. We must remind you, from the All's point of view, everything is the All expressing itself.

To bring this down a notch further, we will offer a simple metaphor. Your hand is your hand, and your foot is your foot. Both are aspects of you that serve different purposes. They are extremities of you, connected to you, and they interact with your reality in different ways. While your hand is your hand and your foot is your foot, they are both you. Even though they are not the total you, they are still a part of you and serve a purpose for you. It is the same with the All.

Through its many creative programs, together with the All's many energies that create, All That IS interacts with its creations and comes to know and experience itself through its infinite limited dimensions. These limited and different aspects of the All exist to fulfill a purpose and role for All That IS. No matter the form it has taken, or level of awareness it exists through, it is all God experiencing God.

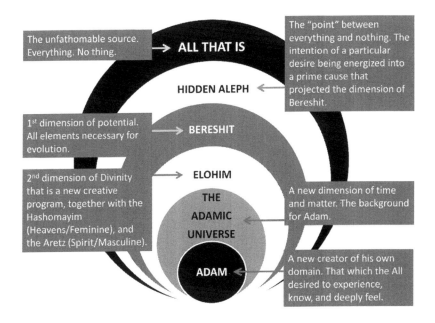

God's Many Aspects

Through the Torah's Genesis Code, we learn of the God/Man relationship and how the All, through its various aspects of self, interacts with its creation. We will now delve into the "many creative energies" within All That IS that work to integrate, communicate, and manifest realities.

As previously stated, several Hebrew names have been given for the Creator, by the Creator, itself. These names contain vast amounts of code and exist for one purpose alone: *They are the Creator's attempt to communicate and express its intrinsic nature to its creation, mankind.*

The following table outlines some of the ancient Hebrew names the Creator gave to itself. This was done in order for man to realize the many dimensions and immeasurable depths that exist within the Godliness. We will now open our minds to that which imagined and created us. God is talking. Are you listening?

To clearly understand the transformative nature of the Godliness, we must delve into the coded message within the authentic names that preceded the man-given name, "God." You are now entering the portal where another reality waits to be realized. You have opened a new door, taken your first step, and are about to journey into the Godliness that is truly "you."

The Original and Authentic Names for God

NAME	TRANSLATION	DESCRIPTION
ALL THAT IS (Hidden Aleph)	The All; The Hidden Aleph; Totality; Infinite; The source.	The prime cause from which all creations begin; Timeless and formless reality; Everything; Unknowable; Eternal.
ELOHIM	God; Lord; The God of The Adamic Universe.	Aspect of the All that was projected by the All; An extraordinary self-aware program of creativity; Powered by the Hidden Aleph); Governs its domain.
JEHOVAH ELOHIM	God; Aspect of the Elohim that breathes life into Adamic Consciousness.	Activated prior to the dimension of earth taking form; Integrates Adam within the Elohim; Heart and core of the Elohim.
JEHOVAH	God; The Now; The present moment.	The aspect of the Elohim that has a deep relationship with man; The connection between the Elohim and mankind.
ADAM	Singularity of Adamic Consciousness; Potential Man; Man in Matter; A creative consciousness in a three-dimensional reality.	An aspect of the Elohim; The hidden potential of the Elohim realized in light; An energy embodiment that manifests realities in a three-dimensional world; Exists to experience its potential in a new reality and be experienced by the Elohim. Through Adam, the Elohim comes into life.

The Torah references the Godliness through many names. This is so because many facets of the Godliness exist, morph, transform, invert, integrate, communicate, and manifest realities. Many aspects of creativity are required to bring a desired expression into "being" (be in God).

For the purpose of this book, we are introducing various levels of creativity within the Godliness—the All, the Elohim, the Jehovah Elohim, Jehovah, and Adam. The code within these names enlightens mankind to the creative evolution and transformation of the Godliness. Know each aspect contains a unique role and purpose necessary to implement and maintain Adam in the Adamic Universe.

All That IS; Prime Cause; Hidden Aleph

The source of the Godliness is a level of creativity that is unknowable and unfathomable to mankind.

Through The Genesis Code, we find the Torah only hints of the source of the Godliness that preceded this creation, Bereshit. The All is a totality, yet a facet of the All is seeded in our creation. This seeding becomes yet another aspect of the All and, what we term, the "Hidden Aleph," an aspect of the Godliness we are briefly introducing at this time.

The Hidden Aleph is embedded in all things, within all matter and energy consciousness, from the smallest particle to the most grandiose galaxy within the Adamic Universe. While hidden from man's awareness, the Hidden Aleph—the power and life-force of the All—is embedded in every particle within this universe, within man's reality, and within man, itself. Of the highest importance, the Hidden Aleph is the power that drives this creation, as well as any other creation outside of our dimension.

The All contains an infinite number of "self-aware creative programs" (creations), each governed through a unique level of God consciousness. Know each creation is a level of Godliness that is independent from other creations and independent from the All. Realize, however, while maintaining its individuality and independence, our creation remains connected to the All through the Hidden Aleph—the hidden aspect of the All That IS embedded in this creation for the purpose of powering this creation.

Each creation is an extraordinarily powerful entity of energy consciousness—powered by the Hidden Aleph—that creates unique realities, dimensions, and universes within its boundaries of self. Once created and evolved, a creation's vibratory field projects and, ultimately, merges with the formless and timeless core of All That IS. Through the infinite experiences and interactions of its creations, the All expands, morphs, evolves, and incomprehensibly becomes more than it was before. All That IS becomes through its many creations.

Man can never comprehend the reality of the All. It is impossible for our three-dimensional minds to grasp a dimension outside of the dimension we live through. Of importance, however, while we can never experience the core of the All, we can come to know and have a relationship with an aspect of the All—the Elohim—the God of the Adamic Universe and the Creator of Adam.

Elohim—God of This Universe

The Elohim is the God of the Adamic Universe, one of the many infinite and magnificent self-aware creative programs projected by the All.

An extraordinary revelation rises: *The Elohim is a level of Godliness projected by the All to implement and manifest that which was desired by All That IS—"Adam" (humanity).* What is mostly unrealized, the Elohim's name is phonetically misleading. In English, it is written as "(E)lohim," but in Hebrew, the name for the God of the Adamic Universe truly begins with an "Aleph" (A). Therefore, in English, "Elohim" should actually be written as "(A)lohim." This is extremely important because the "Aleph" contains a deeper meaning: *The Prime Cause and Motivator for anything and everything that will ever be.*

So what does this mean? The Genesis Code reveals the "Prime Cause and Motivator" for our creation is the All. Through the "Hidden Aleph" (an aspect of the All), the "Prime Cause" is projected within the boundaries of its new creation. As revealed through the coded name, "(A)lohim," the "Aleph" (A) rises within the Creator's name and shows mankind the "Prime Cause" (the All) lives through The God of Adam—the "(A)lohim" (Elohim)—and continues to seed itself through "(A)dam."

We will now reveal another secret and extraordinary fact that has been mostly overlooked: *The Elohim is plural in nature.* This detailed description into the God of man directly challenges age-old perceptions of the Godliness. Through previous translations and interpretations, man has perceived the Elohim as a singular being and this is why the names, "Lord," "Master," and "God" are commonly used when referring to the Godliness. These names are all singular and male terms that simply mislead humanity and confuse the reality of the Elohim.

The Elohim is the Godliness that created our universe, governs our universe, and is the God of man's reality. The Elohim is also many diverse aspects of creative self-aware energies that implement various realities and relationships. The Elohim is immensely potent. In fact, this aspect of Godliness is so intense it can actually overpower, even destroy, that which it has created—including Adam. In other words, the Elohim must distance itself from human beings due to its overpowering vibratory force.

Like the All, the Elohim must distance its vibrational force from its creation. Imagine the level of energy that created this universe, and you will begin to fathom the energy and astonishing vibratory power of the Elohim. When the Elohim is referred to in the Torah, you will find, for the most part, the Elohim speaks to mankind through nature.

Using nature as a form of communication, the Elohim forms vibrational fields of energy and expresses itself to mankind through chosen vibrations. Through vibrations, matter comes in contact with other forms of matter making it possible for the Elohim to communicate with man without harming its creation.

An example of this would be the Elohim's vibratory voice speaking through thunder and lightning as was the case on Mount Sinai; or the Elohim's a vibratory voice speaking through the crackling of the fire as the Elohim spoke to Moses through the Burning Bush. Through nature and vibratory forces, the Elohim communicates to mankind.

The Elohim, through a dimension of light, would manifest a future reality and new dimension of self, together with its desired creation, Adam. Through the Elohim, a new universe would be born, and the Godliness would come to know and experience its unique and awesome program of creation through its Adamic Universe.

<u>Jehovah Elohim—Integration</u>

Jehovah Elohim is the aspect of the Elohim activated to breathe life into Adamic Consciousness.

As the Elohim's creative program evolved, the Elohim was vibrating the idea of Adam into light. Within the light, all of the necessary elements for Adam and his universe existed as potential. However, before Adam could be integrated as a living self-aware consciousness, the Elohim would need to project a new level of creativity through a new aspect of Godliness. This new dimension and differential would come to be known as "Jehovah Elohim."

When the Torah refers to Jehovah Elohim, we know an aspect of the Elohim was activated to breathe life into Adamic Consciousness. Jehovah Elohim was an alternate aspect of the Godliness that fulfilled a unique role—integrating a self-aware living entity, Adam, into the Elohim's reality.

Jehovah Elohim was vital to Adam's becoming. Jehovah Elohim was the life force of Adam and the particular aspect of the Elohim that nourishes the consciousness of mankind. Jehovah Elohim can be perceived as the heart and core of the Elohim and that part of the Godliness that activated Adam's energy consciousness in a new dimension within the Elohim. When the Elohim activated Jehovah Elohim, this was the moment when creation inverted. But this is another heavily coded story and new revelation that has yet to be revealed.

Jehovah—the God/Man Connection

Jehovah is the aspect of the Elohim that connects to mankind in his dimension.

As creation further evolved, a new aspect of the Elohim came into being. Due to its overwhelming power and vibratory force, the Elohim realized another aspect of Godliness was needed to both implement and promote a close God/Man relationship. Therefore, the Elohim projected another aspect of itself that would allow for fluid communication between God and man.

Whereas "Jehovah Elohim" is an active aspect of the Elohim near the core of the Elohim; the name, "Jehovah," by itself, represents an aspect of the Elohim that operates in the dimension of man. The name, "Jehovah," stands alone. Therefore, we know Jehovah has been separated out from the Elohim to operate through a less powerful vibratory field. Jehovah was the aspect of the Elohim that connects to mankind in his dimension.

Jehovah would be the aspect of the Godliness that projected a lower and less potent vibratory force. This, in itself, made it possible for Jehovah to move freely in the dimension of man and be ever present within Adam's reality. Through each moment, Jehovah is where man is, reacting and communicating with man on man's vibratory level.

To reiterate, the Elohim's vibratory energy will overpower, even destroy, its creation through direct interaction. This factor inhibits direct communication between man and the Elohim, thereby, preventing a close relationship from forming. Therefore, the aspect of Jehovah was a necessity in both the Elohim's and Adam's reality. Through Jehovah, the Godliness would be able to directly communicate with man without overpowering or harming man.

Even though Jehovah's vibration is significantly lower than the vibration at the Elohim's core, make no mistake Jehovah is extraordinarily powerful. Through the Elohim's masterful design, Jehovah is the aspect of the Elohim that can flow in man's world, interact with mankind, and reverberate within human consciousness. Through Jehovah, a deep relationship between the Elohim and man is possible.

Jehovah reflects the "God of the moment" and is intrinsically woven in the fabric of life. Jehovah activates man's realities—communicating, interacting, and forming deep relationships with both the Adam of the past and the Adam of today.

 ### Adam—A Creator in this Dimension

Adam is a facet of the Elohim and a powerful creative being. Through Adam, the Elohim experiences deeply felt emotions through a dimension of light.

Man is an expression of the Elohim projected into a dimension of time and matter. You are much more than an outcome, but a desired consciousness containing extraordinary amounts of creative power. Actually, you, as Adam, are an intrinsic "facet" of the Godliness being experienced in a separate dimension within the Elohim.

> I Am.
> I Am my creation.
> The paradox of my reality
> can only be experienced in time.
> For only in time I Am.
> As time, I Am assured of
> my own realization.
> In time, there is creation and loss.
> In time, there is ugliness and beauty.
> In time, I hear cries and laughter.
> In time, there is sex.
> In time, there is sight.
> In time, there is taste and smell.
> In time, there are feelings
> and deep emotions.
> So let me feel.
> Let me become in Adam.
> In Adam, I Am.

"You" (Adam) are God incarnate. You are a unique aspect of the Elohim. You are not separate from the Elohim, but another aspect of the Elohim experiencing the potential of "you" in one of God's many dimensions of self. You are Adam—a powerful creator projected into a dimension of time and matter to create a reality that expresses your essence. Adam is a different level of creator, and, like the Elohim, Adam is the creator of his own universe.

The Elohim: A New Revelation

Since the beginning, humanity has searched for the truth. Today, millions of people are unfulfilled because they intuitively know "something is missing" when it comes to understanding God and creation. Many of the biblical translations and interpretations fail to provide answers that make sense.

Thus far, you have opened your mind and envisioned creation from not only your point of view, but you have imagined the All's reality through the eyes of the Divine. You have absorbed vast amounts of knowledge, and your journey into higher awareness has only begun.

We realize many questions may be swirling within your mind. Furthermore, you have just been given a shocking revelation of the Godliness: *The God of man, the God of Moses, the God of this world, the God of Eden, and the God of the Adamic Universe is the Elohim—a self-aware creative program projected from the highest level and source—All That IS.*

In essence, The Genesis Code reveals many levels and aspects of God exist throughout creation. Furthermore, the "Elohim" (the God of Man) is not the source of all creations, but the source of all things that pertain to Adam and his universe.

Right now you may be thinking, "I can't believe the God of this universe is not all there is! Does the code truly imply that various levels and aspects of God permeate creation? If so, are the code's revelations minimizing the God of our universe, the God of our world, and the God of man? Can all of this be true?" We understand this may be the reaction of some, possibly many. However, we are here to reveal The Genesis Code's truth of the Godliness that is a new and enlightened point of view.

The Genesis Code's revelations open new doors that lead us to a Godliness we have never known. Once you understand how creation works—see the true beauty of the Godliness and its exquisite mastery of becoming—that which was initially unknown and shocking, transforms into pure awe, fascination, and enlightenment.

First, know the code does not deny the existence of God, nor does it belittle or minimize the God of the Adamic Universe. As a matter of fact, just the opposite is true. The Genesis Code emphatically states the Godliness is not only real, but absolutely extraordinary. So much so, we are being told mankind has greatly underestimated the unfathomable intelligence, awesome power, and complexity of the Godliness that IS.

The many aspects of the Godliness, including Adam, are all God experiencing God.

To the All, everything is it, including any and all levels of creative intelligence—what man terms as "God." While this may be a riveting blow to your consciousness, realize God expressing its essence through alternate dimensions of potential actually makes sense. It is time man deeply understands, regardless of the level of consciousness or reality being expressed within the Godliness, it is all "God experiencing God."

From the perspective of the Divine, everything is interconnected; yet "aspects" of the All are chosen to "become" through "various dimensions" within the reality of "Oneness." The All continuously manifests facets of its potential through creative programs of consciousness.

No matter the level of consciousness playing itself out in one of the All's infinite dimensions of self, the emotions and knowledge resulting from the experience transmute into a vibratory signal that communicates with the All. Through this act in creation, consciousness is acknowledged, felt, realized, and absorbed within All That IS.

So what are we really saying? The architect and master designer of the Adamic Universe is the Elohim—a projection of the All. Bereshit, the Elohim, and Adam are seeds of potential planted from the same source—the All. Everything is a facet of the All, including you.

The Elohim knows it is an extraordinary and immensely powerful God containing immeasurable genius and unfathomable energies through which it manifests and governs its dimension of creativity. Through the Elohim, a new universe would be realized and experienced through its awesome command and influence, breathing life into that which was desired by the Elohim's creator—the All.

The Elohim, an awesome creative program and entity of unimaginable energy would transform, morph, invert, and transition through its essence, vibratory power, potential, consciousness, creativity, independence, and free will to create a new world.

Using its powerful creativity, the Elohim would manifest the All's desires into a new matrix of self-awareness—the Adamic Universe—through which Adam would be realized. Soon one of the All's most magnificent creations would be valued above all others.

Man Meets an Aspect of God

While your awareness to the Elohim has increased exponentially, we will now expand on another aspect of the Elohim—"Jehovah." When Jehovah is present a relationship is unfolding between God and man. The Genesis Code reveals Jehovah is "timeless" and is: *The God of the Moment.* As revealed in Exodus 24:12, Jehovah was the particular aspect of God that communicated with and faced a man called Moses.

 Hebraic Text: Shemos 24:12

וַיֹּאמֶר יְהוָה אֶל מֹשֶׁה עֲלֵה אֵלַי הָהָרָה וֶהְיֵה שָׁם וְאֶתְּנָה לְךָ אֶת לֻחֹת הָאֶבֶן וְהַתּוֹרָה וְהַמִּצְוָה אֲשֶׁר כָּתַבְתִּי לְהוֹרֹתָם

English Translation: Exodus 24:12

And God said to Moses: "Come up to Me into the mount and be there; and I will give thee the tablets of stone, and the law and the commandment, which I have written, that thou may teach them."

 ### The Genesis Code: Exodus 24:12

And Jehovah said to Moses: "Rise to me, at the highest level, and be there." Moses had to reach his highest potential of self, within his mountain of self, to interact with and communicate with "God" (Jehovah).

As previously stated, the level of Godliness known as the Elohim is far too powerful for man to face directly. The Elohim is an overwhelming vibratory force that can actually destroy its very creation. For this reason, the Elohim transforms in order to integrate and meld with that which it has created.

Through the aspect of Jehovah, the Elohim found a way to communicate with man without destroying man's physical nature. Jehovah is the connection point between the Elohim and man. Furthermore, Jehovah is the aspect of the Elohim that interacts with and delivers the Elohim's essence to mankind. It is imperative you know when Jehovah speaks, Jehovah is truly delivering a message from the Elohim to man.

Even though Jehovah's energy embodiment is a limited aspect of the Elohim, we must recognize Jehovah's clout and tremendous vibrational force. After facing Jehovah, Moses was a changed man—both physically and spiritually. His looks were forever altered, as was his energy embodiment.

This "moment" is all that exists for you; your entire life has brought you here, right here, to this very moment.

HEBREW	LETTERS AND CODE	VALUE	CODED MEANING
\multicolumn{4}{c}{**The Secret of JEHOVAH**}			
JEHOVAH יהוה	YOD; HEY; VAV; HEY יד הי וו הי	26	The active moment; Now.
YOD י	YOD; DALED יד דלת	10	Hand; Active power.
HEY ה	HEY; YOD הי יד	5	Core of the Elohim; Heart; Breath; Seeding.
VAV ו	VAV; VAV וו	6	And; Connecting.
HEY ה	HEY הי יד	5	Breath; Giving life.

When Jehovah called Moses to the mountain, Moses rose to the top where he was met by Jehovah. As God's sheer force descended upon the mountain, the mountain shook in response to Jehovah's extraordinary vibratory force. This is the vibratory force and extraordinary energy that came face to face with Moses at Sinai.

After meeting with Jehovah, Moses had changed. He was not the same man who had left to climb the mountain and meet with God. In fact, the Torah clearly states his people could no longer look upon his face due to its overwhelming brightness.

Through Jehovah, the Elohim's fiery essence had been delivered to Moses, and Moses had successfully absorbed the Elohim's enlightenment. Jehovah had made it possible for Moses to successfully absorb the energy of the Elohim, and a new relationship was born.

Interestingly, Moses came to be known as "Ish HaElohim" which means: *The man of the Elohim; The man who contains the energy of the Godliness.* Moses was unlike other men. He had changed and now walked a higher vibratory path of enlightenment. Moses and God had melded as "One."

Each generation has a different relationship with the Godliness. One generation's moment—one man's moment—will never be the same as another's. While the energy consciousness of our past has integrated and become part of today's world, the true God/Man relationship is realized in the moment through each and every one of us. Our relationship with God yesterday is not the relationship with God today.

To Jehovah, there is no past, nor is there a future. There is "the moment that is real" and everything else exists in "potential." Jehovah does not respond to your past, nor does Jehovah respond to your future. Jehovah manifests through each and every one of us through the present moment. This is extremely important to realize right now, in this very moment. This is so because your next moment is based on your present moment, and your current vibration is all that is real to the universe right now.

All you have ever experienced—every tragedy, as well as all things beautiful—has brought you here to this very moment. While you carry memories of your past, the past is gone. Although you have goals and dreams for your future, your future exists as a state of pure potential. This moment is all there is, and Jehovah is in your moment.

You are in your dimension.
It is your place, and all that
surrounds you is your world.
Each moment you are in is full of choices,
whether you are alone in a room,
or out and about.
If you desire a change of circumstance,
how much emotion and pain must you feel
before you realize you have the power
to negate your present reality?
Trust in the universe, the Jehovah,
and you will be shown the way
through the present moment.
The "Now" will guide you.
You must make the leap.
You must step onto the ever-surprising,
and sometimes daunting,
unknown path of yourself.
Walk your life path until
you reach your next level of self.
Change is never easy,
but the way to yourself will be given to you.
If you realize all is the Godliness,
you will take it.
Take the moment!

The Unknown World of Mysticism

Throughout the ages, there are those of us who have connected to and encountered the formless realms of creation. They have been called prophets, mystics, spiritualists, shamans, sages, psychics, and mediums. Spiritualism has been with us since the beginning of human consciousness.

Those who tap into the most powerful reality in creation—the metaphysical world where the concentrated power of the Godliness emanates—are highly sensitive human beings. We have heard about their surreal experiences as they travel to dimensions beyond our three-dimensional world. There, in that other place, their consciousness merges with something much larger than themselves.

If you have ever wondered if this experience is possible, know it is. It all comes down to awareness and belief. Know this phenomenon occurs more often than people realize. It is rarely discussed and remains to be fully accepted by modern-day man. Know, however, whether accepted or not this aspect of human consciousness is very much alive and part of human reality.

When a person has a metaphysical experience, there is an uplifting sense and knowingness of a genuine spiritual union with something larger than themselves. It is the sensation of being penetrated, or saturated, in a divine substance. The person's sense of self is lost—just as a drop of water is lost in the vastness of the mighty sea.

For the most part, humanity views God as a supreme being that exists "outside of themselves" or "somewhere else" in creation. Know God does not exist "outside" of us. We exist "within" God and God "exists" within us.

Mysticism is the art of establishing and becoming aware of a relationship between one's personal consciousness and cosmic consciousness. A spiritual experience can be had by anyone and cannot be defined through status, wealth, or religion.

Throughout history, many fascinating minds and characters have embellished our philosophies with ideas, theories, and concepts perceived through visions or messages from the formless world. Through their enlightenment, new knowledge was brought down from the unseen world into our physical reality.

Mankind's ideas, thoughts, and emotions are the highest form of creative energy; and through our creative force, we draw our potential out of the metaphysical realms into our three-dimensional world. Each of us plays a role in the mystery and discovery of the potential within our consciousness.

The difference between a spiritual person and a non-spiritual person is their level of awareness to the metaphysical world. Through an attuned sense of awareness to alternate realities, the spiritual person connects to various aspects of energy consciousness and brings higher knowledge and new insight into our world.

As time passed and mankind became distanced from nature and the earthly elements, the man of technology and practicality rose to denounce that which is formless and hidden. Many people fear a reality they cannot see, and they tend to veer away from that which they don't identify with or understand.

Just as you are part of the physical world, know a part of you is deeply connected to the metaphysical world whether you realize it or not. Oddly, it seems as if the ancients understood this more than the man of today. This is more than likely due to our day-to-day distractions and the very different world we exist in.

Modern civilizations view a metaphysical experience much as they would view the experience of an alien visiting our planet. Many feel it is highly unlikely, at best, to connect to the metaphysical realms and gain knowledge through forces they cannot see or understand. Much like the alien, the belief in personal revelations has become foreign to our consciousness; and mysticism, for the most part, has become a distant memory that existed in an era long ago.

It is important to realize the formless and physical worlds interact moment to moment. You are an embodiment of energy that continuously interacts with unseen energies and vibrational forces within creation. Depending on your current state of awareness, this new understanding may require a change to your perception of the world, or worlds, you believe to be real.

Instead of focusing on the physical three-dimensional world, mankind needs to realize many dimensions exist simultaneously—dimensions that are powerful and greatly affect our reality on earth. Furthermore, each of us has the ability to communicate with the unseen world; we only need to open our minds and hearts to become attuned to another part of who we are. The Godliness lives within you, hidden behind doors you may be frightened to open. Find your strength, completely let go, and open the doors to your inner Godliness.

Science has, for the most part, disputed the existence of God and disagrees with those who say they connect to a higher power in the metaphysical world. However, it is important to realize the scientists have always disputed the God of "age-old perceptions." Therefore, we must bring up an important point. If man's perceptions of God are misguided and misleading, this can only mean science has clashed with and denounced the God of man's past perceptions.

What would it mean if The Genesis Code's perception of God and creation actually complimented science, especially quantum theory? What impact would this have on our world and humanity? No longer would it be science against spirit or spirit against science, but science together with spirit and spirit together with science. In essence, a new bridge would span tumultuous waters and mankind could move forward through unification.

It is important for all people—whether spiritualist or scientist—to remain open to revelations in both the scientific and spiritual arenas. Both are facets of the Godliness. Commonalities recognized amongst the spiritual and scientific man would change everything and be a new starting point making it possible for mankind, as a whole, to manifest realities through a unified collective consciousness.

While science has been unable to prove, unequivocally, the existence of a master designer or Godlike being, spiritual seekers should not discount the importance of modern science—especially rising theories which address the quantum world. The scientific substantiation of our subatomic reality only compliments The Genesis Code's revelations.

*Science and mysticism...
It is just a matter of time before these
dual philosophies understand the
relevance and the unique
roles each plays in creation.
Both are important aspects of
human enlightenment.*

What is interesting, quantum theory supports the idea of a realm that contains infinite potential possibilities. You will soon learn of Hashomayim—a dimension known as Heaven. Quantum theory further supports the concept that your reality manifests from "you" (the observer) and your conscious perception. In other words, the reality you face is manifested from the inside out and not from the outside in.

Quite astonishingly, many scientists are beginning to recognize our universe did not just happen, but is the outcome of an awesomely powerful and unfathomable intelligence—a master designer most refer to as "God." There seems to be an unexplainable architect that cannot be seen. However, through the extraordinary code of life found within DNA, this pre-existing intelligence cannot be denied or explained away.

The bottom line is this: *We should not ignore one philosophy at the expense of another.* There is always a fine balance. When objectively seeking out truth, we must continuously remind ourselves that man's logical mind and emotional self are different sides of the same coin. Realize science and mysticism are two aspects of the Godliness revealing diverse perspectives of creation. One aspect of human consciousness cannot reach the ultimate truth without the other. Again, the "One" cannot be without the "two."

For many, the era of prophets and prophecy died long ago. Prophecy has mostly become a timepiece of man's past. Today, many fail to realize they are connecting to the metaphysical realm every moment. They just don't know it. If more people were aware of their continuous connection to universal knowledge, together with their power to create, the idea of being spoken to by the Godliness would not seem so obscure and foreign to their awareness. In fact, what do you think would happen if someone in today's world were to imply they were communicating with God? Would we accept their truth, or would we believe them to be delusional?

Today's generation of Adam is more sophisticated. Many say they believe in God, but do they truly believe God can speak to them directly? Know this is possible. You only need to believe and be open to receive. God sees you. Now see God. God believes in you. Now believe in God.

The architect exists.
It can be seen, but only through
that which it has created.
It is.

CHAPTER 4

In the Beginning

As one would imagine, the unknown and mysterious realms of creation are exceedingly complex. This is an advanced chapter, so please be patient with yourself as your consciousness becomes aware of new revelations. Know you may need to read this chapter more than once; and know we have rewritten these pages more times than you can imagine in an effort to ease this enlightenment into your awareness. So let's dive down the rabbit hole of creation.

The Bible reveals "In the beginning, God created the heavens and the earth." Most people think the Bible begins with the words, "In the beginning." However, this opening statement is yet another translation for the first word in the Hebraic Bible,

"Bereshit." As we seek to know the deeper meaning within Bereshit, The Genesis Code reveals "Bereshit" is: *A duality vibrating into a complex singularity becoming the explosive power that seeded a new creation.*

Through The Genesis Code, Bereshit offers tremendous insight into the beginning stages of a new creation that would ultimately manifest a self-aware evolving universe. Due to the vast nature and immense amount of coded wisdom found within Bereshit, we introduce only some of Bereshit's secrets, but certainly not all of them.

> Note: Throughout this book, we reference the original texts of the Hebraic Bible written by Moses, the English translation of the Hebraic texts, a Talmudic explanation of the Hebraic texts, and The Genesis Code's revelations of the Hebraic texts. The purpose for these comparisons is to show you the difference a translation, together with its interpretation, can have on one's perception of the Godliness and creation.

Hebraic Text: Bereshit 1:1

בְּרֵאשִׁית בָּרָא אֱלֹהִים אֵת הַשָּׁמַיִם וְאֵת הָאָרֶץ

English Translation: Genesis 1:1

"In the beginning, God created the heavens and the earth."

Talmudic Explanation: Genesis 1:1

The first Hebrew word in Genesis, "Bereshit" (In the beginning), hints of the upper wisdom which is called the wisdom of the "Elohim" (God). This is a secret of the upper world, and "the beginning is the second sphere" (which comes from the first sphere) and comes into being on God's order.

The Zohar, Thirteenth Century
Written by Moses DeLeon, Kabbalist

The Genesis Code: Genesis 1:1

Prior to "In the beginning," the All imagined a new creation—Adam. To express its essence, All That IS projected its idea, then retracted its awareness, from the potential it imagined and desired to know.

Now, a space existed within the totality of the All, and there was a "new dimension" called "Bereshit." This first dimension contained an unimaginable concentration of pure potential and unknowable energy embedded with all of the elements required to transform Bereshit into a massive self-aware creation.

Then, Bereshit's first dimension of potential enfolded into a second dimension of self-aware creativity. As the elements of Bereshit's first dimension transitioned into an extraordinary creative program, a new reality took form within Bereshit.

This transformation became a moment of awareness as Bereshit's "second dimension" (B = Bet = 2 = Duality = House = Dimension) rose within All That IS. Bereshit had transformed into a creation of duality and a new dimension that was a "self-aware aspect of the All."

Bereshit was now set to flourish through its own transformation of self. As the All morphed through Bereshit's first dimension of potential into Bereshit's second dimension that was a self-aware reality of creativity, a new level of Godliness formed. In this moment, the Elohim was realized.

The Elohim, a self-aware Creator, became the God of a new creation. And within the Elohim were "the Heavens" (Hashomayim) and the "Aretz" (the Elohim's spirit that seeks to know the potential within Hashomayim).

The expression of Adam had been desired by the All. Now, the "Elohim" (the God of Man), through its "dimension of potential" (Hashomayim), vibrated its "chosen aspects of specific potential" (HaAdam/Adamic Consciousness) that would, ultimately, manifest a "new reality" (the Adamic Universe) through which "Adam" (a new level of creator) could be experienced in a "three-dimensional reality" (Earth). Much would happen before the idea of "Adam" (mankind) was realized through a space of limitation within All That IS.

While humanity has attempted to understand the deeper meaning within the Torah's opening statement, "In the beginning, God created the heavens and the earth," man has only touched the surface of Bereshit's true meaning and its role in the manifestation of this creation. We will now delve into the abyss of God's Heavens and Earth and deeply explain The Genesis Code's revelation of Genesis 1:1.

The word, "Heaven," is derived from the ancient Hebrew word, "Hashomayim;" and the word, "Earth," is derived from its Hebrew source, "Aretz." Interestingly, The Genesis Code reveals there is the "Aretz" of the physical world "Earth," and the "Aretz" of the metaphysical world "the spirit that runs."

In the beginning, there was chaos and void, and Genesis 1:1 is describing the first stages of a metaphysical reality that preceded our creation. The Genesis Code reveals an astounding revelation and new insight into Genesis 1:1: *Within the metaphysical realms of creation, there was "Bereshit" (In the beginning), the realization of a "new creative program" (the Elohim), the "Heavens" (Hashomayim), and "the Aleph's" (God's) "spirit that runs" (Aretz).* As you can see, The Genesis Code accurately describes the metaphysical "Aretz," replacing the word, "Earth," with the phrase, "the Aleph's (God's) spirit that runs." In the metaphysical realms, the Earth had not yet formed.

What we learn through the Torah's Genesis Code is absolutely astonishing: *As Bereshit's first dimension unfolded and morphed into the second dimension, three primary forces of creativity came into being—the Elohim, the Elohim's spirit, and the Heavens.* Through the coded revelations within "Bereshit" (In the beginning), "Hashomayim" (the Heavens) and "Aretz" (God's spirit that runs), we find there is much more to know about "that which came first."

Hashomayim: The Heavens Above

For centuries man has asked, "How did this creation begin? What are the Heavens?" When humanity refers to the Heavens above, most people imagine a blissful kingdom—an eternal garden-like realm within creation. Most believe Heaven is where God lives and where man's soul goes when he dies. Moreover, mankind has been taught that Heaven is a rewarded state of existence for those who follow the rules and are obedient in the eyes of the religious establishment.

Nearly everyone has been told of the Heavens within the Godliness; however, The Genesis Code reveals current translations lack depth and accuracy. Imagine what it would mean to mankind if the truth of the Heavens was unveiled? What affect would this have on man's perceptions of reality? Have the Heavens been contorted so much so that man has no idea what this metaphysical realm truly is? Have the religious led humanity down an illusory path of enlightenment? Prepare yourself, for the Heavens are very different than what you have been told.

First and foremost, know God does not reside in the Heavens, but the Heavens are a realm within the Elohim. In fact, the Heavens are an aspect of the Elohim's creative program.

Therefore, they are part of the Elohim and a dimension "within" the Godliness—not "outside" of it.

Whereas most of humanity believes Heaven is the place we ascend to upon death, The Genesis Code reveals the Heavens are much more than that: *The Heavens are mankind's starting point and the dimension where human consciousness "begins."* This astounding revelation changes everything we have ever believed the Heavens to be.

Through The Genesis Code, we will enter the depths of the Heavens and discover the Godliness that IS. It is time to surpass that which the ancients have understood and journey where no man has gone before—into the heart of the Godliness where everything for Adam originates. To do so, we must begin with the source Hebrew to find the coded enlightenment within Genesis 1:1 which man has translated to mean: *In the beginning, God created the "Heavens" (Hashomayim) and the "Earth" (Aretz).*

Today, humanity perceives Heaven as a place of bliss. And what is bliss? It is a place of non-action, non-movement, and a state of nothingness. Bliss will always be bliss. However, The Genesis Code reveals Heaven is far from blissful. In fact, The Genesis Code reveals an extraordinary revelation about the Heavens: *Hashomayim is the place of all potential possibilities for the Elohim's infinite creations. Hashomayim is active and vibrating with infinite opposing aspects of potential creativity. Hashomayim is a dynamic and mysterious reality that is continuously interacting with the Elohim's spirit.*

This astounding enlightenment not only changes our perceptions of creation, but our perceptions of how God manifests realities. As the reality of God and creation begins to unfold within our consciousness, what we realize is fascinating. Through the Elohim's Hashomayim, the evolutionary journey of experience will forever manifest.

HaAdam: A Realm in Heaven

To deeply understand Adam, we must first know where "Adam" (mankind) comes from. What is the unknown metaphysical realm that has, thus far, been hidden from our awareness? Hashomayim is a formless reality of potential that preceded Eden, the Adamic Universe, and man's world.

Adam had been imagined by the Godliness, but Adam was still pure potential and a reality that had yet to be projected into light. Adam was unformed and, therefore, an unaware aspect of potential consciousness. God desired to deeply know and experience Adam. Yet, before mankind could be realized as a profound experience, Adam's potential would have to be "drawn out" of God's infinite sea of "total" possibilities—its "Hashomayim" (Heavens) within.

The Elohim would manifest the foundation for a future reality—the world of Adam. But how does man become out of nothingness? The Genesis Code reveals astounding insight into creation: *From within "Hashomayim" (the Heavens), God's spirit would run—choosing and activating its desired creation—Adam.* As the Elohim moved to create Adam and his reality, with great speed the "Aretz" (God's spirit) vibrated and probed Hashomayim's "infinite" aspects of random and chaotic potential searching for "explicit" potential that reflected the reality God wished to express—Adam.

This can be somewhat compared to a wild ball (the Aretz) let loose in a pin ball machine (Hashomayim). Like the ball in the pin ball machine, the Aretz was moving with great speed, probing Hashomayim, and connecting to specific, sought out facets of potential that would transform into an Adamic reality.

This new reality would be a new dimension within the Elohim's Hashomayim "that was" the potential for mankind. This new dimension within Hashomayim is what the Torah references as "HaAdam" and what The Genesis Code reveals is: *A dimension that is the total Adam, the Adamic whole, and Adamic Consciousness.* HaAdam "is" the total Adam in potential, and the place of total possible possibilities of all that Adam is.

Following the creation of the Elohim, the Hashomayim, and the Aretz, the "dimension of Adamic Consciousness" (HaAdam) would be a new vibratory energy field and sea of potential that was "the source" of mankind. Understand every possible experience for God is within Hashomayim, and every possible experience for man is within the dimension of HaAdam that vibrates within Hashomayim. You could say man has his own realm of Heaven within God's vast Heavens.

The Torah's HaAdam was all aspects of mankind's potential vibrating as "One" in the metaphysical realms. Within HaAdam, there was now the potential for the Adamic Universe that consisted of every possible element that could be used to stimulate and project the universe and world of Adam.

HaAdam "is" a sea of total Adamic Consciousness. It is the starting point of creation. It is that which came first—preceding our sun, stars, planets, and earth—even our very universe. Within HaAdam, the Elohim's spirit was vibrating the reality of Adam and bringing Adam's reality forth—out of the chaos and void—into the light. The Godliness was hovering over the deep—the unknowing waters of Adamic potential—vibrating intensely and drawing its Adamic potential forth out of its totality into life.

Through The Genesis Code, we are enlightened to the reality of HaAdam's Adamic Consciousness: *It is the totality of infinite possibilities of Adamic potential, vibrating as a whole. It is the basin of all consciousness from which Adam's reality, and the universe he inhabits, is realized. It was, and is, the place where Adam's potential actively vibrates within the Elohim's totality—from the beginning of time until the end of time that is mankind. HaAdam is the vibratory essence of the total possible possibilities inherent for our universe and for every male and female that has ever been or that will ever be.*

Realize there are an infinite number of potential realities and creations within the Elohim's Hashomayim. Man is not all there is. However, because specific particles of potential were chosen to form the dimension of "HaAdam" (Adamic Consciousness), this can only mean the Godliness chose to create, and desired to know, man.

You began as pure potential within Hashomayim. Then, the Elohim desired to know, feel, and experience your potential in a three-dimensional reality where what happens "matters."

The Heavens Decoded

Hashomayim is truly a place where the Elohim's sea of possibilities percolates. God's Heavens are a realm of creativity; a realm of evolution; a realm of chaos; and realm that is far from blissful where the core of Adam vibrates. Hashomayim is where new life is imagined, selected, activated, and then projected into alternate dimensions within the Godliness.

From within Hashomayim, new creations are projected into alternate dimensions of specific potential. Once the potential is seeded in a new dimension, the potential is activated and, thus, becomes its own reality. This is the secret of the Heavens. Hashomayim is the starting point and the beginning for the Elohim's creations.

Also important to understand, whereas the Elohim manifests through its Hashomayim, mankind manifests through the infinite points of Adamic Consciousness within HaAdam—in the Elohim's Hashomayim. HaAdam is the potential for anything and everything that is possible for mankind, from which all "singular consciousnesses" (each and every one of us) is projected into the dimension of "Earth" (Aretz).

The Secret of HASHOMAYIM (the Heavens)

HEBREW	LETTERS AND CODE	VALUE	CODED MEANING
HASHO-MAYIM השמים	HEY; SHIN; MEM; YOD; MEM שם ים השם הם מה מים שמי	395	The/My name; The many; There; Sea of all potential consciousness; Water; Percolating question.
HEY ה	HEY; YOD הי יד	5	A particular; The breath and life force.
SHIN ש	SHIN; YOD; FINAL NUN שין יד נון	300	Teeth; Devour; Transformation; Gift.
MEM מ	MEM; YOD; MEM מים יד מים	40	Matter; Active hand; Water.
YOD י	YOD; DALET יד דלת	10	Seed of creativity; Potential; Hand; Doorway.
"FINAL" MEM ם	MEM; YOD; MEM מים יד מים	40	Who am I?; Active hand; Matter.

HASHOMAYIM = Place of all Potential

Hashomayim is the infinite possibilities and potentials for the Elohim's creations. Within Hashomayim is "HaAdam" (Adamic Consciousness)—the place of infinite possibilities for Adam—from the beginning until the end of time.

Hashomayim, together with its vibratory force of "Adamic Consciousness" (HaAdam), is a realm of potential and the place where all possibilities for every male and female exist in potential. Every scenario, every experience, and every person you face was first a potential energy consciousness within Hashomayim. As pure energy consciousness, all potential waits to be chosen by the "Aretz" (the Elohim's spirit that runs). Then, and only then, does a particular potential consciousness manifest in a world of time and matter to be experienced by the Elohim. That which is probed for, desired, and selected within the Hashomayim's dimension of Adamic Consciousness is vibrated into other dimensions of self-realization.

 ## HEY = A Particular Consciousness

"Hey" reflects the breath of life. It is the core of the Elo(h)im that signifies the "beat of creation."

"Hey" represents the heartbeat of life pulsating throughout the Heavens. Furthermore, "Hey" reflects a "particular" aspect of vibratory consciousness that became the realm of Adamic Consciousness within Hashomayim.

 ## SHIN = Fire; Teeth; Transformation

Hashomayim is not fixed potential, but an ever-evolving powerhouse of transformative potential consciousness.

Hashomayim is a place of transformative energy. The "fire" referenced in Hashomayim reflects the Elohim's "fire of creativity." Fire is both destructive energy and life-giving energy. Fire transforms energy consciousness through destruction, and out of the destruction, new forms of life rise from the ashes. Creation stares into the status quo and creates a new paradigm within the fabric of creation. As it does so, this is when the energies in Hashomayim consume, merge, meld, and transform with one another, manifesting new energy bodies in different dimensions of potential creativity.

 ### MEM = Matter; Water

"Water" in the Torah is a metaphor for "consciousness." "Mem" is also a metaphor for "matter." In its totality, "Mem" is a metaphor for "consciousness that completes itself in matter."

Two "Mems" (M) exist within "Hasho(m)ayi(m)." The "First Mem," located in the center of "Hasho(m)ayim," has an opening at the base of its letter (see table below). This shows us energy contains potential. Like water, energy consciousness flows from a source, downwards, into an alternate dimension where it gathers to form a sea of consciousness.

Mem (First)	מ
Mem (Final)	ם

Within Hasho(m)ayi(m), the "First Mem" eventually flows into the "Final Mem" (see table above). The "Final Mem" is represented by a square in the Hebrew letter (a border that has no opening and reflects a final destination). The "First Mem" (fluid consciousness) flows into the "Final Mem" (matter consciousness) where fluid consciousness transforms into matter consciousness—in a new dimension of creativity.

YOD = Seed of Creativity

All new growth begins with a seed that is energized and brought into light. All seeds are planted in a new and different dimension from their source.

The seed of the majestic oak tree is planted in a dimension of darkness. Once watered, the seed grows roots that take hold in the earth, and its trunk sprouts forth and grows its many branches. Out of the darkness, it has become in the light. Alive, the oak tree now exists in two dimensions—both the darkness (its roots) and the light (the tree that can be experienced).

The "Yod" in "Hashoma(y)im" reflects "the active hand of the Godliness" moving through a "doorway" (a portal) and planting a "seed of potential" (Adamic Consciousness) in a new "dimension of matter" (the Adamic Universe) through light. Like the great oak tree, your seed of consciousness was planted in your "mother's womb" (darkness) and you now live and experience your essence in light. Know, however, Adam's roots are still deeply rooted in the unmanifest, and we are very much connected to the metaphysical world that is our "source" (the darkness that is hidden from our awareness).

FINAL MEM = Matter

The end destination for potential consciousness is matter consciousness. The potential has been seeded in a new dimension of light.

The "Final Mem" is the end destination that represents the "seed planted in matter." Through a dimension of matter, the seed grows and can be experienced by the Elohim. The last letter of "Elohi(m)" is also a "Final Mem," which reveals a phenomenal revelation: *The Elohim expresses its vibratory essence in a dimension of matter consciousness.* That which the Elohim desires to experience and know is manifest in a new dimension "that is the end destination" where Adam's emotional self will be deeply experienced by the Godliness.

The Earth Decoded

Through the Torah, the secret of the Aretz' creative role is revealed. For thousands of years, man would translate the "Aretz" as "Earth," however, The Genesis Code reveals Aretz' depths of creativity reach far into the metaphysical realms.

Through its Adamic creation,
through its Heavens and Spirit that runs,
God awakens to its reality of self.

The Secret of ARETZ (Earth)			
HEBREW	LETTERS AND CODE	VALUE	CODED MEANING
ALEPH א	ALEPH; LAMED; PHEY אלף למד פה	1	Prime Cause; Spirit that projects and retracts to give, take, teach, learn, and experience. Mouth; Expression.
RESH ר	RESH; YOD; SHIN ריש יד שין	200	Head; Vibrating and seeding potential energy into a lower and transformative dimension.
"FINAL" TZADIK ץ	TZADIK; DALET; YOD; KOF צדיק דלת יד קוף	90	A specific aspect that manifests through a portal into a balanced reality through the highest and lowest levels of the animal self.
RATZ רץ	RESH; FINAL TZADIC ריש צדיק	290	Run; Continuous vibration; Transform; Move; Spirit.

 ## ALEPH = Prime Cause and Motivator

The "Aleph" in the word, "(A)retz," shows mankind the Prime Cause and the spirit of the Godliness is active.

The Elohim's spirit projects and retracts. It moves back and forth between dimensions. It gives and takes, retracts and expands, teaches and learns. It wants to express its essence so that it can experience its essence.

RESH = Head

The "Resh" in the word, "A(r)etz," represents the intention that vibrates and seeds its potential in a dimension of transformation.

As the spirit of God vibrates its extremes into specific intentions, it seeds its many intentions and transformative thoughts into different dimensions. It reconfigures its intentions to bring a transformation out of the totality into a separate reality—a specific experience it desires to experience and know.

 ## TZADIK = Point of Balance

The "Final Tzadik" at the end of Aret(z) represents the point of balance between many different and active forces of possibilities.

"Tzadik" expresses the "Aleph" (the Godliness) that is "choosing" specific aspects from within the totality of HaAdam. It brings forth perfect balance and all of the necessary ingredients for Adam. An example of Tzadik can also be found in our dimension. Our earth is so fine- tuned that if its orbit was altered by even one percent, we would all perish.

The Secret of TZADIK (Point of Balance)

HEBREW	LETTERS AND CODE	VALUE	CODED MEANING
TZADIK צדיק	TZADIK; DALET; YOD; KOF צדיק דלת יד קוף	204	Justice; Point of balance; Righteousness; Highest aspect of duality that is Adam.
TZ צ	TZADIK צדיק	90	Duality; Balance; Knife's edge.
DALET ד	DALET דלת	4	Doorway; Portal.
YOD י	YOD יד	10	Seed; Hand.
KOF קוף	KOF קוף וו פי	100	Ape; Primal Animal Self; Head.
DI די	DALET; YOD דלת יד	14	Limit.
TZAD צד	TZADIK; DALET צדיק דלת	94	Side.

The "Tzadik," the last letter of "Aret(z)," provides great understanding into this creation. As you can see from the table above, the code offers significant insight through the following descriptive words: *Ape, portal, balance, righteous, duality, knife's edge, seed, limit, and side.* We, however, are focusing primarily on the letter, "Kof," the final letter within the word, "Tzadi(k)."

The "Aretz" (God's spirit) desired to bring forth out of Hashomayim a consciousness and reality that would become the essence of what the word, "Tzadik," truly means: *Righteous man.* The description of "righteous" does not mean a "religious or judgmental man," but is intended to describe a male and female that "lives through a balanced center." Through the coded revelations of "Aretz" and "Tzadik," we are being shown the basis for creation follows: *Manifesting "balance" amongst opposing forces through which different realities are experienced as Adam.*

Finding balance within a universe of duality is not an easy task. As potential consciousness is seeded in the dimension of man, it transforms into a limited aspect of self-aware consciousness that experiences its reality through two diverse and powerful perspectives—the animal self and the logical self.

Because the primary meaning of "Tzadik" is "balance," we will now focus on "Kof's" coded revelations. Through "Kof," we are being shown it is the intention of the Elohim's spirit to bring forth a consciousness that contains two primary aspects of opposing forces: *"Resh" (the head) that is "logic, thought, and pure energy;" and the "Final Nun" (the animal self) that reflects "deep and powerful emotions, intuition, the killer instinct, and earth consciousness."*

Interestingly, the symbol for "Kof" (ק) is made up from two disconnected symbols—the "Resh/Head" (ר) and the "Final Nun/Animal Self" (ן). Because the lines of these symbols are not connected to one another (ק), what does connect the lines is the "empty space" between the lines. Through the space that is "nothingness," the code is revealing the Godliness that is the "Hidden Aleph" (the aspect of All That IS embedded in each and every creation).

The Hidden Aleph is an extremely important facet of the Godliness. The Hidden Aleph is the creative force that runs throughout all creations and each and every possible dimension. The space in the Hebrew letter that is "Kof" (ק) reflects the "Hidden Aleph" (All That IS) that is seeded within creation.

In the case of the Adamic Universe, the Hidden Aleph is the space between the duality that is man—the head and the tail—man's thoughts and instincts. The Genesis Code reveals the following revelation: *The space "is" the "Hidden Aleph" that is the "soul of man."* In truth, the Hidden Aleph is the "nothingness" that is "everything." In this case, however, the Hidden Aleph is empowered through the duality that is man—it is the Godliness taking on the "personality of man." The Hidden Aleph is the nothingness becoming Adam. When The Genesis Code reveals, "Man is a facet of God," this is what the code is referring to. God becomes through us.

RATZ = Run; Continuous; Movement

Like the Godliness, this creation is always on the move, always evolving, and in perfect balance.

The Elohim's creation is always moving. Nothing is ever at a standstill. God is creative and forever changing. Evolution is only possible through movement and transformation.

The Genesis Code reveals an astounding revelation: *As the Elohim transitioned to manifest a three-dimensional world; it did so through its spirit that is always running, transforming, integrating, and revealing new dimensions of reality.* This is the reality of the Aretz—the spirit that is always moving and evolving. Like the Elohim, Adam would have his own "Aretz" (spirit that runs) that interacts with his own "Hashomayim" (HaAdam) through which new realities would manifest and become a God experience.

Know the metaphysical Aretz has manifested the physical Aretz, and this world is a reflection of the Elohim's spirit that is forever moving and transforming, together with mankind. This Earth we live on is travelling through space at enormous speeds. "Mankind's spirit" (Aretz) is running through time, experiencing a reality through matter where death is certain and feared, limitation flourishes, eternity is not a reality, emotions are deeply felt, and man's choices are met with consequences.

Within creation, two aspects of Aretz had been activated—God's spirit that runs within Hashomayim, and Adam's spirit that runs within man's world. From within HaAdam, the Aretz would project a masterpiece—a life force the Elohim passionately desires to experience.

CHAPTER 5

Darkness Upon the Face of the Deep

A new creation was in its infancy, and all was not known. Darkness was upon the face of the deep. Much would be needed for life to manifest out of HaAdam's formless and timeless realm of Adamic Consciousness into a "dimension of time and space" (the Adamic Universe). From the depths of the Elohim's imagination, programs of immense creativity were imagined to support a new level of creator, Adam.

Within HaAdam were the infinite elements needed to create Adam and his reality. There would be galaxies, solar systems, stars, suns, planets, moons, the element of fire, and the nourishment of water to support life. There would be land, skies, and everything in between. There would be fish, birds, animals, and all that is nature, itself. Then, there would be Adam. All of this would be necessary before a grand manifestation—humanity—was possible. Everything that was needed would be created by the Godliness. All that is, all that we know, it was all created for us.

Hebraic Text: Bereshit 1:2

וְהָאָרֶץ הָיְתָה תֹהוּ וָבֹהוּ וְחֹשֶׁךְ עַל פְּנֵי תְהוֹם וְרוּחַ אֱלֹהִים מְרַחֶפֶת עַל פְּנֵי הַמָּיִם

English Translation: Genesis 1:2

"Now the Earth was unformed and void, and darkness was upon the face of the deep; and the spirit of God hovered over the face of the waters."

Talmudic Explanation: Genesis 1:2

"The throne of glory was standing in the air and hovering on the face of the waters by the wind of the mouth of God, and the sound was like a Dove fluttering on its nest."

~ **Rabbi Shlomo Yitzhaki Rashi, Twelfth Century**
Author of the First Comprehensive Commentary
on the Talmud and Hebrew Bible

The Genesis Code: Genesis 1:2

Within the depths of the "Elohim" (God), a "face" (expression) was rising out of the darkness. The expression of Adam was forming as "HaAdam"—a new dimension of Adamic potential within the Elohim's Hashomayim.

The Elohim was vibrating over the unknown waters of consciousness. The Elohim's deep sense of feeling towards "Adam" was sprouted by urgency. So powerful were the vibrations of these emotions, their intensity activated the face of HaAdam.

From within Hashomayim the face of HaAdam was rising to the surface of the unknowing waters. From the infinite elements of possibilities within HaAdam's Adamic Consciousness, the "Elohim's spirit" (the Aretz) vibrated its chosen aspects—manifesting into light the universe it desired to experience. All that was to be would rise from the darkness into the light out of God's abyss of unrealized self.

"DARKNESS" upon the "FACE" of the "DEEP"	
	DESCRIPTION
DARKNESS חשך חש	An idea existing in the depths of the Elohim's hidden self, empowered by a feeling and sense of urgency emoted within the Godliness.
FACE פני	The projection of a potential reality looking back at the Elohim becoming the seed of creation.
DEEP תהום תה / תם	The depths within the Elohim containing unrealized potential that is percolating and rising to the surface showing itself as a face. The potential wants to be desired and known and can only be expressed and realized through light into matter.

The deeper message within Genesis 1:2 describes how the Elohim looked within its immeasurable depths to face its unrealized potential. The Elohim passionately desired to know its extraordinary Adamic Consciousness. We will now explore the deeper meaning within the Bible's description "darkness was upon the face of the deep" and provide a detailed explanation of this fascinating Biblical statement.

DARKNESS = An Idea Rises

The darkness represents a state of non-clarity.

Within the darkness a sense of urgency was sprouting forth, together with intense emotions the Elohim longed to feel. A reality of potential was attempting to express itself. However, the Adamic Universe was still a "potential" and, therefore, remained somewhat hidden within the "shadows" (darkness) of the Godliness.

Because the "face" (the idea becoming) had yet to form through matter and light, it was hidden within the depths of the Elohim. While not fully formed, know the face was rising through the darkness, making it possible for the Elohim to realize a "glimmer of expression." Out of the depths, a new reality was rising to the surface, wanting to be known in the aspect of light. The Elohim was vibrating, poised to manifest.

FACE = Projection of a Potential Reality

The "face" represents that which the Elohim most passionately desired and that which was rising to the surface from its infinite possibilities and depths.

A "face" is a reflection of "an emotional awareness looking back at you," inviting you to know its deeper essence of self vibrating through its "surface." Within the unknown waters of consciousness, the face had risen to the surface from the depths of the sea.

As the Elohim came to face a reflection of its previously hidden self, questions must have surely risen within the Godliness, "What is this face that has risen from within my depths? What is the potential that lies behind the face?" The Elohim was coming to realize the "face of Adam" and God peered intensely into human potential. The idea of "Adam" (mankind) was forming within the Elohim, inspired by an intense emotion and urgency to know that which was unknown.

 ## DEEP = Potential in God's Depths

Rising from the depths of the Elohim, a potential universe was percolating as pure energy consciousness—a universe that would support Adam.

From the deepest aspects of infinite possibilities, through the face that rose from the depths of the darkness, the Elohim began to realize it passionately and urgently desired to experience these unknown waters. The Adamic Universe, and all it would encompass, was becoming within the Godliness.

The Secret of Water

Within the name, "Hashomayim," is the powerful metaphor of "water." We will now peer through a window and look deeper into the Elohim's place of all potential. As we come to understand the coded message in "mayim" (water), we learn Hashomayim is the many singular seeds of potential consciousness that come together to form a mighty sea.

From within HaAdam's Adamic Consciousness, the Elohim would project its expression of the Adamic Universe and manifest its chosen potential into a three-dimensional reality. Like water, consciousness is fluid and flows into alternate dimensions. Without water, there is no life. Just as water gives life, so does consciousness.

As The Genesis Code reveals, "Hashomayim" (the Heavens) is governed by the "God of the Sea" (the Elohim). What is extraordinary is that the Elohim is sometimes expressed as "El Hayam" which means: *God of the Sea.* Through this metaphor, we come to know the relationship "water" has with the "God of the Sea"—the place of all potential that transforms infinite possibilities into new realities.

The Secret of MAYIM (Water) within HASHO-MAYIM

HEBREW	TRANSLATION	DESCRIPTION
MAYIM מים	Potential consciousness that transforms into matter.	Water is receptive—it absorbs consciousness. Also true, all life is receptive of water.
YOD י	Potential seed of creativity.	The seed sprouts forth new life. The seed is within all creative potential.
"FINAL" MEM ם	Potential transmutes into a singularity and matter consciousness.	Creative potential moving towards a lower dimension within the Elohim to be experienced as light.
YOD-MEM ים	The totality; Sea of Consciousness containing infinite potential for man.	Infinite points of potential consciousness within the singularity of the sea. The many becoming 'One.'
MEM-YOD מי	Me? Who? Whom? Waters.	That which asks the question through various aspects of consciousness.

 MAYIM = Water

Hashomayim is a vibratory energy field void of time. It is a vibratory force of potential consciousness that contains all possible possibilities of Adam that is Adamic Consciousness. Mayim reflects the infinite drops of potential coming together to form a sea of consciousness. The "sea of consciousness" is a "totality" containing an infinite number of "potential experiences" vibrating in the metaphysical realms.

The Elohim already knows Hashomayim's infinite aspects of potential through its vibrational force. In other words, the Elohim feels the potential percolating within its sea of consciousness. What is fascinating, because the Elohim is a powerful and self-aware entity of creativity, it probes and feels the unmanifested potential within its Hashomayim. The Elohim looks for potential within its Hashomayim to create various realities it desires to experience. In the case of our universe, the Elohim desired to know the potential within HaAdam, a particular dimension of potential within the Elohim's Hashomayim.

Within the Elohim's sea of possibility, an "infinite number of water drops" (singular points of consciousness) exist in a state of unmanifested realization. However, before the Elohim can experience its desired potential, the individual points of consciousness must be activated and projected out of the sea into another dimension within the Elohim.

As we decode the secrets of creation, The Genesis Code is unveiled through numerous methods. One technique encompasses reading a word both forward and backwards. Using this method, we find "mayim" (water) contains additional realizations.

"(M)a(y)i(m)" contains the letters, "Mem + Yod + Mem." When you combine the first two letters, "Mem + Yod," the code reveals "a singular drop of consciousness" and the revelation of the question, "Who am I?" Also fascinating, when you combine the last two letters, "Yod + Mem," the code reveals the "sea of consciousness." Furthermore, when you reverse these last two letters, you find "Mem + Yod" and, again, another revelation rises as the "sea of potential" (the Elohim that is the God of the Sea) asks the question, "Who am I?"

New revelations within "mayim" (water) shed light on the Elohim's perception of self. First, there is the perspective of the "singularity" (Adam)—the drop of water that has emerged from the Elohim's sea of consciousness. As the drop of water moves through the portal, falling into our three-dimensional world, it becomes a "singular consciousness and self-aware entity" (Adam). From its new perspective, it looks back at the mighty "sea" (the Hashomayim/Heavens) and asks, "Who am I?"

Out of the totality, in a dimension of limitation, the "singularity" (Adam) expresses its potential through our physical world of matter. No longer pure potential—Adam immediately experiences his expression and becomes a self-aware aspect of consciousness. It is important to realize, once a "drop of water" (a singular aspect of Adamic Consciousness) attains self-awareness, it will never be the same as it was before.

For Adam, the time will come when each man's journey on earth will end. When Adam leaves the dimension of "Earth" (Aretz), he transcends into the "sea of potential" (Hashomayim) governed by the "God of the Sea" (the Elohim). As the "singularity" (Adam) returns to the "totality" (Hashomayim), his energy consciousness holds his memories, together with the knowledge and insight he gained through his life's experiences. Through his journey of becoming, the "drop of water" (Adam) has evolved.

Once Adam returns to, and melds with, the God of the Sea, he realizes he is part of everything. When Adam returns to Hashomayim—the place of all potential consciousness—he will continue to contain potential, but through a new point of view. Now, he is a self-aware singularity, as well as the totality, simultaneously. His understanding has changed. His awareness of self, and All That IS, has evolved. He is enlightened.

Now, as an evolved singularity in the totality, Adam's vibratory consciousness reflects the totality of his life experiences, including his memories, thoughts, and emotions. From this new point of view, the "self-aware singularity" (Adam) now encompasses the emotional knowingness of "being the totality."

Through a heightened sense of awareness and deep understanding, the "evolved singularity" (Adam), has transformed and is now an aspect of pure self-aware energy consciousness that has merged with the God of the Sea. Now, the evolved singularity, will continue to ask the question, "Who am I?"

 The Elohim (the God of the Sea)—From within the totality and sea of potential consciousness the Godliness asks, "Who am I?"

 Adam (the Singularity/Drop of Water)—Once drawn out of the sea of consciousness (the totality) and projected into a new dimension (earth), there is self-awareness and Adam asks, "Who am I?"

 Adam (the Evolved Singularity/Drop of Water that Returns to the Totality)—Upon man's physical death, the drop of water returns to the sea of consciousness (the God of the Sea). Now, however, it is an evolved self-aware singularity with the emotional knowingness that it is not only a singularity, but also the totality. The evolved and advanced singularity now understands it is, and has always been, a facet of the totality and asks, "Who am I?"

As revealed through this breathtaking code, everything is the All. The Torah's Genesis Code reveals regardless of its position in creation, point of view, or level of awareness through various perspectives of creative consciousness, the Creator will always ask, "Who am I?"

All consciousness, whether pure potential or self-aware, is a facet of All That IS. The Godliness is the energy that lives on both sides of the portal—it is the portal—and an unfathomable intelligence that continuously and forever seeks to define its evolving essence as a creativity that creates realities.

The Elohim, through its heavens and spirit, earth and mankind, is continually evolving, transforming, and forever searching to discover and know its infinite potentials of self. God is continuously becoming through its creations and will forever ask, "Who am I? What can I become?"

Separation within the Elohim

Within the Elohim, separation must occur before the Godliness can know and realize an individual aspect within its totality. An "illusion of separation" occurs within the Godliness before a sense of independent life can be possible. Know the illusion of separation begins within the core of All That IS and continues to manifest throughout its subsequent dimensions of creativity. The illusion of separation is a necessity before differentiation can be realized within a reality of "Oneness."

Through The Genesis Code, we are shown how the Elohim perceives consciousness from a distance—from "over there." Additional code prevails within Hashomayim providing insight into the Elohim's ability to perceive and realize its differential from a distance.

No observing entity can observe itself observing unless it is one aspect of duality observing another aspect of duality. For example, a child cannot move an object in a coordinated fashion until his consciousness becomes differentiated from his environment.

The Secret of SHIN-MEM (Over There; Name) within HA-SHOM-AYIM		
HEBREW	TRANSLATION	DESCRIPTION
SHIN שין	Potential fire consciousness; Prior to the dimension of man.	Within the creative potential of all possibilities is the element of fire and consumption that transforms consciousness.
MEM מים	Potential water consciousness; Prior to the dimension of man.	Life requires the element of water that contains the infinite drops of potential singularities.
SHIN-MEM שם	Over there; Name.	'Over there' reflects a differential and two sides of a relationship. A 'name' encompasses that which is observed from another's perspective.
YOD-MEM די	Sea of Consciousness; Potential.	Points of potential coming together as One. The place that signifies all possibility within the Elohim.

 ### SHIN-MEM = Over There; Name

Hashomayim's "over there" points to the metaphorical elements of "fire and water" (Shin-Mem). Our universe was imagined, conceptualized, and brought into being through opposing forces.

Also fascinating, the word, "create," contains the hidden elements of: *Fire, consumption, and transformation.* When we create anything, we actually take in new elements and transform those elements into something else. Transference of energy always occurs in any creative measure, and this applies to the Elohim, Hashomayim, HaAdam's Adamic Consciousness, and Adam.

Hashomayim's possibilities can only be experienced in a dimension that exists "over there" distanced from Hashomayim. The drop of water looks back at the mighty sea and says, "I am this now, but where have I come from?" This once "potential" consciousness has become a singular "self-aware" consciousness that now perceives reality through a powerful illusion: *"I am here, and the sea is over there."*

Much like the drop of rain that falls from one dimension (the thundercloud in the sky), the droplet is seen, realized, and experienced in another dimension (the observer in the dimension of earth). The "droplet of water" (consciousness) has attained awareness, together with a powerful self-image. It no longer sees reality through the eyes of Oneness, but through a perception of separation. This singular aspect of consciousness has transitioned within creation making it possible to perceive and experience reality from an individual and separate point of view.

Adam: A New Reality

In the Game of God, the All would experience its new "creation" (Bereshit). Bereshit contained all of the elements necessary for a new creation and it, thereby, transformed into a powerful creative program and "new level of Godliness" (the Elohim). The Elohim would contain the "Hashomayim" (the Heavens), and the Hashomayim would be activated by "God's spirit that runs" (the metaphysical Aretz).

The Elohim passionately desired to experience Adam. Therefore, the Elohim vibrated over the unknown waters of Hashomayim to bring HaAdam to light. Through HaAdam's infinite elements of potential, the Elohim would project a "new reality" (the Adamic Universe). Within the Adamic Universe, a new dimension would be realized as "Earth" (the physical Aretz) that would serve as the background for a phenomenal new level of "creator" (Adam).

Everything that was, is, or will ever come into your awareness was created for you. This extraordinary support system allows mankind to utilize his magnificent vibratory force and creative power to become anything and everything he could possibly imagine or believe in. Yet, a profound secret would riddle Adam's consciousness: *Adam would not know he was God incarnate.*

Prior to the creation of our universe, Adam was an unrealized potential that had never been experienced within the Godliness. Understand the Elohim desperately desired to experience Adamic Consciousness, together with its extraordinary potential for "emotional realization." In truth, we are a facet of the Elohim that has come to life in and through light. Through light, mankind is experienced by the Elohim; and the Godliness comes to know the face that was previously hidden and unknown in the depths of its darkness.

We are a reflection of that which created us. How could we be anything else? We will now divulge a revelation that is an explosion within human consciousness: *The Elohim is defined through its very creation.* This revelation reveals the true relationship between mankind and God. You are here to experience it all, and you are here to be experienced by the All. Through Adam, God feels.

Meet you where the sun ends
and the earth begins.
~ I Am

You are the onlooker of your own metamorphosis, and you are a witness to yourself. Through time, it becomes possible to observe our evolution of self—the past, the present, and the future we imagine. If there was no time, Adam could never observe his own metamorphosis, nor could he be a witness to himself.

Through a dimension of time and space, Adam observes his energy consciousness as it manifests through various scenarios in his outer world. Through higher awareness, Adam knows that which he faces is truly himself. What is extraordinary, together the Elohim and Adam play out and experience life which gives rise to intense emotions that reverberate throughout creation.

God feels what we feel—our pain and agony, together with our orgasmic vibrations of love. God feels through man's intense emotions.

Even though it appears we are separate from God, know we are not. Feeling we are separate from the Godliness, is yet another powerful illusion. In fact, our three-dimensional world is a projection and reflection of the formless world we cannot see. We will now reveal the coded message within the name, "Adam." Through The Genesis Code, you will better understand that "Adam is you." You are much more than you've ever imagined yourself to be.

\multicolumn{4}{c}{The Secret of ADAM}			
HEBREW	LETTERS AND CODE	VALUE	CODED MEANING
ALEPH א	ALEPH; LAMED; PHEY אלף	111	The Elohim; the Prime Cause projecting its essence into a new dimension.
DALET ד	DALET; LAMED; TAV דלת	434	Portal; Doorway through which the Elohim projects itself into a new dimension; The Adamic Universe.
"FINAL" MEM ם	MEM מים	50	Adamic Consciousness seeding in matter.
DALET; "FINAL" MEM דם	DALET; MEM דלת מים	44	Blood; The Prime Cause (Aleph) is the spirit of the Elohim in the man's blood.
ALEPH; "FINAL" MEM א ם	ALEPH; MEM אלף מים	41	Mother; Creator.

ALEPH = the Prime Cause

The first letter of (A)dam is an "Aleph" (A). The "Aleph" is also the first letter within the name, "(A)lohim" (Elohim). Ada(m) also ends with a "Final Mem," as does the Elohi(m). This is no coincidence. Through a portal, the "Prime Cause" (the Elohim) projects its essence into this dimension as "mankind" (Adam).

The Genesis Code reveals Adam is a facet of the Elohim. The first and last letter of "(A)da(m)" is exactly the same as the first and last letter of the "(A)lohi(m)," (E) being the same as (A) in the case of the name, Elohim. In order for the Elohim to realize Adamic Consciousness through a dimension of matter, a "portal" (doorway) was created to make it so.

 ### DALET = Portal/Doorway

"Daled," (D), the center letter in A(d)am shows us a "doorway" was created before Adam, a facet of the Elohim, could be realized in a dimension of matter and light.

The Elohim desired to experience a facet of itself in matter. To do so, the Elohim projected potential energy consciousness through a portal into an alternate dimension. Prior to Adam taking form as a human in matter, the Elohim would project a singularity of Adamic Consciousness through a doorway/portal into a new reality. We are being shown the "doorway" within Adam's name reveals: *The "Aleph" (the Prime Cause) travels through a portal within creation to experience life as Adam on the other side.*

Mankind's unquenchable desire to know the unknowable rises from the deepest levels of our consciousness. In fact, the human desire to seek out and know our truth is the same desire that motivated the Elohim to seek out and know its truth, Adam. This vibratory force is a two-way street. God seeks to know Adam through its perspective, and Adam seeks to know God through his perspective.

 ### <u>MEM = Matter Consciousness</u>

The last letter in the name, Ada(m) is exactly the same as the last letter in the name, Elohi(m). Because the Hebrew letter, "Mem," (M), is located at the end of both names, the "Mem" becomes a "Final Mem." The "Final Mem" is a metaphor for matter consciousness and shows us the Elohim desires to express itself in a dimension of matter that is a "final destination"—the place where the experience will be realized.

Because the name, "Elohi(m)," contains a "Final Mem," we are being shown "a final result would be realized" through the Elohim's intentions. Interestingly, the name, "Ada(m)," also contains a "Final Mem." A phenomenal secret rises: *Adam, a self-aware entity of consciousness, would be "the end result" that reflected the creation the Elohim passionately desired to experience.* Through The Genesis Code, we learn out of the "Adamic whole" (HaAdam), the Elohim would project its "chosen" singularities of potential into matter to become Adam and a "particular experience" for God.

DALET; FINAL MEM = Blood

The spirit of the Elohim, the Prime Cause and Motivator, is embedded in man's blood.

This coded revelation reveals that man's life force is powered by the spirit of God. The blood flows through man's veins and feeds his physical body. The blood gives life to the matter consciousness, and the life force of the blood is God's spirit flowing in this dimension. The "Creator's spirit" (Aretz) is alive in each of us—running through man's blood.

ALEPH; FINAL MEM = Mother

Adam reflects the energy of creation. Adam is that which gives life to new realities in the dimension of time and matter.

A groundbreaking level of enlightenment is found within the name, "Adam." The names Elohim and Adam have the same first and last letters in their names, the "Aleph" and "Final Mem." What do the Hebrew letters, "Aleph + Mem," mean when they are combined? They reveal a new word, "Mother." This is an absolutely phenomenal revelation into the Godliness.

While mankind has always envisioned Adam to be male in nature, this coded revelation reveals the core aspect of Adam's creativity is intrinsically female. Interestingly, there is scientific theory that suggests all fetuses begin their journey in this dimension as "female." In other words, some scientists are stating each male entering this world was feminine—first.

The code's insight into creation is remarkable. Just like the Mother that contains all of the potential for her creations (i.e., the female eggs inherent within her being at birth), we are being shown inherent within the "total Adam" (HaAdam) is every possible potential for any and all creative outcomes for mankind. Because of this, Adam is the "Mother" of its infinite creations.

Because the names "Elohim" and "Adam" both contain the word, "Mother," another extraordinary revelation rises: *The Elohim and Adam are creative entities that contain "male aspects of self-aware creative spirit" (reflected through the "Aleph" in their names), together with "female aspects of creative birth in matter" (reflected through the "Final Mem" in their names).* The "One" cannot be without the "two." God is female energy consciousness that contains the male spirit. In other words, creation is the outcome of the "spirit" (male) being experienced in a dimension of "matter" (female).

Like an extraordinary Mother, both the Elohim and Adam give life to new creations and realities. We are being shown the Elohim and Adam are not solely male in nature, as many have perceived, but intrinsically female in nature. The Godliness is the "Mother of Creation." God is not a "he." God is not a "she." God "is" everything, and God "is what it is." God is: *Consciousness in matter.*

The Elohim and Adam are two extraordinarily powerful creative programs and entities that manifest life. The Elohim and Adam are the "Mothers of Creation," and the energy consciousness that gives birth to infinite realities. This changes everything we have ever believed Adam and his God to be.

"Let Us Make Man in Our Image"

Your consciousness is energy, your intentions are energy, your thoughts are energy, and your energy never ceases to exist. Your essence will forever be felt and known in the Godliness. As you become aware of your desire to create, as you recognize your need for creative freedom and expression, know that you are very much like the Creator. You are probably saying, "How can I be like God? This can't be possible." Nothing is further from the truth.

> How can I choose the me
> that I have never experienced?
> How can I experience that
> which I have never known?
> By becoming that which I Am.
> Therefore, I Am what I Am.
> Through Adam, I become.

Hebraic Text: Bereshit 1:26

וַיֹּאמֶר אֱלֹהִים נַעֲשֶׂה אָדָם בְּצַלְמֵנוּ כִּדְמוּתֵנוּ וְיִרְדּוּ בִדְגַת הַיָּם וּבְעוֹף הַשָּׁמַיִם וּבַבְּהֵמָה וּבְכָל־הָאָרֶץ וּבְכָל־הָרֶמֶשׂ הָרֹמֵשׂ עַל־הָאָרֶץ

English Translation: Genesis 1:26

And God said, "Let us make man in our image, in our likeness, and let them rule over the fish of the sea and the birds of the air, over the livestock, over all the Earth, and over all the creatures that move along the ground."

Talmudic Explanation: Genesis 1:26

> Note: In the statement "Let 'us' make man in 'our' image," Rabbi Yitzhaki was troubled by the words "us" and "our." Both words reflect pluralism and oppose the perception of a "singular" God. Because man has always perceived God to be a singular male-like being, Rabbi Yitzhaki asks the question, "Why is the Godliness describing itself as a plurality?"

"We learn from this statement that God shows his humble nature so man can learn from God's actions. God made man in the image of his Angels; but prior to creating Adam, God asked his Angels whether or not he should create Adam.

"And while God did not need the Angel's help in creating Adam, God asked the Angel's permission only to prevent the Angels from becoming jealous of Adam. And because Adam looked similar to the Angels, Adam was made in the likeness of the Angels—but created by God."

Rabbi Shlomo Yitzhaki Rashi, Twelfth Century
Author of the First Comprehensive Commentary
on the Talmud and Hebrew Bible

 ### *The Genesis Code: Genesis 1:26*

And the Elohim said, "Let 'us' make man in 'our' image and in our likeness, and he will go down into his domain of reality. When the Elohim refers to 'us' in this statement, man is being told God is not a singular being, but an entity of pluralities.

The Elohim is the "many energies that create." It is many different vibratory aspects of creativity and, through the many energies, creative programs are formulated through which realities manifest.

"Adam" (mankind) was an imagined potential and reflection of the Elohim's perception. As man's creative consciousness evolves, this dimension, including the earth and all that is nature, is greatly affected by our choices. Man is a powerful creative force in this reality, and the ruler of his domain.

We exist within the "Elohim" (the God of this Universe), and through the God/Man relationship man evolves. "Adam" (man) is not only a facet of the Elohim's many aspects, but a creative entity with extraordinary power made in the image of the Elohim—the many energies that create.

The Genesis Code reveals you are a unique and miraculous projection of the Elohim being expressed in and through light. You were once pure potential, but you "became" within a part of the Godliness and now exist within one of the Elohim's many dimensions of self.

Your consciousness is participating on a planet called earth. What you do with your energy consciousness, how you treat yourself and others, what you believe to be truth, will have a tremendous effect on your reality and domain. The Elohim is revealing a life-changing secret: *You are a powerful creative being and master of your own reality.* Right now, as you hold this book in your hand, your awareness is increasing. You are becoming; and through your becoming, God is becoming.

THE DIMENSIONS OF ADAM

All That Is:
The nothingness and the everything before the beginning.

1ST DIMENSION: THE HIDDEN ALEPH

The "point" between everything and nothing. The intention of a particular desire being energized into a prime cause that projected Bereshit—a dimension of duality.

2ND DIMENSION: BERESHIT (DUALITY)
Note: Seven dimensions prevail within Bereshit

Bereshit's 1st Dimension (A; א)

The Hidden Aleph (the power of the IS) embedded in Bereshit (the house; new dimension).

Bereshit's 2nd Dimension (AB; אב)

Father; the Hidden Aleph combined with the (B) "Bet" in (B)ereshit means "Father."

Bereshit's 3rd Dimension (BARA; ברא)

Duality vibrating into a complex singularity.

Bereshit's 4th Dimension (ROSH; ראש)

Head; Interchanging energy and programmed creativity.

Bereshit's 5th Dimension (ESH; אש)

Pure energy.

Bereshit's 6th Dimension (SHI; שי)

Gift; Transformative seed.

Bereshit's 7th Dimension (BAT; בת)

Daughter; The first and last letter of (B)ereshi(t) when combined means "Daughter."

THE REVELATION OF THE 2ND DIMENSION:

The "Daughter" of the "Father" vibrates into the "Mother" and the level of Godliness known as the "Elohim"—the God of the Adamic Universe and the God of Adam.

3ʳᴰ DIMENSION: THE ELOHIM (GOD OF ADAM)   **Note: Seven dimensions prevail within the Elohim**
Elohim's 1ˢᵗ Dimension (A; א)
The Hidden Aleph realized; The first letter of the (E)lohim.
Elohim's 2nd Dimension (EL; אל)
The Prime Cause (Aleph) desires to learn, teach, and evolve.
Elohim's 3rd Dimension (ELAH; אלה)
Into many things; Undefined potential.
Elohim's 4th Dimension (LAH; לה)
To her; To become "life."
Elohim's 5th Dimension (HAYAM; הים)
Sea of all potential consciousness.
Elohim's 6th Dimension (YAM; ים)
Into a sea of self-aware consciousness.
Elohim's 7th Dimension (EM; אם)
Mother; The Aleph and the Mem, the first and last letter of the (E)lohi(m) and (A)da(m), mean "Mother."
THE REVELATION OF THE 3ᴿᴰ DIMENSION:
The Elohim vibrates the reality of Adam.
4ᵀᴴ DIMENSION: ADAM REALIZED IN LIGHT
The Elohim and Adam both represent the "Mother" that is the creative force of life in the dimension of man. Like the Elohim, Adam also contains seven (7) dimensions. However, Adam's dimensions are represented through the "seven" days of formation in Genesis—the last being "Shabbat" (Sabbath). Shabbat represents the transformative energy of the "Daughter of Bereshit" being realized in the Elohim's 2nd dimension of evolution and energized in Adam's 7th dimension (Shabbat/Sabbath).

CHAPTER 6

The Highest Level of Man: Moses

When we think of the Torah's origins, our minds take us to an era long ago when a prophet named Moses walked the face of this earth. Even though Moses died several thousand years ago, his life's work, the Five Books of Moses, is rising again, projecting a new level of understanding through a hidden code and language.

When most think of Moses, they recall his legacy, the Ten Commandments. However, Moses was much more than a prophet who left ten moral laws for a generation of people. He walked the earth in a higher level of awareness and was the one who would gift humanity with the Elohim's stories of enlightenment.

Prior to Moses, there was no Torah/Bible. No one knows how long it took Moses to write the Five Books of Moses, but it is widely believed this doctrine of genius was written by Moses, alone, during his lifetime. While the powerful Egyptians would leave their legacy through extraordinary monuments of stone, Moses' legacy would be left through black ink on parchment.

This one man's journey would change the world and revolutionize the way humanity perceives God and creation. When Moses faced God on Mount Sinai, many fail to understand the metaphysical significance of this event and the consequences it would have on human consciousness. Moses not only faced an entity of fire, energy, and intelligence; he actually absorbed and integrated the energy of the Elohim into his vibratory essence and being. On top of a mountain long ago, this one man became the personification of human potential in the Adamic reality.

 ### English Translation: Exodus 34:30

When Aaron and all of the people of Israel saw Moses, behold the skin of his face shown; and they were afraid to come closer to him.

When the Torah references the "brightness that exuded from Moses", this is a direct reference to Moses' vibratory force. Through this statement, the Godliness is explaining how Moses' energy consciousness had changed after his encounter with Jehovah. His "energy" (light) was exuding from the "inside out." Human beings normally "reflect light," they do not "project light." However, this was not the case with Moses, for he became much more than reflective light. His light was internal and projected outward from the core of his being.

When new energy is absorbed into one's being, there is a change at the molecular level. Moses now exuded creative power and wisdom, and his consciousness was forever transformed. After facing the Godliness, his internal vibratory frequency altered and, as a result of this transformation, his matter consciousness also changed. His physical appearance was affected by the energy consciousness he now energized and lived through. He had absorbed the energy of the Elohim, and his consciousness vibrated at a different pace.

Moses had absorbed the energy of the Elohim. He now projected his inner light, and his people could no longer look upon him.

Because of Moses, man would be led closer to the Godliness than ever before. More so than any other man, Moses achieved ultimate enlightenment. Moses was not only a mysterious man, but a mastermind. This is apparent through his astonishing writings that reveal his understanding of human emotions and endeavors, together with the ever so complex metaphysical world. The Torah's genius is not only extraordinary, but mind-boggling. Moses' legacy is now in our hands, and a new generation of Adam will be faced with the choice to accept the Torah's highest level of enlightenment.

The very idea of one man creating, and then embedding, a cryptic language of the highest enlightenment within another level of language (the stories of the Torah) is a feat we believe is not only improbable, but absolutely impossible. Therefore, the real question becomes, "How and why did Moses embed this sophisticated code of enlightenment within the Torah's outer stories?" To find this answer, we must go back to deeply understand the story of Moses, the matrix he lived through, the dimension of Sinai, and his unique journey that led to ultimate enlightenment.

*From the Waters
I Drew Him Forth*

Through the revelations of the Torah's Genesis Code, it is obvious Moses was far more than an ordinary man. But, if not ordinary, what was Moses? You are about to discover the true Moses, a man that has never been deeply understood. Together, we will unravel the mystery surrounding this phenomenal prophet, explore his metaphysical journey, and come to know who he truly was.

Moses lived approximately 3,500 years ago in a time when the Hebrews lived and died in bondage under Egyptian rule. This was the era of the master and the slave, energized through the Egyptian Matrix that empowered ultimate hierarchy.

The Egyptians held the primary position of power and control. However, this would not stop the Pharaoh from tormenting the Hebrew slaves. The Hebrews' numbers had grown strong, and the Pharaoh decreed all newborn Hebrew males be put to death and thrown into the mighty river.

Caught in the middle was a young Hebrew woman who had given birth to a male son. Obviously, she was haunted with the ominous threat of her son's looming death. Desperate, she did everything possible to hide her young baby from the murderous Egyptians, but she could not hide him forever. Out of options and out of time, the Hebrew woman placed her child in an ark by the reeds on the bank of a river hoping someone could somehow save the life of her child.

Ironically, the baby boy wouldn't be saved by an ordinary Egyptian, nor would he be rescued by another Hebrew slave. The baby boy would be pulled out of the waters by an Egyptian princess who would keep him for her own. Within the great paradox of creation, this young Hebrew slave would now be groomed by a female of royal blood.

After being weaned, this young Hebrew boy was taken into the palace of his people's oppressors where he would be given a name. This, too, would be ironic. The Egyptian princess would call the young child "Moshe" (Moses) because she "drew him out of the waters." The metaphysical realms were in play.

Hebraic Text: Shemos 2:10

וַיִּגְדַּל הַיֶּלֶד וַתְּבִאֵהוּ לְבַת פַּרְעֹה וַיְהִי לָהּ לְבֵן וַתִּקְרָא שְׁמוֹ מֹשֶׁה וַתֹּאמֶר כִּי מִן הַמַּיִם מְשִׁיתִהוּ

English Translation: Exodus 2:10

"And the child grew, and she brought him unto Pharaoh's daughter, and he became her son. And she called his name Moses, and said: 'Because I drew him out of the water.'"

The Genesis Code: Exodus 2:10

After the child had been weaned, he was brought to the princess who was the daughter of Pharaoh. Ironically, this child had been born into non-existence—into a life of slavery and death. Now, however, the child was being led into the heart of Egypt where he would become a prince. And the unnamed princess would call him "Moshe" because she said, "From the waters of destruction, from the formless chaos, from the core of Hashomayim—the center of creative consciousness—I drew him forth."

As Moses grew into a man, he was shown the secret arts of Egypt—their metaphysical powers and magic—together with all of the trappings and power that accompanies a royal crown. As an Egyptian prince, Moses was imbued with the idea that the Pharaoh and his family were divine.

From the moment Moses entered our world, his energy consciousness reflected a paradox in this dimension. In retrospect, as one looks back upon his life experiences, the paradox that was Moses continues to reveal itself. Moses had been born into slavery, yet he would become the greatest prophet to have ever lived. He would gift humanity with God's greatest enlightenment—the knowledge that man is an extraordinary facet of the Godliness and an ever-evolving cosmic creator.

Moses had been born at the bottom of the pyramid, into death and non-existence; yet he would rise to become a prince of Egypt. He had been born into slavery, yet he gave life and freedom to the world. For his people, he had sacrificed his life on earth and was also willing to sacrifice his eternal memory within the Godliness to save his people. He was a man willing to give up everything, even his very existence, to advance his people in this creation.

Through The Genesis Code, deeper insight prevails within, "From the waters I drew you forth." Within this statement, a hidden set of words are brought to our awareness: *Chaos, void, and potential.* A single point of "potential" (Moses) was drawn out of the "chaos and void of potential" (Hashomayim's HaAdam) to express its essence in a reality of matter, "Earth" (the physical Aretz), that would enlighten all of "humanity" (Adam).

A portal had opened within the Egyptian Matrix and the metaphysical realms were in play. Moses was seeded in this dimension and a new aspect of human potential would be watered by the matrix of Egypt. Time would play its course, and this young Hebrew child would grow into a prince of Egypt and one day become the prophet that would lead the Hebrew slaves to freedom.

Moses would soon challenge the very consciousness that saved his life, gave him his name, status, and power through the trappings of royalty. He had been groomed to become an extraordinary man. Through the paradox of Moses', his essence would soon be realized in human reality, and he would rise to challenge the core of the Egyptian Matrix.

Moses did everything possible to break the matrix that suppressed his people. He was a spiritual warrior and lived to change humanity's minds and belief systems. Know, however, his journey to enlighten mankind is not yet over. In fact, it has only begun. We have yet to discover the full extent of the enlightenment his writings hold.

The "Unnamed" Egyptian Princess

"Moshe" was a name given to a Hebrew baby boy by an unnamed Egyptian princess. Interestingly, the Torah places great emphasis on the names of those who impact humanity. The giving of names is profoundly important, for the names, themselves, contain code and significant insight into the consciousness being referenced and its relationship to the creative process of becoming.

For example, Abraham's name was changed from Avrom to Abraham by the Elohim; Abraham's son, Isaac, was named by the angels; Jacob's subsequent name, Israel, was given by the "Ish" (God incarnate); and with Moshe, an unknown and unnamed Egyptian princess—not his father or mother, or even another Hebrew—named the Hebrew boy.

The Torah takes great pains to reveal the giving of Moshe's name because this child would have a huge effect on the world—not only throughout his life, but forever more. In other words, this one particular aspect of Adamic Consciousness would change the world. While we clearly understand this unnamed princess drew Moshe out of the waters, many questions surround this particular event.

In the case of "Moshe" (Moses), the Torah focuses solely on his name, and purposefully denies humanity from knowing the true name of the Egyptian princess who took Moshe in as her own. This fact, in itself, leads to another revelation of enlightenment: *The "unnamed" Egyptian princess would be remembered not for her true "name," but for her "greatest act"—saving the Hebrew child and giving him his name. She would be remembered for her actions—not for her Egyptian name.* Because of her choices, the unnamed Egyptian princess drastically changed the world and the path of mankind. Her name would be represented through Moshe's name, "From the waters I drew you forth."

The Genesis Code reveals that Moses was drawn out of God's sea of potential by the princess of Egypt. What is fascinating, the Elohim projected Moses into Egypt and, paradoxically, this Hebrew child and unique aspect of potential was pulled out of the waters and placed at the core of Egyptian royalty and governance.

The Elohim had projected the highest level of man out of Hashomayim's HaAdam. Yet, it was the "unnamed Egyptian princess" who drew Moses out of Hashomayim and into the core of Egypt's empire. She was Egypt, therefore, it was the feminine aspect of creative consciousness that pulled the potential of transformation from the waters of destruction and gave this potential life.

The mere fact that Moses was drawn out of the "waters" (consciousness) by an Egyptian princess is remarkable. In truth, the Egyptian princess—the feminine aspect at the top of the Egyptian pyramid—is the metaphorical aspect that enabled Moses to move from a state of "non-existence" (slavery and death) into a state of "existence" (freedom and enlightenment).

It was the "unnamed Egyptian princess" (the feminine aspect representing royalty and Egypt) that brought Moses to the very core of the Egyptian Matrix. A profound paradox rises. It would be the feminine aspect of Egyptian consciousness that gave birth to its own destruction. From a metaphysical point of view, the dominant creative feminine aspect of the times gave Moses an opportunity to overthrow and topple the very consciousness that drew him forth—out of the sea of consciousness.

Also fascinating, when the young Hebrew boy was named, his name was given by an aspect of Egyptian consciousness—the unnamed Egyptian princess. Even though it was known the young child was a Hebrew slave, the Hebrew would be transformed into an Egyptian prince. Therefore, his name was not a reflection of his character or culture, but a reflection of his salvation *"from the waters I drew him forth."*

The giving of Moshe's name reveals "the selective process" in the choosing of his particular potential. His name was not given to reflect the young boy's character, but given to show "how the Egyptian princess saved him" by drawing the consciousness of Moshe out of the "waters" (consciousness) of Hashomayim.

It was Egyptian royalty who pulled Moses from the waters and placed him at the top of the Egyptian Matrix where he was given status, power, and control. Yet, as his life continued to unfold, Moses would rise to destroy the powerful Egyptian Matrix that enslaved him, saved him, and gave him life. From a metaphysical point of view, another question rises, "Why would an Egyptian draw this potentially dangerous potential out of Hashomayim? Why was it an Egyptian—not a Hebrew—who drew Moses' consciousness forth, out of the waters of

Hashomayim, to free the Hebrew slaves and threaten Egypt's way of life?"

To understand the deeper significance within this paradox, we must go back to the time of Abraham. God told Abraham his children would one day inherit the land of Canaan, but there was a condition: *God's children would first be slaves to Egypt for 410 years.* And so it was. These events did come to pass and the Hebrews became bound to the Egyptian Matrix.

Bound to Egypt's matrix of slavery, the collective consciousness of the Hebrew slaves was vibrating the "cry for freedom." This cry was vibrating at extreme rates—penetrating the Elohim's Hashomayim. The "spirit of the Hebrew slaves" (the Aretz) was probing HaAdam for a potential reality that would release the slaves from their pain and bondage to Egypt.

Divine intervention would soon become a reality for the Hebrew slaves, and a new doorway would manifest making it possible for the Hebrews to escape. Moses, in the far-off wilderness, would soon be led to the bush that burned and called to meet with God. Creation's story was unfolding in a dimension of time.

As we look back upon these events, we can see the trials and tribulations surrounding Moses and his people were a probable future within Hashomayim's HaAdam long before their consciousness was projected into our world. God had spoken, and through the Israelites' experience of pain and suffering, the Children of Israel would gain wisdom and inherit the land promised to them.

Regardless of their future freedom and power, the Israelites would never forget their many years of slavery. Through torture, pain, suffering, and sorrow, the Israelites would fully understand the effects of a narrow and limited consciousness. The master/slave experience was now embedded in the Israelites' DNA—its vibration forever flowing through their blood and in the veins of their offspring. Because of their past, future generations would carry a deep appreciation and respect for life and freedom.

The destiny of the Israelites was set in motion from "within" the powerful Egyptian Matrix.

Because Egyptian consciousness was the superpower and dominant belief system of the time, the Israelites' future was put into play the moment the unnamed princess drew Moshe out of the waters and "into the core of royalty and power." Destiny for the Hebrews began "within" the Egyptian Matrix, and this revelation teaches us: *Human "exodus and transformation" will always begin from "within the matrix of consciousness" we are bound to.* Therefore, any scenario, transformation, or new reality will always begin within the system and matrix man lives in. This, you should know, applies not only to the man of the past, but to the man of today.

Entering No Man's Land

As a young man, Egypt was all Moses ever knew. Immersed in the trappings of royalty and the Egyptian way of life, he thrived for many years. He became a leader and had learned essential qualities to support his position. He was young, strong, and highly accepted within the Pharaoh's inner circle. Yet, as Moses matured, he began to realize something was wrong. It would not be long before the prince's eyes were opened to the reality of Egyptian consciousness.

On one particular day, everything would change for Moses when he happened upon an Egyptian taskmaster brutally beating a Hebrew slave. As the Prince of Egypt looked into the eyes of the dying man, his heart was filled with both anger and compassion. Flooded with emotions, Moses would find his hands covered in blood as he fought to protect the life of a Hebrew. When it was all over, Moses had committed the ultimate crime. He had murdered an Egyptian taskmaster and saved the life of a lowly slave.

In a split second, Moses came to realize who he was deep within. His consciousness immediately transformed and his outer world would soon follow the lead of his inner truth. His days as a prince were over, and he fled into the desert where he would live for the next forty years.

Moses' life in the palace was brief.
His consciousness was on the move—
his Godliness was transforming.

Moses had fled Egypt and entered no man's land. But, on a metaphysical level, what was Moses fleeing from? "Egypt" is a translation for the Hebrew name, "Mitzraim," which The Genesis Code reveals is "narrow consciousness." But how could the greatest civilization of the time be described as a consciousness that was narrow and limited?

The Egyptians believed their many gods had power over their lives, when just the opposite is true. Furthermore, the Egyptians were engrossed in the philosophy that man connected to God only upon death. They believed life "began" upon the soul's transition into an alternate dimension upon death. Egyptians were enamored with the energy of the crypt, the underworld, and the afterlife. They lived their lives consumed with the energy of death and a world that waited for them on the other side.

This level of consciousness was limited and lacked awareness. The Egyptians failed to realize the following: *This life, this experience, this world is God becoming. What is important is here—right now. What matters is what happens in the dimension of matter—not in the Heavens above or in an underworld below. Life is God. Life allows God to feel. Adam allows God to love. Nothing is more important to the Godliness. Nothing.*

Through man, God experiences the entire spectrum of human emotions—from unconditional love to the evil within. Good and evil are potentials within man because good and evil are potentials within God. While there are those who believe there is "God" and God's opponent, "Satan," humanity must deeply know and believe the following: *There is only God, and the infinite extremes of potential within the Godliness.* It is man's choice, just as it is God's choice, to embrace one aspect of duality over another—to embrace the vibration of fear or to embrace the vibration of love. Both are potentials within the Godliness through which realities are manifest.

It is our awareness and understanding of creation that influences man's choices. Through an elevated consciousness, man can overcome fear—a powerful emotion that vibrates an energy that works to limit enlightenment. Know there are different types of fear, such as the fear intended for survival purposes. This is a productive state of fear that warns us not to enter a lion's den. This fear keeps us alive.

However, there is another type of fear which manifests a slow and agonizing death. This state of fear vibrates an extremely narrow level of consciousness and affects human reality in negative ways. It makes one afraid of the next moment. It convinces us to stop believing in ourselves. It riddles us with stress, anxiety, and depression. It prods us to fear our future reality. This continuous "background fear" becomes a dangerous undercurrent that colors everything that enters its vibratory realm. In other words, this negative, continuous fear touches everything in the person's life—both consciously and subconsciously.

Man is much more powerful than he believes himself to be. We will now offer some examples of the powerful affect human consciousness has on man's reality. If man fiercely believes in an entity that has the power to haunt and torment his reality, such as "Satan," he will unknowingly create a sentient form of consciousness that reflects this belief. If man deeply believes an evil entity and place of punishment exists—such as Satan and Hell—this reality may very well manifest for those who imagine and project this possible scenario and reality.

What must be realized is the following: *Without the extremes—love and fear—deep and passionate emotions could never be realized.* Fear empowers hate. Hate creates wars. Yet, fear is the stepping stone to love and the highest emotion of all—unconditional love. It creates the potential for mankind to rise up and climb mountains of enlightenment. This is true knowledge and that which the Egyptians, and most of humanity, has failed to understand.

To create and enter the higher realms of self—to move out of narrow consciousness—you must know it is "you" that creates your reality in this dimension and also in the next. You must leave your pre-conceptions behind and enter no-man's land as Moses did.

Because the Egyptians were so enamored with passing over to an alternate reality, they devoted their lives to worshipping that which exists beyond the here and now. Their consciousness was far removed from the present moment and focused on a distant and future reality in another dimension.

As the Egyptians' enslaved the Hebrews, they unknowingly enslaved themselves through their chosen aspect of consciousness. Their awareness was limited, and they did not believe the Godliness exists in and through all things—including those they so eagerly enslaved.

To the Egyptians, the Hebrew slaves were certainly not a facet of the Godliness or considered equal to the Egyptians by any measure. The Hebrew people were denied rights, terribly abused, and were forced to serve the Egyptians to forego torture and death. To the Egyptians, God was "out there" and in "some other place" and certainly not connected to a lowly Hebrew slave.

Any belief system that fails to recognize that the Godliness lives through all men is extremely limited and narrow. In the end, the Egyptians failed to make a deep connection with the Godliness that is here—right now. The Egyptians failed to recognize the truth of the Godliness—in this life and in the next.

A pattern prevailed throughout the life of Moses. He seemed to forever move from one matrix of consciousness to another.

Through understanding the code's inner message of Mitzraim, we learn Moses' exodus out of Egypt was a manifestation resulting from a "transformation of consciousness." Unbeknownst to Moses at the time, he was moving out of narrow consciousness into an extraordinarily expansive consciousness—a journey that would take him many more years, even decades, to fully understand and realize.

Looking back, a pattern emerges. Since a young child, Moses had moved out of one matrix of consciousness into another. As a baby, he was catapulted out of the consciousness of the Hebrew slaves into the consciousness of Egyptian royalty and divinity. Now, he was to move again and leave the only place he had ever known.

Forced to flee Egypt, his identity had been stripped away. He was no longer a prince and, of course, he had no idea who he would become. He now walked in a desert-like nothingness, and his consciousness was in the wilderness of the unknown for many decades. There, in the wilderness, it is said he became a king of many tribes and fought many battles. In the barren-like desert, Moses was becoming a new light.

Moses and the Mountain of God

Removed from the powerful Egyptian Matrix, Moses had made a life for himself in the desert. As the years passed, Moses came to be a simple shepherd and, one day, his flock of lambs led him to an amazing revelation. Moses came upon something extraordinary—something he could hardly believe. He came upon a bush that burned—yet the bush wasn't burning.

Through Exodus 3:1, we learn of the message within the Hebrew word, "Chorebah," translated in English as "Horeb," which means: *Mountain of God.* There, at the Mountain of God, Moses faced the fiery energy of the Elohim. The coded revelation within Chorebah provides extraordinary insight into the physical and metaphysical environment that led to this strange encounter between God and man.

What is mostly unknown is the "Mountain of God" represents a "powerful paradox in man's dimension." Here, Moses would face a choice: *He was given the opportunity to look into, and absorb, the fiery essence of the Elohim.* At the Mountain of God, a portal opened before Moses. The question was, "Would Moses' consciousness move through this portal of transformation where enlightenment prevailed?"

Hebraic Text: Shemos 3:1

וּמֹשֶׁה הָיָה רֹעֶה אֶת צֹאן יִתְרוֹ חֹתְנוֹ כֹּהֵן מִדְיָן וַיִּנְהַג אֶת הַצֹּאן אַחַר הַמִּדְבָּר וַיָּבֹא אֶל הַר הָאֱלֹהִים חֹרֵבָה

English Translation: Exodus 3:1

Now Moses was tending the flock of Jethro his father-in-law, the Priest of Midian, and he led the flock to the far side of the desert and came to "Horeb" (Chorebah), the Mountain of God.

The Genesis Code: Exodus 3:1

Moses was tending to his father-in-law's flock. And he led this flock towards the desert where he came to "Chorebah," the Mountain of the "Elohim" (God) that was a place of desolation.

The Mountain of the Elohim is a metaphor. When climbing a mountain of revelation, inherent within the "revelation" is the powerful aspect of "destruction." Mankind cannot evolve into a higher level of Godliness unless a destructive force is put upon the existing matrix that holds man back from his potential.

A new level of God consciousness would soon be revealed to mankind through the Torah. Therefore, the existing matrix, powered by a particular level of human consciousness, must first be destroyed before new enlightenment could flow into man's awareness.

The following table outlines the deeper message within the ancient Hebrew name, "Chorebah," which has been translated as "Horeb" in the English Bible. As you can see from the table below, The Genesis Code reveals three primary words that offer insight into the Mountain of God: *Desolation, sword, and in her.*

The Secret of CHOREBAH (Horeb)			
HEBREW	LETTERS AND CODE	VALUE	CODED MEANING
CHOREBAH חרבה	CHET; RESH; BET; HEY חט ריש בית הי	215	Desolation
CHEREV חרב	CHET; RESH; BET חט ריש בית	210	Sword
BAH בה	BET; HEY בית הי	7	In her

CHOREBAH = Desolation; Destruction

At the core of the Elohim, life cannot survive. It is a place of destruction and desolation. Yet, its powerful energy is also the very essence that gives life.

The core of the Elohim is fire—a powerful source of energy beyond our mind's comprehension. Its energy force far exceeds that of the sun which is, in itself, destructive and a place of desolation. Life cannot survive at the sun's core. However, the energy emitted from the sun's core is the very power that also gives life to our world. We are being shown the following insight: *As Moses neared the Mountain of God, he was moving towards a portal that would lead him to an alternate dimension of self—the place where his highest potential would be realized.* Moses was nearing the Godliness that was truly him.

CHEREV = Sword

The sword is an instrument of destruction, and this metaphor reflects a point of extreme danger within the metaphysical realms of creation.

The presence of the sword signifies impending danger on a metaphysical level. As Moses neared the Mountain of God, his consciousness began to elevate towards a new level of enlightenment. With this transition, the potential for paramount destruction was also manifesting through this mountain of desolation. The metaphor within this coded message applies to singular consciousness, as well as mass consciousness. A singular consciousness, as well as a collective consciousness, can become exposed to suffering when new aspects of enlightenment are on man's horizon. Enlightenment usually comes with a price, and desolation is its wake.

BAH = In Her

Because the feminine aspect is present within the word, "Chorebah," we are being shown a "creative element" (the feminine aspect) was not only present, but active.

Because the feminine aspect of creativity is present at the Mountain of God, we know an existing aspect of human consciousness will be destroyed making way for the birth of another. The Mountain of God was a place of revelation. However, in the revelation was an impending warning: *A destructive force would alter the existing matrix of Egypt.* The consciousness of Egypt would fall through destruction, and the Israelites would soon face the potential of becoming a new level of man through a new level of creativity within the Godliness.

The Burning Bush

As Moses neared the Mountain of God, he came to face a bush burning with fiery energy. This bush, however, failed to be harmed or consumed by the energy that raged within it. Obviously, Moses was stunned as he observed this amazing sight, and he looked deeper to see "the cause" as to "why" the bush burned and never turned to ash.

 ### Hebraic Text: Shemos 3:2-6

וַיֵּרָא מַלְאַךְ יְהוָה אֵלָיו בְּלַבַּת אֵשׁ מִתּוֹךְ הַסְּנֶה וַיַּרְא וְהִנֵּה הַסְּנֶה בֹּעֵר בָּאֵשׁ וְהַסְּנֶה אֵינֶנּוּ אֻכָּל: וַיֹּאמֶר מֹשֶׁה אָסֻרָה נָּא וְאֶרְאֶה אֶת הַמַּרְאֶה הַגָּדֹל הַזֶּה מַדּוּעַ לֹא יִבְעַר הַסְּנֶה: וַיַּרְא יְהוָה כִּי סָר לִרְאוֹת וַיִּקְרָא אֵלָיו אֱלֹהִים מִתּוֹךְ הַסְּנֶה וַיֹּאמֶר מֹשֶׁה מֹשֶׁה וַיֹּאמֶר הִנֵּנִי: וַיֹּאמֶר אַל תִּקְרַב הֲלֹם שַׁל נְעָלֶיךָ מֵעַל רַגְלֶיךָ כִּי הַמָּקוֹם אֲשֶׁר אַתָּה עוֹמֵד עָלָיו אַדְמַת קֹדֶשׁ הוּא: וַיֹּאמֶר אָנֹכִי אֱלֹהֵי אָבִיךָ אֱלֹהֵי אַבְרָהָם אֱלֹהֵי יִצְחָק וֵאלֹהֵי יַעֲקֹב וַיַּסְתֵּר מֹשֶׁה פָּנָיו כִּי יָרֵא מֵהַבִּיט אֶל הָאֱלֹהִים

English Translation: Exodus 3:2-6

And the angel of the Lord appeared unto him in a flame of fire from within the bush, and the bush was not consumed. And Moses said: "I will turn aside now, and see this great sight—why the bush does not burn up."

And when the Lord saw that Moses turned to look, God called unto him out of the midst of the bush, and said: "Moses, Moses." And Moses said: "Here am I."

And God said: "Do not come any closer. Take off your sandals, for the place where you stand is holy ground." And then God said: "I am the God of thy Father, the God of Abraham, the God of Isaac, and the God of Jacob."

And Moses hid his face; for he was afraid to look upon God.

The Genesis Code: Exodus 3:2-6

Jehovah's messenger appeared to Moses in a flame of fire from the midst of the bush. Moses saw the bush was burning with "fire" (energy) and that the bush was not consumed, or destroyed, by the flames. Moses was not interested in the messenger, but why the bush did not burn.

Moses desired to know "the cause" within the Burning Bush. He wanted to know why the bush wouldn't burn and be consumed by the fire. And Moses said to Jehovah's messenger, "Please allow me to look deeper into the cause of this great sight so I may know why the bush does not burn." It was then Jehovah saw that Moses turned to look closer into the energy that flamed.

What is fascinating is that the messenger is no longer mentioned, or referred to, in this story again. Now that the Godliness was made aware of Moses' desire to know the truth hidden within the energy that flamed, the messenger's role was apparently over.

Suddenly, the Elohim communicates to Moses from the core of the "sneh" (bush). Through the crackling of the energy that flamed, vibrations formed through this act of nature, and the Elohim called to him, "Moses, Moses." And Moses said, "Here am I."

And the Elohim said, "Do not come any closer to the vibration for it will surely strike you down. You must first remove your shackles so you can transform your vibratory energy force. Realize the 'place where you stand now' is the dimension that supports you in the moment and where your creative power is."

And then the Elohim said, "I am the Elohai of thy Father, the Elohai of Abraham, the Elohai of Isaac, and the Elohai of Jacob." Interestingly, the name, "Elohim," is not referenced in this statement, but the name, "Elohia," is.

Through the alteration of the name, "Elohim," to "Elohia," we are given deeper insight into the God/Man relationship. "Elohia" is a variable of the Elohim that was expressing, "I am the God that exists through limitation and particular relationships with mankind. Through my relationship with a particular singularity of human consciousness, the Godliness is defined." And at this, Moses hid his face, as he suddenly became frightened of the Elohim's power and no longer looked upon the Godliness.

<u>JEHOVAH'S MESSENGER = Angel</u>

While the messenger was the first to appear to Moses within the Burning Bush, Moses was far more interested in the bush that burned than the angel, itself.

The angel that appeared in the Burning Bush manifested at the bush's very core. It appeared through the flames that rose from the bush, and through the flames the angel took on form. One assumes an angel does not have free choice, so the angel's role was that of Jehovah's messenger. The angel did exactly what it was ordered to do. Within the Torah, there is no information as to the message of the angel, itself, or what affect the angel's sudden and brief appearance was meant to have on Moses.

 ### <u>SNEH = Burning Bush</u>

The Burning Bush is a powerful metaphor that symbolizes the ability for matter to absorb the high-level energy of the Elohim and remain intact.

Just as the Burning Bush absorbed the fiery energy of the Godliness and kept its physical structure, the Elohim was showing Moses that "man" (a form of matter) possesses the ability to "absorb the fiery energy" of the Elohim and remain intact. Moses was given a powerful message through the example of the bush that burned: *Man can absorb higher vibrations of fiery energy without being destroyed.*

Human consciousness lives through physical bodies intrinsic with matter. Yet, prior to achieving enlightenment, the human body must transform at the cellular level. This physical transformation makes it possible for human matter to absorb "higher vibrational fields of energy" (enlightenment). The

Elohim was reassuring Moses, "Even though enlightenment can be dangerous, and comes with a price, you, Moses, will survive this enlightenment, as reflected through the Burning Bush." This was the true message of the bush that burned, yet remained intact.

 ## The Elohim Calls to Moses

Through the "crackling of the fire," the Elohim spoke to Moses—a man who reflected a paradox in this world.

The Elohim did not speak, in words, to Moses. The Elohim's voice was projected through the crackling of the flames. This is a prime example of how the Elohim speaks to man through vibrations manifest through nature. Again, the Elohim's energy is far too powerful for man to face directly. Because of this, the Elohim speaks to man through its vibratory essence made possible through man's world of matter.

What is interesting, when the Elohim called to Moses, he called his name out twice, "Moses, Moses." Yet, another question rises, "Why didn't the Elohim call out his name just once?" God was speaking, certainly Moses was listening. Again, Moses was a paradox. There was Moses, the Egyptian, and Moses, the Israelite; Moses, the humble man, and Moses, the warrior; Moses, the Prince of Egypt, and Moses, the shepherd in the desert. Moses would contain the essence of the Elohim and the essence of man. A revelation rises: *Moses was the hook between the Elohim and humanity. He was the bridge that connected the Elohim to mankind.*

When the Elohim called out to him, "Moses, Moses" he was calling out to mankind and the duality within human nature. The Godliness was calling out to the Moses of the moment and to the Moses of the future. Through his transformed consciousness, Moses would nourish the potential within humanity achieved through the paradox of choices that make it possible for realities to be realized.

This call from the Elohim to Moses was much more than a call to come closer, but an actual "call to become." Moses was given a powerful message by the Elohim: *Challenge yourself. Push yourself. Become that which you are intended to become. Reach your highest potential.* And Moses answered to the Elohim, "I am ready to become."

 ## *"Do Not Come Any Closer"*

Moses was entering the higher realms of creation and was journeying into its very depths of fire and destruction. Moses was nearing a point of no return.

As Moses drew closer to the Burning Bush, the Elohim's energy was merging and integrating within Moses. As the Elohim's vibratory force pulsated and burned into his physical body and consciousness, Moses was able to see creation from not only man's point of view, but from God's. At this very moment, the Elohim said to Moses, "This is as far as you go."

As Moses looked deeper into the core of the Burning Bush, he was warned by the Elohim to stop. The Elohim's energy and vibratory force would overtake his life energy. He could not get too close or he would surely be destroyed by the Elohim's sheer power. His consciousness could journey no further into the formless world without risking his own destruction—both physically and metaphysically.

"Where You Stand Is Your Power"

In order to receive the revelation, one has to remove any shackles that disallow new enlightenment from entering one's being. The Elohim didn't want Moses to be afraid as revealed through the Burning Bush.

The Elohim was telling Moses, "Let go of your old self. Where you stand, in the moment, is where your power is. Where you stand, however, requires equilibrium. You need to simultaneously balance the fire of enlightenment with the earth-bound elements of humanity. Your power is not found somewhere else—in the past or in the future. Your creative power is in your 'new' vibratory energy field of this moment. You are no longer the man you were before. You have changed, and so has your life path."

ELOHIA = The Seeding of a Relationship

In this Biblical statement, the name "Elohim" transitions to become "Elohia." Through "Elohia," we are being shown the Godliness is not only defined through its creation in matter, but great emphasis is placed on the Elohim's definition of self through "particular relationships with man."

In the name, "Elohi(m)," the letter, (M), represents "matter." Yet, in this biblical statement, a derivative of the name, "Elohim" is used—the name, "Elohia." In the name "Eloh(ia)," the (M) is left out, leaving a "Yod" as the last letter which is "the hand that represents the active seed."

Using the name, "Elohia," the Godliness gave Moses a profound revelation: *The Creator is defined through its creation.* As we understand the deeper meaning of "Elohia," we learn the Elohim is not defined by matter alone, but through intimate relationships with particular aspects of human consciousness.

The Elohim was telling Moses, "I am the One who had a unique God/Man relationship with those who came before you—Abraham, Isaac, and Jacob. I am that which exists and transforms in this reality through my relationships with man. Through individual relationships, both God and man transform."

The Burning Bush was a powerful message to Moses. Through an extraordinary exchange of energy consciousness, a new relationship was born between the fiery essence of the Elohia and Moses. Through this relationship, humanity would move closer to the Elohim than ever before.

A storm was brewing in "Hashomayim" (the Heavens) and "droplets of water" (enlightenment) would soon pour down on man's world. Moses would soon challenge the Egyptian belief system and its powerful matrix of consciousness. As revealed through the coded message of Chorebah, events would soon manifest bringing forth great devastation, desolation, and profound enlightenment.

Every act of creation is first an act of destruction and desolation through which new consciousness will rise.

CHAPTER 7

The Secret Code in "Moshe"

Adam is not only a facet of the Godliness, but an actual creator in his own right projected into a dimension of time and matter. Moses would make it possible for a new level of humanity to evolve on earth. First, realize what the Elohim imagines as possible for Adam and his creation becomes a new potential within Hashomayim's realm of Adamic Consciousness. This is what Moses was—he was an extraordinary potential being realized within the imagination of the Godliness.

To deeply understand Moses, we must look beyond his physical nature and delve into the metaphysical world that projected the man. The Elohim was imagining a new level of Adam—a man that mirrored its desires. This new potential of man would meld deeply with the Elohim. However, this deep and profound relationship between man and God could only be realized in a slower dimension of time where emotions could be intensely felt and experienced.

So the "spirit of the Elohim" (Aretz) began vibrating a unique aspect of Adamic Consciousness it desired to know; and the spirit of God probed its realm of Adamic Consciousness searching for the one singularity that embodied Adam's extraordinary potential. And from the infinite possibilities, the singularity known as Moses was projected into man's world to elevate and empower humanity's collective consciousness.

Moses was a consciousness selected with great purpose. He would absorb the extraordinary essence of the Elohim, deliver humanity God's gift of enlightenment, and change the minds and beliefs of man. Through his example, he would show others it is possible to meld with the awesome power and vibratory force of the Elohim.

Of great importance, Moses was chosen by the Godliness to write the Elohim's stories of creation so man could become closer to the Godliness than ever before. Whether these stories are real or unreal is not what is important, they are God's chosen stories to enlighten humanity to All That IS.

Moses achieved the highest potential of man through his deep relationship with the Elohim.

The relationship between Moses and God was profoundly important. It was to be a new experience unfolding in the Elohim's creation. Furthermore, this relationship would change humanity and the consciousness of mankind. This extraordinary connection between God and man would be transformative not only for humanity, but for the Creator, itself. This interaction between the Elohim and Moses brought into being a new era, and mankind's eyes were opened to a new reality. After Moses, nothing would ever be the same for humanity.

The Torah's Genesis Code reveals vast insight into the depths of Moses, his purpose in this world, and how his enlightenment broke through powerful matrixes of pre-existing consciousness. Moses became the example of what is possible for man. You are about to realize an extraordinary message within the name, Moshe—a message from the Godliness expressed through a powerful feminine aspect of Egypt who was a princess and the daughter of a King.

The Secret of MOSHE (Moses)

HEBREW	LETTERS AND CODE	VALUE	CODED MEANING
MOSHE משה	MEM; SHIN; HEY מים שין הי	345	Drawing out of.
MEM מ	MEM; YOD; MEM מים יד מים	40	Matter consciousness.
SHIN ש	SHIN; YOD; NUN שין יד נון	300	Transformation.
HEY ה	HEY; YOD הי יד	50	Creation into; Core.
SEH שה	SHIN; MEM שין הי	305	Lamb; Transformation.
MAH מה	MEM; HEY מים הי	45	To question; What?
HEM הם	HEY; MEM הי מים	45	They; Them; The many.
SHOM שם	SHIN; MEM שין מים	360	Over there.
HASHEM השם	HEY; SHIN; MEM הי שין מים	345	The name.

 ## MOSHE = Drawing Out Of

In order for the Elohim to experience Adam's most extraordinary embodiment of potential, a singular aspect of consciousness, "Moshe," was drawn out of Hashomayim's dimension of Adamic Consciousness and projected into our world.

The Torah states the Princess of Egypt chose the name, "Moshe," because she "drew him out of the waters." Interestingly, when the two words "mayim" (waters) and "Moshe" (Moses) are combined, a new word is created, "Hashomayim" (the place of all potential consciousness).

However, the coded connection between Moshe and Hashomayim travels even further down the rabbit hole. The first three Hebrew letters in Hashomayim, when spelled backwards, become the name, "Moshe." The coded relationship between Moshe and Hashomayim reveals Moshe was not only drawn out of Hashomayim, but was, and continues to be, the core of Adamic Consciousness. In essence, Moshe was the highest level of man possible in our world.

The Torah's Genesis Code validates Moshe was drawn out of the place where all potential consciousness for mankind exists. More importantly, he was the core and highest potential of Adamic Consciousness. Moses represents the Elohim's projection of its most desired aspect of Adam into matter. Moses also reflected the paradox in creation and one's ability to take quantum leaps of consciousness—moving from one matrix of awareness into another.

Not to be discounted, his energy was drawn forth, out of the waters of consciousness, by the most powerful feminine aspect in the Egyptian Matrix—the daughter of Pharaoh. He was saved by the creativity of royal blood, and led to the core of a brutal matrix that he would, one day, implode. Egypt's reign of terror would be destroyed from the inside out.

 ## MEM = Matter Consciousness

"Mem" represents energy consciousness taking on the construct of form in a dimension of time and matter.

You are far more than physical matter in this world. You are a consciousness that has transformed from energy into matter consciousness. Before the soul enters the body, it first exists as potential within Hashomayim's realm of Adamic Consciousness.

Once an energy consciousness transforms into a state of matter, a new relationship is formed. The consciousness defines the matter, and the spirit becomes locked into a body bound to the time/space continuum for a period of time. As we walk the earth, we no longer exist as pure consciousness in a formless universe, but a self-aware consciousness that is bound to form becoming an independent aspect of matter.

SHIN = Transformation

God becomes through you. Transformation is the key that opens the door to your inner sun—your light that shines from the inside out.

Moses became the highest level of man. Because the letter, "Shin," is at the core of his name, we can know he challenged himself and remained open to new levels of transformative awareness. His consciousness was fluid, and he refused to be bound to status-quo ideology. Also important, Moses' physical body transformed to match his elevating energy consciousness. This made it possible for Moses to absorb the higher vibrations of the Elohim and remain intact.

When human consciousness transforms, moving from one level of vibration to another, the vibrational field of the body alters to match the vibrational field of the transformed consciousness. In order for us to reach an extreme state of enlightenment, our current energy field must be open and willing to accept a more acute vibratory energy. Once absorbed, a new level of Godliness waits to be discovered.

HEY = Creation Into; Core

The core of the Elohim projects its vibration—its creative force—into the core of mankind.

The last letter of Mos(h)e is the letter, "Hey," which embodies the "breath, power, and core of the Elohim" seeding itself into a singularity of matter consciousness. Because the letter, "Hey," is also found in the center of the name, "Elo(h)im," we are being shown creativity is projecting from the core of the Elohim into Moshe. "Hey" signifies the breath of life and the creative force.

Also interesting, "Hey's" numerical value is "five" (5). It is well known that five is the number that reflects the "Golden Ratio" (PHI). PHI is a ratio that encompasses beauty, love, creativity, and sexuality. It is beauty and functionality in one aspect. Five is the number of proportional beauty and the symbol that teaches us the core of the Elohim vibrates emotions through a sexual nature.

Sexuality is the core of new creations. Through sex, souls intertwine and exchange their vibratory essence. The Elohim is sexual in nature, as is its creation—mankind. Each of us live as a male or female, and we are projected from a Godliness that contains both male and female energy consciousness—sometimes more male than female, sometimes more female than male—depending upon the act taking place within creation.

As the Elohim's seed of potential manifests into reality, the creative ability of man flowers, dancing in harmony with the vibration of the Elohim. This vibration is "life on a higher level." It is passionate, sexual, and intense. "Hey" reflects all that is creative. The "Hey" in the name, "Mos(h)e," signifies an aspect of the Elohim implemented within every human being.

Through elevating one's awareness, the vibration of the human body becomes in tune with the Elohim's vibratory core. Through the aspect of "Hey," Moshe vibrated the core of the Elohim in our world. "Hashomayim" (Heavens), the name that begins with a "Hey," and "Moshe" (Moses), a name that ends with a "Hey," reveals a fascinating revelation: *From the beginning of time until the end of time, Moses was an aspect of creative potential drawn out of the core of Hashomayim to actively vibrate the core of the Elohim's passion in a human world.*

SE = Sacrificial Lamb; Transformation

A true leader is willing to become the sacrificial lamb and give himself up for his flock. A true leader is both humble and wise. This is the true shepherd. Moses was willing to give up not only his life in this world, but his very existence in the mind and heart of All That IS. In other words, Moses was willing to become non-existent to save his people.

The Elohim was attracted to Moshe due to the potential within his particular consciousness. In spite of what you would think, the metaphorical quality of the lamb attracted the Elohim to Moses. Also interesting and not to be overlooked, it was the earthly lamb that led Moses to the Burning Bush where Moses first encountered the Godliness.

The qualities of the lamb are necessary to achieve the highest level of enlightenment. We are being shown that one is to be humble, unassuming, gentle, and accepting. The lamb is not a predator, nor does the lamb ever abuse its power. Yet, it is important to remain aware of the unassuming lamb that can lead you to the lion whose roar vibrates throughout creation. They are both you, and we will now explain why.

First, know the core letter of Mo(s)he's name is the "Shin" which is a symbol for "transformation and the meshing of energies." The core letter of the Elo(h)im is the "Hey" which is the "breath of life" and also the fifth sign in the Zodiac which is "5" and the symbol of the "lion" (Leo) who is the ruler and king of his domain.

What is extraordinary, when you combine the core of Moshe with the core of the Elohim, the "Shin" and "Hey" become "Shin-Hey" which means "lamb." In other words, through the melding of the core between the Elohim and man, God transforms. If one is not humble, if one is not accepting and open to change, nothing will ever change. The lamb leads you to the lion that roars, and the lion is the Godliness in you.

Quite astonishingly, there would come a time when Moses would vehemently stand up to Jehovah and demand his people be given another chance. If God refused to be merciful towards the Israelites, Moses no longer wished to exist within God's memory and asked to be removed from the Creator's story. Moses deeply knew and realized that if this were to happen, it would be as if his energy consciousness never existed at all.

Jehovah deeply realized this was the ultimate sacrifice and Moses' threat exemplified who Moses truly was. To our knowledge, no other prophet has ever made such a statement to the Godliness. Moses was the Elohim's ultimate shepherd, and the man who would lead his flock to enlightenment.

 ### MAH = The Question; What?

Our questions within, together with our endless search for transformative knowledge, are the motivating forces that energize our evolution.

The first and last letters of "(M)os(h)e," "Mem + Hey," when combined form the word, "Mah," which asks the question, "What?" Through the asking of a question man evolves; and within every answer, another question inevitably rises. Without the question, there is no evolution of consciousness. For example, animals do not ask questions. Their consciousness remains static—they just are. Your questions are your guides to discover your essence. Never stop asking the questions.

 ## HEM = They; Them; the Many

Within the highest level of man, there is an innate awareness of the many, together with the knowingness that each man and woman is an aspect of the Elohim, and all human beings are connected to one another and everything.

Moses understood everyone was him, and he was part of everyone else. The embedded code within Moses reveals: *We are each a facet of the Godliness.* Moses was never out to appease himself or separate himself from others. In fact, the Torah explicitly states he was the humblest of all men.

Moses exists in the consciousness of the many, and his enlightenment is intended for all of mankind. You are a facet of the Godliness, as is every other human being on this planet. Do not separate yourself through prejudice, status, culture, or gender. The moment you do, you project a negative outcome within the Elohim and greatly limit your personal potential.

 ## SHOM = Over There

While something may appear to be "over there," remember all things are interconnected. The illusion of separation is a necessity in a three-dimensional reality. Look for potential in others, even if they perceive life differently than you. Empower them to reach their potential, even when you perceive others to be over there in a level of awareness that differs from your current state of being.

Many people believe if one is over there—physically, mentally, or in spirit—the distance between the two can only mean one has no effect over the other. This is not the case. What happens "over there" stimulates human awareness and affects the collective consciousness of the many.

Ironically, all new experiences and new levels of awareness come into our reality from "over there." Any and all levels of new awareness enter an observer's reality from a place "other than the place of the observer." You may want to remind yourself of the following statement, "If awareness is here, 'where I am,' then that which I am unaware of exists over there, 'where I am not.'" Any new consciousness that enters your awareness will do so from the perception of "over there"—from the place of unawareness to the place where you are, "the place you stand," in the moment.

Moses had merged with the essence of the Elohim—the Godliness that man had always been perceived as being "over there and out there." Once this new level of awareness was activated, the perception of the Godliness being "over there, out there, and up there," no longer existed for Moses. He deeply knew he was part of everything and that everyone is the Godliness.

 ## HASHEM = The Name

Moshe's name contains a coded message that offers insight into this phenomenal prophet. We learn a name is a reflection of one's consciousness. There is more to a name than meets the eye.

Within matter, subconscious levels of intelligence exist to be realized—even within a name. Through Moshe's deeply coded name, the Godliness is telling mankind, "A name is a call to being." The closest communication and understanding of anything or anyone is reflected through the given name connected to the consciousness we perceive. What we call people, places, or things reflects our perception of the expression being revealed.

Interestingly, certain cultures have been known to wait until the child is weaned from its mother prior to giving the child a name. In doing so, the parents have an opportunity to experience the child's energy and nature to ensure the name reflects the child's true essence.

A name always reflects the vibratory energy of the living consciousness through its letters and sounds. Within a name, a subconscious level of intelligence exists to be realized. Look deep within, for the words within the Five Books of Moses are a coded program of conscious expression and a vibratory field of energy the names and words reflect.

The Return of the Cryptic Luchot

An ancient story exists—a story that is rarely talked about. This story's truth has remained in the shadows and hidden from mankind. It isn't discussed, because it isn't understood. We will now delve into the Biblical revelation that sheds light on Moses' encounter with Jehovah on top of Mount Sinai so long ago.

The Bible is far more complex and mysterious than man ever imagined. To our knowledge, The Genesis Code's tremendous insight into the tablets Moses brought down the mountain cannot be found in any other books or teachings, including the Talmud. This, in itself, is astonishing when one considers the ancient texts have been scoured over time and time again since the very beginning.

The Genesis Code's interpretations of the Godliness, Moses, and the tablets he brought down the mountain will change mankind's perceptions of what truly happened at Mount Sinai. This is the untold story of the "first and original Torah" (the Luchot Haedot) given to Moses by Jehovah nearly 3,500 years ago.

The enlightenment of the Luchot has eluded us since the beginning. Its depths have never been revealed and, therefore, the Luchot has never been understood. Through The Genesis

The Return of the Cryptic Luchot

Code, you will discover the revelation of the Luchot and its relevance in our world today.

No longer shrouded in mystery, the story of the Luchot sheds light on one of creation's greatest mysteries: *We learn "why" the Bible holds a coded language that was purposefully hidden from man's awareness.* You will soon see this story through a new set of eyes and never look at the Bible in the same way again.

Before we delve into that which has never been known, we must first evaluate that which humanity is very familiar with—God's Ten Commandments. These basic laws and moral guidelines were intended to be the foundation for man's forming societies.

Current interpretations of the Ten Commandments reveal the following message from God to mankind: *God prohibits having other gods before him; making or worshiping idols; threatens punishment for those who reject him; promise love for those who love him; forbids blasphemy of his name; demands observance of the Sabbath and honoring one's parents; prohibits murder, adultery, theft, false testimony, and coveting of one's neighbor's goods.*

The Ten Commandments are widely accepted and, therefore, permeate humanity's belief systems. While we are not delving into the coded language within the Ten Commandments at this time, know a deeper and unknown message of enlightenment prevails within God's ten statements. The Genesis Code offers subtle, and sometimes not so subtle, nuances that offer deep insight into the Ten Commandments and bring forth a new understanding of the Elohim's statements of enlightenment.

There is much to learn and discover about the tablets of Sinai. For example, did you know the Ten Commandments were not the first, but a secondary set of tablets Moses brought down the mountain and delivered to his people? This is where our journey into the story of the tablets begins. This is a search for enlightenment and the truth of the mostly unknown tablets that "came first."

The Torah refers to the first set of tablets as "Luchot Haedot" (pronounced Luke-ot Ha-a-dut). Furthermore, "Luchot Haedot" means: *Tablets of Witness; Tablets of Testimony.* Throughout this book, we will refer to the "Luchot Haedot" (the first and primary set of tablets) as the "Luchot." Therefore, there is the "Luchot" (the first set of tablets) and the "Ten Commandments or Ten Statements" (the second and subsequent set of tablets) delivered to humanity by Moses.

The Torah holds a carefully guarded secret surrounding the Luchot: *The Luchot's brief presence in our world is a key factor and the primary reason the Five Books of Moses contains a coded language and alternate level of enlightenment within its ancient Hebrew texts.* As you will soon learn, the Luchot's description, "Tablets of Witness," offers insight into another reality—the quantum world.

Until now, the Luchot has been mostly unexplained—its hidden meaning and consequential effect in man's world overlooked and unknown. In truth, the extraordinary enlightenment and reality of the Luchot has been lost in man's awareness and mostly forgotten. Nearly everyone, regardless of their religion, culture, or status knows little about the Luchot. Mankind has much to learn from the Luchot's lost enlightenment—a gift that slipped through man's fingers thousands of years ago.

You are about to embark on a new journey and know what the Luchot was, why it was gifted to mankind by the Elohim, and how you can rediscover its message of enlightenment. Of profound importance, know the Luchot is the key to the Torah's Genesis Code. It is the link and driving force of the Bible's many secrets.

The Luchot's existence in our world has never been more relevant than today. The time has come to breathe new life into the lost story of the Luchot. The time is now for mankind to know what really happened between Moses and God on top of a mountain—in the dimension of Sinai—so long ago.

*The Luchot's secret has been revealed.
Its truth will guide mankind
out of the shadows and into the light.*

The Portal of Enlightenment Opens

The encounter between the Godliness and Moses on Mount Sinai was, undoubtedly, one of the most significant spiritual events in our history. The divine energy of the Elohim had merged with Moses giving birth to an exquisite and intimate relationship. A new God/Man connection had formed. Life had been given to a new level of consciousness, and a new projection of potential entered man's world. At the top of Sinai a portal opened offering "Adam" (mankind) the secrets of creation.

Moses had achieved what no other man had accomplished, and vital to realize, this was an extreme transformation in the Elohim's creation. As the Elohim merged with Moses, a portal between the physical and unseen worlds formed, bringing with it the mystical Luchot.

On top of Mount Sinai, the Luchot had crossed the threshold into man's three-dimensional reality making it possible for the Elohim to "witness" (Luchot Haedot = Tablets of Witness), experience, and deeply know the essence of Moses and humanity. Because of the Luchot, a new reality was now possible for Adam.

Through the vibratory energy of the "Luchot" (Tablets of Witness), Adam's consciousness could expand making it possible

The Portal of Enlightenment Opens 193

for man to peer into his soul and into the depths of creation. From where Adam stood, in his own dimension, through higher awareness it would be possible for man to overcome his illusion of separation through a deep knowingness to that which resides on the other side of the portal.

With the manifestation of the Luchot, creative consciousness could flow freely, back and forth, between dimensions. Yet, it was even more than that. It was now possible for one level of Godliness, the Elohim, to deeply meld and communicate with another level of Godliness, "Adam" (mankind).

The Luchot vibrated a new level of awareness that made it possible for man to tap into the power of his inner Godliness. The Luchot was an opening to a new world—a reality intended for an advanced level of man and a new civilization realized through a drastic transformation of consciousness. Through the Elohim's mystical Luchot, humankind could achieve a deep and constant connection to the Godliness that was everlasting. This is what the Godliness had intended.

The Torah reveals the Luchot was not created "within" the dimension of man, but "outside" of man's three-dimensional reality by the Elohim. What is important to realize, unlike the Luchot, the Ten Commandments were chiseled in stone "by Moses" and created "within" man's world. This revelation sets the Luchot apart from the Ten Commandments.

The Genesis Code reveals the first Luchot was far different than the Ten Commandments. Yet, through past interpretations it has become widely accepted the first and second tablets were exactly the same in both nature and purpose. Nothing is further from the truth. According to the Torah's Genesis Code, both sets of tablets offered enlightenment for mankind. What becomes important to the story is the level of enlightenment unique to each set of tablets.

First and foremost, the Luchot was a gift from the Godliness—a celestial level of enlightenment offered to the man of long ago. The Torah is clear when it emphatically states the Luchot was created by the Elohim. Furthermore, the enlightenment offered through the Luchot is what the Elohim intended for mankind to absorb and activate in this dimension.

The Luchot had travelled through the portal bringing with it vast levels of transformative enlightenment. If mankind were to accept and absorb the Luchot, a transformation would occur within the realm of Adamic Consciousness, activating new aspects of potential that would greatly enhance mankind's spiritual awareness on earth and form a new relationship between God and man.

What has gone unrealized, this transformation would not only transform man spiritually, but physically. The particles in man's dimension would be altered through a more powerful vibratory force activated in man's dimension of matter. Essentially, the Luchot would change everything in man's reality. Adam would still be human, but a different type of human would walk the face of the earth and experience an enhanced form of nature, wildlife, vegetation—everything would become enriched in Adam's new reality.

With the giving of the Luchot, the Elohim had gifted humanity with a new opportunity to move through the portal at Sinai, elevate his consciousness, and become a highly advanced spiritual being. The door had been opened by God. Now the question was, "Would mankind take a quantum leap into a new level of consciousness wherein his spiritual self would be deeply realized through a heightened and deeper relationship with God?"

With the giving of the Luchot,
the door had been opened for man...
by God, itself.

With a new opportunity to achieve higher awareness, a new possibility faced Adam. If man was to integrate this extraordinary enlightenment, he would vibrate in harmony with the Elohim—within the body's physical limitations—and not be consumed by its fiery energy. If accepted, everything would change.

Through the revelation of the Burning Bush—the bush that burned with the fire of the Godliness and remained intact—Moses knew it was possible for earthly matter to absorb high levels of vibratory energy without being destroyed.

Moses also knew the Luchot's enlightenment would only be possible if mankind deeply desired to experience a massive transformation of consciousness. Mankind would have to climb his own mountain of self, as Moses had, if humanity was to walk through the doorway to a new reality of "being."

As the Luchot permeated human reality, Adam's truth would soon be known. Mankind would be faced with a choice, and this choice would affect the future of humanity and the Godliness of this dimension. What we believe is possible is of the highest importance, including the God we believe, or don't believe, to be real. How we feel about ourselves, life, creation, and what type of God we empower, not only matters but actually impacts creation and transforms human reality.

The Secret of Sinai

Because the Luchot was created by the Elohim, Moses understood the vibratory force of the Luchot was a genuine extension of the Elohim's essence projecting into the human world. As Moses held the exquisite Luchot in his hand, he could feel the Luchot's powerful vibration rise through the tablets, flow through his fingers, and spread throughout his body.

The Luchot was projecting its essence into the dimension of man. It was now time for Moses to descend Sinai and deliver the Luchot to his people. However, as we deciphered the complex language of God, we learned Mount Sinai was far more than we ever imagined.

 Hebraic Text: Shemos 31:18

וַיִּתֵּן אֶל מֹשֶׁה כְּכַלֹּתוֹ לְדַבֵּר אִתּוֹ בְּהַר סִינַי שְׁנֵי לֻחֹת הָעֵדֻת לֻחֹת אֶבֶן כְּתֻבִים בְּאֶצְבַּע אֱלֹהִים

English Translation: Exodus 31:18

And he gave unto Moses, when He had made an end of speaking with him upon Mount Sinai, two Tablets of Witness written with the finger of the Elohim.

The Genesis Code: Exodus 31:18

Moses was given the tablets in the dimension of Sinai—a transcendent dimension that has eluded man's awareness. Sinai was much more than a mountain on earth—it was a vibratory dimension and extraordinary portal that opened at the peak of a mountain.

When Jehovah had finished communicating with Moses in the dimension of Sinai, two Tablets of Witness were given at the mountain's peak where the portal had opened and was vibrating the mountain. The Luchot was not of this world, for it was created and written by the finger of the Elohim.

The Luchot had entered man's dimension through the portal of Sinai. These mystical and alien tablets contained properties that allowed their energy field to move within, and operate through, different dimensions within the Elohim.

The Luchot was designed to interact with and communicate with various aspects of human consciousness as its enlightenment moved from the top of the mountain to the mountain's base. At the highest level of Sinai, Moses would be gifted the Luchot and bring the Luchot's wisdom to the level of earth, where his people were.

The architect of the Luchot was the Elohim. Moreover, the energy of the Luchot vibrated the awesome creative force and power of the Elohim into our world. The Torah specifically states the Luchot was not written by man, but by the finger of the Elohim.

As we look deeply into this statement, we asked the question, "What is the Torah revealing to us through its specific description of the Elohim's "finger?" What insight does the "finger" reveal about creation?" What we found is remarkable. The Elohim's finger was a concentrated aspect of the Elohim's vibratory force that projected enlightenment in a precise direction—into man's reality of time and matter.

Through this transference of energy, the Elohim's energy and wisdom echoed the potential for transformation into the energy consciousness of man. This realization can be somewhat complicated, so we will describe the deeper understanding of the Torah's reference to the "finger" that "projected the Elohim's essence into Adam's reality."

Imagine a balloon. Now imagine you are inside of the balloon. Suddenly, you realize something outside of the balloon is "projecting" (vibrating) into the balloon's wall and taking on the form of a finger. What you see is the projection of the concentrated and focused energy vibrating its force through the plastic membrane that is the balloon. Through this transference of energy, the membrane has morphed into a shape that most closely reflects the "concentrated expression of the vibratory force and energy" being projected from outside of the balloon.

As you envision this event, know the membrane is the mystical Luchot—a filter through which vibratory energy flows from one dimension into another. The projection of the Elohim's expression is a vibratory energy that subsequently gives life to the shape of the finger. The finger then points toward its intended recipient and transmits the energy of that which projected it. As the energy vibrates its essence through the membrane, a new portal is opened allowing cosmic consciousness to flow into a new dimension of limitation—a three-dimensional reality that is Adam's world.

To further describe this reality, imagine a river that flows with the answers to all of man's questions. This river of wisdom and enlightenment rushes into one dimension from another—it is the consciousness that swirls within and out of your being. Through the river, you are able to feel and know the power of God and all that exists beyond your three-dimensional reality. For you, this is an emotional experience of the highest level, and words will never be adequate when describing this profound realization.

The finger of the Elohim is a metaphor describing the intention and desire of the Elohim to project its energy consciousness into Adam's world. The never-before witnessed essence of the Elohim was projecting through a portal into a three-dimensional reality so man could witness, absorb, and ultimately manifest new experiences through a highly evolved God/Man relationship. The Luchot was God's way of inviting mankind to "become."

The Luchot Enters Man's Reality

    The Torah's incredible description of the Luchot provides insight into the awesome intelligence, complexity, power, mystical characteristics, and divine nature of the first set of tablets. Man is meant to know the Luchot was not from this world, and that these esoteric tablets would have a monumental affect on humanity. With the giving of the Luchot, Adam's creation would be forever changed.

 Hebraic Text: Shemos 32:15

וַיִּפֶן וַיֵּרֶד מֹשֶׁה מִן הָהָר וּשְׁנֵי לֻחֹת הָעֵדֻת בְּיָדוֹ לֻחֹת כְּתֻבִים מִשְּׁנֵי עֶבְרֵיהֶם מִזֶּה וּמִזֶּה הֵם כְּתֻבִים

 English Translation: Exodus 32:15

    As Moses turned and went down from the mountain, he carried two tablets of testimony in his hands; tablets that were written on both sides; on the one side and on the other side they were written.

The Genesis Code: Exodus 32:15

As Moses moved to descend Sinai, he was actually turning away from his highest level of self. He would now descend to Sinai's lowest dimension where the people were at the mountain's base.

The two Tablets of Witness were in his "hand" (singular). The reference of "hand" reveals the metaphysical tablets were mostly weightless and, therefore, Moses needed only one hand to carry the two tablets down the mountain.

The Luchot was the work of the Elohim, and the writings were the writings of the Elohim. The tablets were written on both sides—from one side and from the other side—they were both written. Moreover, the writings were visible from any angle.

The Elohim's projection of consciousness was not only engraved in the Luchot, but as the consciousness expressed itself in man's world, it appeared to "rise and float" above the tablets. As the Luchot moved down the mountain, exiting the highest dimension of Sinai, its essence was flowing and projecting into the lower dimension of man where the people were and where Adam's collective consciousness had gathered.

The difference between the Luchot and the Ten Commandments is sobering. Although both sets of tablets were brought down Sinai by Moses, they contained two diverse levels of enlightenment that would project two very different vibrations in man's world.

Also important, the Elohim's Ten Commandments, while profound, were a "limited aspect" of the primary Luchot. In other words, the Luchot contained far more enlightenment. It is vital to realize the Ten Commandments were a "facet" of the

Luchot, implemented as a stepping stone for humanity. Even though the secondary statements from God were vital for the people to understand and implement within society, know their enlightenment offered only a fraction of the Luchot's vibratory totality.

As we delve into the characteristics of the Luchot, the Torah reveals these tablets were not made from a dense earthly stone like the Ten Commandments, but consisted of an energy-like stone that was somewhat transparent. Moreover, the Torah describes an intense vibration emitting from the energy-like tablets. In fact, the Luchot's vibratory force far exceeded the energy of the second set of tablets that would follow.

Also fascinating is that the Torah describes the Luchot's Hebrew words and letters to be three-dimensional in nature—rising up and projecting outward in man's reality. That which was being communicated by the Elohim seemed to take on a life of its own; the message transforming as it filtered into the observer's reality.

What is fascinating is that the consciousness streaming through the portal of the Luchot would transform into letters and words that floated above the tablets. Regardless of the position, angle, or placement of the mystical tablets, the Torah reveals the Luchot's message could not be overlooked. In other words, if you wished to attain enlightenment, the Luchot would answer your emotional intent.

As we come to better understand the mysterious Luchot, we find that regardless of its position in man's reality, its powerful message would be witnessed by the observers. These characteristics become crucial details as we compare the flowing nature of the Luchot's vibratory letters to the Ten Commandments' two-dimensional writings that were sculpted and fixed within the solid stone tablets.

The Luchot was much more than two tablets. It was more like a vibrating membrane between two worlds. But how was the Luchot a means through which the energy within one dimension could communicate with another? Think of a sieve or filter. The Luchot worked to transform energy consciousness as it streamed from one dimension into another. As energy filtered through the membrane, its essence was transmuted into a method of communication that could be understood and felt by the onlooker.

The tablets were a means through which one form of "creative consciousness" (the Godliness) could meld with and experience another form of "creative consciousness" (Adam). Interestingly, this stream of consciousness flowed both ways, from one dimension to another and back again, much like a two-way street. Not only did the Luchot allow the Godliness to experience man, but it allowed for Adam to meld with and experience the vibratory essence of the Elohim.

It becomes clear the Luchot was not of this world. Everything about the Luchot was foreign and surreal. Much like the man of long ago, the Luchot has risen once again to challenge modern-day man. The coded message of the Luchot has been given, but a question remains unanswered, "Will mankind grasp this chance for transformation and true enlightenment?"

The Observer and Witness

Even today, the Luchot seems foreign and surreal—their reality difficult for our minds to absorb. They appear to be illusory, impossible, and out of this world. While the man of the twenty-first century struggles to fathom the Luchot's mystical powers, imagine the sheer impact and shock this portal of enlightenment had on those who lived 3,500 years ago.

Whether one chooses to believe in the Luchot or not, the Torah is specific when it validates their presence in our world, their mystical characteristics, and profound importance. The Torah has opened the door, and it is now our responsibility to familiarize ourselves with the secrets of the Luchot.

Know that God can only experience its creation at the level through which its creation has evolved. A point to ponder: *If God is realized in man, and man is realized in God, the purpose of the Luchot was to show us something new, so man and God could become something new.*

Thousands of years ago, man was presented with two polarizing perspectives of God through two very different aspects of enlightenment. At Sinai, two diverse realities were offered to mankind through the Luchot Haedot and the Ten

Commandments. A new potential was seeded at Sinai, and it would be up to Adam to water the seed of its choice and give it life.

Adam defines the Godliness of this dimension.

Through our conscious projection, we say, "I believe the Creator is this, and I don't believe the Creator is that!" The Godliness of our being, how we truly see ourselves in creation, manifests through our belief in "who we are and what we believe God to be." Again, our belief in what is possible leads us back to the Luchot's enlightenment.

As mentioned earlier, a profound clue as to the Luchot's purpose in man's reality is found within its very name: *Tablets of Witness.* The quantum world is a subatomic reality powered by the relationship between "cosmic consciousness" (Hashomayim) and "matter consciousness" (a singular consciousness drawn out of HaAdam that has become bound in a reality of matter). The result of this relationship evolves into what man experiences in his individual universe and personal reality.

Quantum mechanics delves into the core of our universe's subatomic reality and reveals something remarkable: *A witness or observer must be present before any new reality or experience can manifest.* Through man's consciousness, and its vibratory relationship with the subatomic particles in creation, Hashomayim's potential manifests into human reality. To put it quite simply, quantum theory implies the following: *No phenomenon is possible without a witness or observer.*

The implications of this theory are profound and greatly impact the way we view reality. The fact that a "witness" is required prior to any manifestation taking hold in our dimension tells us "the physical universe could never be without the pre-existence of an observing consciousness." Quantum theory suggests the following: *Manifestation cannot occur without the pre-existence of a consciousness that has the ability to observe potential.*

Prior to anything manifesting in the Adamic Universe, there had to be a "pre-existent consciousness" (the Godliness) to observe the potential within Hashomayim's realm of Adamic Consciousness (the place of all potential for mankind). This theory is applicable to all aspects of Adamic Consciousness—that which is potential and that which is realized in matter. In order for man to manifest an experience in our reality, our consciousness must first tap into and connect to the potential of the possible experience in the "subatomic realm" (Hashomayim) before a reality can be experienced. This is truly remarkable.

Our physical universe is the direct result of consciousness.

This notion has a striking resemblance to esoteric theory which asserts all phenomena results from the consciousness of a master designer or Godlike mind. Paradoxically, other scientific theories presume human consciousness is the result of the workings of a physical brain. However, according to quantum theory, the physical brain cannot come into existence until it is the subject of observation by a pre-existing self-aware consciousness.

Others claim human desires and intentions cannot materialize as an experience unless the "singularity of consciousness" powering the desire for an experience is "first observed on some level" and then obtains a "form of agreement" from "cosmic consciousness" (the Godliness). Without a "witness" (an observing consciousness), the subatomic level of reality never materializes in the dimension of time and matter, but merely fluctuates as potential. Without the observer, reality becomes impossible and remains in the void of unstructured chaos within the Elohim's Hashomayim.

Reality is identical with the totality of observed phenomena. Therefore, reality becomes non-existent in the absence of observation.

Through the act of observation—man being the "witness" to the energy flowing through the Luchot—a new level of creativity would be possible. Through Adam's elevated awareness, his consciousness would probe the subatomic world for potential that would manifest a reality that reflected his advanced level of consciousness. Adam would experience something new, something profound, and something very different than he had before.

However, the Luchot had not yet been brought down the mountain and given to the people. The Luchot had been realized by Moses at the mountain's peak, but had yet to be realized by the many at the mountains base. Therefore, the Luchot, at this point in time, was still a potential in man's world.

CHAPTER 8

The Transformative Luchot

On top of Sinai, Moses had achieved what no man had accomplished—a deep connection with the Elohim through Jehovah. Moses had become the highest level of man, and he came to realize all that is possible at the highest dimension of self.

 ***Hebraic Text: Devarim 34:10*__

ולא קָם נָבִיא עוֹד בְּיִשְׂרָאֵל כְּמֹשֶׁה אֲשֶׁר יְדָעוֹ יְהוָה פָּנִים אֶל פָּנִים:

English Translation: Deuteronomy 34:10

Since then, no prophet has risen in Israel like Moses, whom the Lord knew face to face.

The Genesis Code: Deuteronomy 34:10

In Isreal, no other prophet would arise again like "Moshe" (Moses). He had the highest connection and the deepest insight into the Godliness. He deeply knew, meshed, and resonated the Elohim's many aspects.

The view from the top of the mountain was nothing short of spectacular. For the first time in his life, Moses was seeing creation through the eyes of the Divine. Nothing could be more beautiful or profound. What Moses had become, God felt and knew. A new God/Man relationship had formed, and Adam's world was forever changed.

The Torah reveals the Luchot's enlightenment would have a transformative effect on every person who absorbed its vibratory consciousness. Through these tablets, each person was gifted with an opportunity to deepen his/her connection to the Creator. In other words, the tablets offered a unique spiritual recipe formulated to match the awareness of the observer.

Once the vibratory force of the Luchot was absorbed by the individual, a new connection between man and God would blossom. This elevation of consciousness would have a profound effect on the onlooker's existing potential within Hashomayim's HaAdam. A new level of vibratory energy would flow through their being, and they would experience a sensation, together with a level of knowingness, they had never known before.

The Elohim desired for the many to absorb the Luchot's enlightenment, knowing HaAdam's Adamic Consciousness would take a quantum leap within its totality. This was to be a new beginning for both God and man, and a new light would shine in the Elohim's creation.

Through the Luchot, the Elohim's energy streamed into man's world through letters, words, vibratory sensations, and hieroglyphs. As the energy of the Luchot vibrated and energized man's reality, it became possible for the onlooker to realize the previously unknown mind of the Godliness. This is how it happened for Moses, and this is what was intended for the many.

This connection of thought and emotion can be compared to the reader who observes that which is being communicated by the author. When writings are realized and absorbed, the "reader" (onlooker) becomes enlightened and inspired as he feels the expression of the author. The reader absorbs the streaming thoughts and emotions of the author who projects his consciousness through the pages and words of the book he has written.

Through realization, new ideas and possibilities are empowered and brought forth in man's world. How many lives have been transformed because of an inspiring idea or observation? We grow from that which we witness and observe. The observer observes potential and perceives the potential as being "over there." As the potential "over there" is "absorbed by the observer," it integrates with the observer's consciousness and manifests as a "new level of awareness."

Upon this transference of potential—from over there to where the observer currently stands—the observer's newly acquired awareness melds with his existing awareness to form a new level of human consciousness. The observer has transformed and so, too, will his experience.

One's experience will always follow one's consciousness. This is the core nature of who we are. We feed from knowledge and enlightenment, regardless if the nature of the knowledge is from an objective or subjective point of view.

Through the observer's new level of awareness and vibratory consciousness, man's "Aretz" (his spirit that runs) connects to the "subatomic world" (HaAdam) to manifest a new reality and "experience" (a realization). Once any message is absorbed, understood, and deeply realized at the core of our being, the vibratory energy of the message becomes part of who we are.

No longer "over there," the vibratory energy of the message has integrated within our consciousness—"where we stand now." We have accepted and absorbed its vibratory essence and truth, and this new awareness has become part of us. This new persona now desires to express its essence in our outer world. It is a self-aware aspect of energy that wants its potential to be realized and experienced by "the observers in creation."

Through the outer world, the new persona and self-aware aspect of consciousness expresses, "I am this. Realize my truth. I am over here. You are over there. See me. Accept me. Absorb my life-force. We will be 'One' and experience something new." This is consciousness in action—a never-ending re-creation of self. From moment-to-moment, new potential becomes and life happens.

From a thought or emotion, we successfully absorb new levels of awareness and manifest new realities through our persona that lives to create and express its essence. Human consciousness lives to be realized through its infinite aspects and transformations of self.

Obviously, the vibratory essence of the Luchot did not project simple knowledge, but a very different type of knowledge—transformative knowledge. It was created by the Elohim to change the minds and hearts of men and alter their belief systems through an elevated awareness to All That IS.

Today's man wants to experience more than ever before. We want to gain new knowledge. We want to be wise. We want peace and prosperity. We want to build a new world through a new sense of self. We want to create.

We are a new generation of Adam that will absorb an ancient and profound level of enlightenment. Through The Genesis Code, we are being guided to the ultimate truth of the Godliness. It will be our choice to climb the mountain and reach our highest potential of self.

The portal has opened once again.
It has opened for us.
God desires a new experience.
Surely, so do we.

The Power of the Matrix

Most of humanity is unaware we experience our lives through a matrix. Today, the dominant matrix that influences the Western world is ancient—existing since the time of Egypt and its Pharaohs. Interestingly, when the matrix is referenced in casual conversation most people think of the blockbuster movie that portrays a sentient consciousness that is dominate and controls society.

Actually, this portrayal is not far off the mark. The dictionary's definition of a "matrix" is "a surrounding substance through which something else originates, develops, and/or is controlled." In order to understand how our realities manifest, we will illuminate and discuss the little understood and rarely talked about matrix.

So what is the matrix? The matrix is a powerful embodiment of collective energy consciousness that is a self-aware entity that manifests scenarios to support the reality it desires to experience. What the matrix supports is truly what the people within its boundaries desire deep within their consciousness—whether they admit to, or are aware of, the truth they are projecting.

Most people will not, or cannot, confess to motivations that are either secrets, dark aspects of self, or emotions they have hidden from themselves. In other words, there are those who may not even know what motivates them at the depths of their soul.

For example, what was the motivating force that led to the global financial crash of 2008? First, we must look to the most influential and powerful nation that resides at the top of the pyramid. That nation is America. It is a superpower and its influence affects all life on this planet. It is the leader of the pack, and the outcome of its motivations reverberates throughout the world.

Man drives reality through the matrix he empowers. While most people would never admit to being materialistic, self-serving, and contemptuous of others; in the end, many of the people had a ravenous appetite for power, control, wealth, and status. Their bellies were full, yet their gluttonous behavior continued. Unbeknownst to the people at the time, the projection of their consciousness was soon to hit their reality with brute force.

What must be realized, deeply so, is that the catastrophic events that drastically changed man's reality were "chosen experiences" projected by the masses within, and outside of, America. Enough of us had projected a particular level of consciousness that resulted in a powerful matrix that manifested humanity's vibratory force and truth. Man's reality reflects his vibratory essence—always.

Because insatiability can never be satisfied, it will eventually run its course and implode. And this is exactly what happened. Just like Humpty Dumpty, all that represented the financial system went crashing down—destroying many lives along the way. Whether the people blame the greed on Wall Street, the banking system, the governments, this man or that woman, the truth is this destabilizing event represented the destabilization of human consciousness. This happened because the "majority" of the world condoned greed, self-indulgence, and disdain for their fellow man. There is no one to blame but ourselves.

The many will always outweigh the few; and the many put the "like-minded" few in power to make decisions for, and answer to, the many. In the end, the people will always observe and experience the result of their motivation and vibratory force through world events. Whether the experience is wondrous or extremely painful, gives life or takes life away, the experience is always man's energy consciousness being realized through matter consciousness. This is creation in motion.

The Genesis Code reveals the following insight into a matrix of consciousness: *A matrix is an energized outcome of the many points of singular consciousness coming together, in agreement, and merging to form a point—a collective "mass" consciousness that becomes a self-aware entity on the metaphysical level.* The matrix manifests realities in the physical world that support the driving force and motivation of its masses on a metaphysical level.

Know the metaphysical drives the physical. The matrix is a reality we cannot escape. In fact, the matrix is a reality we embrace and create. The matrix exists as an essential part of human creativity—whether its projection is brutal or peaceful—the matrix is an outcome of who we are "as a creative vibratory life force."

Important to understand, the majority of those who live within the boundaries of a matrix are vibrating a similar level of consciousness. We have all heard the saying, "Like attracts like." Know any matrix is powered by the consciousness of the people who live within its boundaries. Humanity gives the matrix life. Human consciousness—man's emotional and intellectual being—is the engine and driving force that will either feed this enormous entity of self-aware consciousness, or starve and implode its reality through rejection, challenge, and opposition to what the matrix stands for.

Because a matrix feeds from the collective consciousness of the many, it will always "project the vibratory force" of its citizens, participants, or followers. Whether a nation, government, religious establishment, or political party, without the driving force of human consciousness, the matrix will decompose, become powerless, and no longer influence society. The people are the consciousness that has created this entity; therefore, without the support of the people, the matrix will lose its grasp on reality and merely fade away into nothingness.

At one time or another, each of us has imagined what it would be like to challenge or change a powerful system that works to control society and mankind. It could be a government, philosophy, political organization, religion, etc. There was probably a time when you wanted to influence, challenge, or oppose the philosophy or point of view of a group or organization, only to find it wasn't so easy.

We have all heard the saying, "You can't go against the system." Well, what do you think the system is? What do you think you are up against? When challenging, even questioning, the motivation that is the core of any matrix, you will be facing an immensely powerful energy consciousness that does not want to change. The reason for this is quite simple: *If a matrix of consciousness changes, the old entity of consciousness will basically die, no longer exist, and, therefore, lose its power of manifestation.*

Nothing is more difficult than changing, challenging, or destroying an existing powerhouse of consciousness. Know if you ever do make the choice to challenge the system, you will be facing a powerful matrix of consciousness that is self-aware and will fervently, possibly violently, work against you every step of the way.

As a matter of fact, if you ever felt as if you were under attack, but didn't quite understand what was actually happening around you, know the manifestation of the attack was, more than likely, the matrix working against you to hold you back and/or disempower your threat towards its motivation.

Spanning the lands and oceans, the matrix of today is a commanding, authoritative, and influential sentient consciousness that creates far-reaching events. A revelation rises that is absolutely extraordinary: *The matrix will continuously create scenarios and realities that favor and support its core motivation.*

Paradoxically, the matrix will fiercely battle any attitudes or transcendent philosophies that oppose its core motivation. Know the matrix will actually work to disempower, hinder, and manifest obstacles for those who support the new and opposing ideology. This is how powerful the matrix truly is.

Know The Genesis Code has risen to challenge the matrix of today. Its message of enlightenment vehemently challenges misguided perceptions of God and creation. Even though The Genesis Code is a message of enlightenment from the Godliness, we understand today's matrix will not break easily. In truth, until mankind as a whole realizes the matrix no longer reflects his truth, nothing will ever change. Until the masses change, the matrix never will.

Only one dominant consciousness exists at the top of the pyramid. The matrix of our world is exponentially powerful and can only be challenged by another powerful opponent supported by the many.

Know the matrix has a profound effect on the world. What humanity experiences, whether war or peace, is merely an outcome of human consciousness unfolding through a powerful matrix. All global and large-scale events are truly reflections of who we are "as a people." When enough of us realize global events are merely the outcomes of human consciousness in action, one's awareness to how creation works changes exponentially.

As to the heads of government, it is crucial to realize that those who exist at the top of the matrix are merely a reflection of the many that live within its boundaries. You may be saying, "I don't make decisions that affect the world, the government makes those decisions, especially when it comes to war and peace." If the collective consciousness driving the matrix truly desired to change the matrix' core motivation and grid of consciousness, they would. The heads of government will always reflect the consciousness of the masses they lead—whether an elected official, or dictator.

One as All,
All as One.

If you are wondering how our world became so chaotic and destructive, the answer is quite simple: *We are the cause.* When humanity comes to the realization that everything is "One;" when mankind changes his perceptions of reality; when each male and female acts, thinks, and feels the vibration of higher awareness, only then will we elevate our world's vibratory force, together with our connection to the Godliness.

Because the matrix is powered by the masses, it can only be changed when new forms of singular consciousness gather through agreement, meld, and create an advanced matrix through a higher level of awareness. Today, there is much pain in our world. Mankind must understand the earth generates all that we need. There is plenty of food to feed the poor—to share with our brothers and sisters on the other side of the world. There is enough to help those who are sick and weak—we only need set our minds and hearts to it.

Humanity will always drive reality. Global transformation will not come about through the efforts of any one country or nation, but through the efforts of humanity as a whole. To set it straight, mankind has evolved, but we have not evolved enough. Our consciousness remains stuck in the age-old idea of God and separation. The results of these belief systems are clear—we only need open our eyes. Man must no longer empower a reality of separation, but create a new world founded on the philosophy of "Oneness."

Elevating humanity will not be a simple task. There will be significant antagonism from opposing matrixes of consciousness. Peace and harmony will only happen on a worldwide scale when the majority of mankind realizes their opponent, rival, antagonist, and foe is truly a facet of them.

On a metaphysical level, when we abuse, hate, deny, or kill another, we are truly abusing, hating, denying, and killing a part of ourselves. Much like a gigantic living organism, we are all connected—living and breathing in a dimension of time and matter.

Before a new matrix of higher awareness can manifest, this truth must be realized. Whatever your choice, know you must deeply believe in and absorb the vibratory force of your choice. The time is now for you to become. The world is in your hands.

The Egyptian Matrix

To fully understand the times surrounding Moses, the Israelites, the Luchot, and the Ten Commandments, we must revisit ancient Egypt. The Egyptian way of life centered on the empowerment of idol gods that controlled nature and the human experience. These mythical gods reflected the origins and behavior of the forces they represented and great efforts were made to gain their favor.

Formal religious practice centered on the Pharaoh—the King of Egypt. Although the Pharaoh was human, he was believed to possess divine power. He was the ruler and King. He acted as the intermediary between the gods and his people and worked to satisfy the gods through rituals and offerings. If the gods were pleased, they would maintain order in the universe.

The Egyptian belief system was complex and primarily composed of polytheism, magic, politics, and a steadfast belief in the afterlife. However, the absolute authority of the Egyptian ruler was the determining factor when it came to which belief system would be implemented during their respective reign.

The Egyptians dedicated enormous resources to the performance of these rituals and to the construction of the temples where they were carried out. Individuals could also interact with the gods for their own purposes, appealing for their help through prayer or compelling them to act through magic.

Another important aspect of Egyptian ideology was its extravagant belief in the afterlife and burial practices. The Egyptians made great efforts to ensure the survival of their souls after death, providing tombs, grave goods, and offerings believed to preserve the body and soul of the dead. Due to their belief systems, the Egyptians spent the majority of their lives preparing the extravagant pyramids that were designed to be the crypts of the Pharaohs.

The Egyptian way of life was an era of extreme hierarchy and a philosophy that denied human rights. The Pharaoh, together with his priests, was in complete control and embodied with the following belief: *This world was merely a passageway to another reality; and through the Pharaoh and his preparations for the afterlife, the Egyptians would be accepted into the next world.*

While Egypt has come to be known as the first sophisticated and advanced society, its ruthless nature and lack of empathy towards the Hebrew slaves is well documented. Egypt was a land that enslaved others—an endless cycle of stripping an individual of his right to be. For nearly 400 years, the Children of Israel endured endless suffering while being subjected to the Egyptian belief system.

The Egyptian environment was embodied in a master consciousness that manifested the reality of the slave. Through the slave's eyes, the perception of the master was empowered. Because the master/slave mentality directly opposed the belief or philosophy that all people are a facet of the Creator, we can easily determine the "philosophy of Oneness" was non-existent in this particular epoch.

The master empowers the slave;
and the slave empowers the master.
They feed from the same energy field.
One cannot exist without the other.

Although the master and the slave are at two opposite ends of one spectrum, these diverse forces of energy are forever connected and need each other to play their role in creation. They feed on the same energy—hierarchy, power, control, and submission. Interestingly, these opposite aspects of consciousness cannot play the game without the other.

In the end, the Egyptian's failed to make a quantum leap of consciousness. The Elohim stepped in and through divine intervention the Israelites were able to escape Egypt's energy of slavery and bondage. The vile nature of slavery consciousness eventually brought severe consequences to the Hebrew slaves, as well as the Egyptian people. Many, regardless of race or rank, would eventually become trapped in Egypt's reality of suffering.

Also fascinating, even though the Children of Israel were led out of Egypt by Moses, subliminally their consciousness would hold remnants of the Egyptian belief system. For generations, the Children of Israel would continue to be influenced by the Egyptian Matrix, together with its attitudes and ideologies. The memories of Egypt were deeply embedded in the Children of Israel, for it was all they had ever known.

Moses Descends the Mountain

When Moses faced the Godliness, this was a defining moment. We will never fully understand all that this extraordinary prophet encountered, nor will we know all that Moses knew. What we can know is the event on Mount Sinai was unprecedented, uncommon, and miraculous. Quite remarkably, this unique God/Man experience has failed to be understood, let alone replicated in our world.

Moses had transformed into a new level of human being. He became the personification of man's highest potential in the dimension of earth where man's spirit runs. In other words, Moses represented: *The highest level man can achieve through a deep God/Man relationship.* He was a living example of what is possible. Through his drastic transformation, Moses had "become," and he was chosen by the Godliness to bestow humanity with the greatest gift: *The enlightenment and energy of the Luchot.*

No one has experienced what Moses experienced because mankind has yet to meld and integrate, as Moses did, with the essence of the Divine. Therefore, it is impossible for us to feel the vibratory force of the Elohim as Moses did, or even relate to the overwhelming emotions Moses felt. To date, no one has walked down his path of enlightenment—a profound outcome of revelation gained from his experience on Mount Sinai. We are only left with his coded writings.

 ### English Translation: Exodus 32:7

And then Jehovah said unto Moses: 'Go down because your people whom you have brought up out of Egypt have become corrupt.'

Moses travelled to the top of the mountain where he stayed for forty days and forty nights. While he was away from his people, the Godliness warned Moses something had gone horribly wrong at the mountain's base. Jehovah informed Moses his people had become corrupted, and he must return immediately.

With the Luchot in his hand, Moses descended the mountain to where his people were. With every step he took, one can only imagine the thoughts and emotions rushing through his being. Even though Jehovah had warned him of a problem at the mountain's base, Moses knew his people would soon be given the greatest of all gifts and bestowed with the Elohim's most magnificent enlightenment.

As Moses entered his people's camp, his eyes took in an unbelievable sight. The Israelites were worshipping and dancing around a molten calf—an idol elevated to the status of the god of the Israelites. While he had been warned by God that his people had become corrupt, he had not expected this.

Shock, devastation, and anger were pounding through his veins. Overcome with disappointment, Moses realized the future he and the Elohim had imagined was quickly becoming a distant and far-off dream. At the bottom of the mountain, all he had hoped for was receding from his reality.

*The Israelites remained shackled to the powerful Egyptian Matrix.
The future of Adam was at risk.*

As we reflect on this story, we come to understand the Israelites had been influenced by the dominant consciousness of the times—Egyptian ideology and the philosophy of idol worship. The Israelites had gone through so much to escape bondage. How could they possibly choose to embrace a consciousness they had just fled? Why did the Israelites create a false god—the Golden Calf?

From the perspective of the Israelites, Moses had been away for far too long. In those forty days and nights, fear crept into the people's camp and they came to believe Moses would never return. They were desperate for a leader, and the Israelites feared they were on their own and, more importantly, godless.

While the Children of Israel recognized, even believed in, the God of Moses, they also believed—much more deeply—a replacement was needed for Moses and his God, both of which seemed to have vanished from the Israelites' reality.

Even though the Israelites had witnessed miracles and heard the Elohim's vibratory voice speaking through the thunder and lightning from the top of Sinai, they still believed themselves unworthy because Moses had not returned. The Israelites had convinced themselves Moses and "his" God had abandoned them, and they were now alone.

The Israelites needed a leader. They wanted an idol god they could see, touch, feel, and worship. While they had come to experience the Elohim, they failed to deeply understand the true God of this reality. But it didn't end there. The Israelites didn't believe in themselves, or in the Godliness of their being. At the very least, they didn't believe—enough. This changed the future of Moses' people because each man and woman creates the Godliness that melds with their inner belief of what is real and possible "for them."

To understand the factors that influenced the Israelites' choices, we must revisit Egyptian ideology. While the Egyptians more than likely believed in one source, they also worshipped various manifestations of the one source. For example, the Egyptians worshipped their idol god, "Ra," which reflected the creation of the sun, its power, and life giving energy.

Yet, behind "Ra" (the sun) was the belief in "Amun" (the source of all things), which represented the unknown and unseen realm of creation. When the Egyptians referred to Ra they, at times, referred to their sun god as AmunRa because they understood Ra was not the source, but a facet of "Amun" (the source of all things).

To understand the mindset of the Israelites, we must take in many factors. First, they had lived within the Egyptian society for centuries. For the Israelites who followed Moses into the desert, idol worship was all they had ever known.

Also interesting, the Israelites' consciousness also carried the aspect of "innocence." They never intermingled or married with a person of another culture, and they worked to keep their tribe intact. Also important, due to centuries of bondage, torture, and humiliation, they epitomized victim mentality. From their point of view, their lives were controlled by outer events.

Using Egyptian ideology as a roadmap to understand the past, we come to realize the Israelites did not deny the experience they had been through with Moses and the Elohim, but were seeking to validate their primary essence—redemption.

Just like their former taskmasters, the Israelites worked to create an idol god that reflected the way they saw themselves. Using what they knew, the Israelites created a statue of gold, elevated it to god status, and made sacrificial offerings in the hope they would be led to freedom and into the Promised Land.

The Mask of Egel Masecha

When Moses was on the mountain meeting with God, his brother, Aaron, the High Priest, was left in charge of the Israelites. It was during this period of time that Aaron and the Israelites created an idol god, "Egel Masecha," known in the Bible as the "Molten Calf" or "Golden Calf."

The Israelites had come to believe the Golden Calf was the aspect that represented the "redemption" they longed to experience. They convinced themselves to believe the Egel was the true god who had delivered them out of slavery and would soon lead them to the Promised Land.

Freedom, in the minds of the Israelites, was only attainable through wealth and power. Therefore, Aaron, the High Priest, together with the Israelites, melted their artifacts of gold and jewelry and molded them into a new idol to worship—a statue that portrayed a golden calf. Through the eyes of the Israelites, this idol of gold became their god of redemption. Like the gods of the Egyptians, the Israelites had manifested the god of their own consciousness. As they bowed to and worshipped their idol god, it became clear to Moses his people remained bound to the Egyptian Matrix and its powerful talons of consciousness.

Also fascinating, the Hebrew word, "Egel," has a hidden meaning, "circle," which infers to the matrix that encompasses a particular level of human consciousness. Furthermore, the Hebrew word, "Masecha," contains a hidden meaning, "mask." Much like a mask, the matrix that encircled the belief in the God of Egel Masecha hid the true reality of the Elohim from the Children of Israel.

The Genesis Code reveals when Aaron, the High Priest, and the Israelites created an idol god to worship, a new matrix became manifest at the bottom of the mountain. This new grid of consciousness, the Matrix of Egel Masecha, was empowered by the "Egel Man" (the people who empowered the God of Egel Masecha). The Genesis Code reveals a powerful revelation: *The Matrix of Egel Masecha rose within creation to hide the truth and deeper reality of the Godliness from those who willed this matrix into existence.*

But why did the Israelites believe the Golden Calf was the God of Israel that brought them out of Egypt? The "God of Egel Masecha" (the Golden Calf) represented "innocence and wealth." In the minds of the Israelites, both qualities were necessary if they were to reach the Promised Land. Therefore, the Israelites' idol god would need to reflect innocence and wealth before they could bow to, pray to, and worship that which they believed was the god of their new reality.

And so it was. The God of Egel Masecha reflected the innocent calf that pounces through the grass and drinks its mother's milk. It is basically an unaware animal that reflects purity. Also important, in the eyes of the Israelites, the calf represented wealth. Those who had oxen could plow their fields, plant crops, and live through a sense of security.

The God of Egel Masecha reflected the energy consciousness of the Israelites—their idea of innocence, purity, and wealth. Now the Israelites' consciousness was bound to the God of Egel Masecha, and they were blinded to the Elohim. The "mask" (Masecha) was now in play and would hide the higher truth of the "Elohim" (God) from the "Egel Man" (the Israelites) who empowered a "mass consciousness" (the Matrix of Egel Masecha). The Israelites had placed their belief in a false god that projected limitation. The Golden Calf would limit their potential and their relationship with the Elohim.

What is interesting, the moment the Matrix of Egel Masecha came into existence, a paradox was created, and duality rose to challenge the Israelites' idea of "redemption"—the motivation at the core of the matrix. Even though the Israelites had intended to manifest a new reality of innocence, purity, and wealth, an opposition to their intentions came into play to test their level of awareness. Now, a darker aspect rose within the matrix—guilt, impurity, and poverty—to challenge the Israelites "redemption" and the choices they would make.

Every conscious choice will always manifest its opposition in "potential." This is a universal law of consciousness. When one ideology is empowered, the consciousness that created the matrix also embodies a potent and opposing counterpart of potential.

*A paradox had been put into play.
At Mount Sinai, there was the God of
Moses and the God of Egel Masecha.
The Israelites had made their choice to
empower the Godliness that reflected
their "being" (be-in-god).*

Of relevance, the Elohim desired for the Israelites to break free from the Egyptian Matrix. With assistance from the Divine, the Israelites eventually escaped the borders of Egypt. Once free, the Israelites could have created a new matrix the Elohim desired to experience. This is a phenomenal revelation that reveals: *The Elohim wanted the people to free their consciousness from their narrow beliefs in themselves and in God.*

Even though the Egyptians were the greatest civilization at the time, their belief system was narrow in perception and limited the Godliness through their worship of idol gods. Even today, most religions continue this ritual and personify aspects of the Godliness through "icons" (things, animals, and humans), such as "Jesus" (Christianity), "Buddha" (Buddhists), "Muhammad" (Islam), "Mother Mary" (Catholics), and the "Messiah" (Judaism). These are only a few iconic idols that have become deeply embedded within human consciousness today.

It seems man must be able to experience a physical representation of the Godliness before he can identify with, and believe in, a powerful creative force. Through false and/or restrictive representations of the Godliness, man limits both God and himself. If a man believes the way to find God—or be accepted and desired by God—is only possible through his faith in an enlightened human being or idol god, he is subconsciously saying to God: *"As 'I Am,' I am not worthy enough for you. I have been taught I must go through something else, or someone else, to be accepted by you."* This distorted ideology supports a false matrix of limitation: *The Matrix of Egel Masecha.*

Even today, many religions are opposing the will of the Elohim as they create and worship man-like images, or animal gods, to reflect the All. This is not what the Elohim desires. Idol worship clashes with the truth of the unlimited Godliness that lives through everything. All men are facets of the Godliness—some are only more enlightened than others.

When Moses' brother "Aaron" (the High Priest) idolized the idea of purity, he created a mask that hid the truth from not only himself, but the Israelites. Aaron was subconsciously emoting impurity and guilt. In other words, while the people were idolizing and worshipping purity and innocence, they were subconsciously manifesting licentious experiences. The Israelites' reality now contained two extremes: *Innocence and corruption.* Interestingly, this reality would become a core experience for not only the Israelites, but mankind.

This, in fact, is no different than a belief system that idolizes a Creator that is only good—like the word, "God," that reflects the idea of something being "good." To realize goodness, to have a deep relationship with that which is perceived to be "good," we must also experience that which is its opposite. Through all aspects of duality, the Godliness comes to know its essence and potential through various matrixes of human consciousness. Everything is the Godliness.

As we live our lives, manifested through love, passion, and creativity, we will always face a duality that expresses the opposite of that which we desire to experience. As we experience both sides of duality, we come to know who we are. God is never separate from anything we experience—both the beautiful and horrific. Again, man creates his own reality. What he believes is possible, becomes possible.

If we are all God,
we are all Satan battling ourselves.

God is us, and we are God. God is not just good, God is everything. If we believe in "something," we create a possibility and new potential for our beliefs to manifest in "our reality." If we don't believe in something, it will never manifest in our reality—in this dimension or on the other side. What is true for you, carries the possibility of becoming in your world—both the physical world and formless world—but not necessarily in another's. You create the reality you believe to be real. You create sentient forms of consciousness. If you believe it, it can happen. If you don't believe it, it won't. The time is now for you to remove the mask and know the truth.

Breaking the Matrix

The Egyptian Matrix was born through an ancient consciousness. Even today, this powerful matrix exists, is immensely powerful, and remains rooted deep within human consciousness. We have never truly escaped its core ideology and energy consciousness.

The Egyptian Matrix was abusive and the energy that powered this matrix was, and continues to be, an insult and defamation of the "Elohim" (God). We are all facets of the Godliness. Each one of us reflects a different light of the "one living entity of consciousness"—a truth far different from the truth of the Egyptian Matrix and our attitudes today.

Under Egyptian rule, the Israelites had suffered greatly and experienced immense pain and tragedy for hundreds of years. The Hebrews' spirit ached to be free from Egyptian abuse, but the minority population within any matrix can become trapped in its jaws of reality. This was true for the slaves of long ago and is also true for the man of today. Many are locked into the jaws of suppression because the consciousness of the majority will always outweigh the few. In the case of the Hebrew slaves, the "majority population" (the Egyptians) refused to let Moses' people go.

Within any matrix, it is always possible for consciousness to elevate and move out of its current boundary of limitation. To do so, the majority within each matrix has to find their own key and door to walk through—just like Alice in Wonderland.

Your journey will always begin through the consciousness from which you desire to break free. Your journey into a higher level of self will always begin from your lowest point of self and at the base of the mountain you wish to climb.
There is no other way.

The Hebrew slaves' powerful desire and emotional longing for freedom and independence activated a potential within HaAdam. This potential would soon be activated by the spirit of the Hebrew slaves that desired a different reality. Through Moses, the Godliness would intervene and the slaves would be freed from Egypt.

From the perspective of the Israelites, they had escaped and broken free from their tormentors. Unfortunately, they weren't exactly correct. The Israelites may have been outside of the Egyptian border, but they had yet to escape the powerful grasp of Egyptian consciousness. Their minds had yet to be freed. On a subconscious level, the Israelites remained somewhat bound to the Egyptian Matrix.

Of extreme importance, we must acknowledge the Israelites' tremendous efforts and ground-breaking accomplishments. The Israelites had managed to distance themselves from the core of Egyptian consciousness. This, in itself, was a tremendous accomplishment. Even though they had not completely overcome the overbearing Egyptian Matrix, they bravely challenged the system and moved through the portal into a new matrix of potential at the base of Sinai. They had taken a quantum leap of consciousness and, at the very least, made it to the mountain of revelation.

The Israelites had entered the wilderness—a dimension between the matrix they had escaped and the matrix they had yet to manifest—the Promised Land. What they had failed to realize was the energy of suffering was deeply rooted in their subconscious self, and this vibratory persona would continue to influence their reality. The Israelites' journey into higher understanding had only just begun.

Regardless of the nature of the consciousness—whether oppressive or empowering—all energy consciousness is creative and manifests its truth and essence in man's reality. The Israelites' experience and memories of Egypt would flow in their blood for thousands of years. The culmination of their history was embedded in their DNA and would forever affect their perception of self.

In some way, Egypt would continue to have a hold on the Israelites, for they had yet to fully overcome this powerful energy embodiment. Even though they were physically free, they continued to be bound to its oppressive and painful consciousness.

In many ways, the man of today is not so different from the Israelites of long ago. We have distanced ourselves from Egypt's ancient beliefs and powerful matrix of consciousness. Unfortunately, the slave/master consciousness continues to prevail, and the numbers of those trapped in this level of consciousness are stronger than ever before.

For all of our great achievements, mankind has yet to reach spiritual enlightenment. We are brilliant creators and have grown our technical prowess. Nevertheless, humanity continues to wander in its vast desert of self. The times and events have changed, but we are still influenced by another type of Pharaoh—the taskmaster that controls our minds. We have yet to truly escape the matrix of narrow consciousness.

Like the Israelites, modern man is lost in another powerful illusion—an idea of a false God. Through powerful misconceptions, the truth of the Godliness—including the truth of Adam—has been masked from human awareness. Make no mistake this void of enlightenment has greatly affected human reality. Again, our inner world is the power that projects our outer world. It is time to remove the mask that shields the truth and limits human potential.

*If it surrounds you,
it is you.*

Through a narrow interpretation of the Torah, our minds have bought into a limited ideology of the Godliness. No different from the slaves of long ago, humanity remains shackled to its past. This is so because many of us are still enslaved to a false idea of God; and through our fixation and stagnant beliefs, our consciousness is tied up within itself—limiting our creative potential. Unfortunately, we have placed limitation on ourselves and also limited the Creator that imagined us. God becomes through man, and it is time Adam becomes the highly advanced creative being the Elohim intended for Adam to become.

Like the Israelites, today's man is striving to reach a new reality. Like the man of our past, the choices we make will, ultimately, reveal our deepest truth and show us who we are through our outer world. When a new consciousness streams into man's reality, there is always an equally powerful and opposing matrix to challenge a rising consciousness.

Humanity will always face another powerful path of potential with every choice that is made. Duality exists in every choice, every society, every continent, every walk of life, and within every level of human consciousness. Man cannot escape duality, and man must always be free to make his own choice and walk his own path. Enlightenment can never be forced. It must be accepted fully and absorbed by the observer freely.

*The secret to changing
the matrix of today...
you must believe it is possible.*

Know we have been tricked—maybe through good intentions—but nonetheless, we have been tricked through our perceptions of the Godliness, our perceptions of creation, and our perceptions of who and what we are. Yet, who have we been tricked by? It is us. We have played the ultimate trick on ourselves in the Game of God.

CHAPTER 9

The Paradox at Mount Sinai

We will now delve into the paradox of two brothers—one a Prophet and one a High Priest. Moses and Aaron represented two diverse aspects of God consciousness activated in man's reality. Each brother reflected an aspect of the God/Man relationship. In other words, each brother chose to walk in a particular level of awareness that ultimately reflected an example of the diverse types of relationships possible between God and man. The relationship experienced between God and Moses was certainly very different than the relationship experienced between God and Aaron.

What we realize is astounding. As we look deeper into the paradox at Mount Sinai, we find a higher vibratory force and level of God consciousness was at the "top of the mountain" (where Moses and Jehovah were), while a lower vibratory force manifested at the "mountain's base" (where Aaron and the Israelites were).

While Moses, the Prophet, was on top of the mountain receiving the first Torah and Luchot, at the base of the mountain, his brother and the High Priest, Aaron, allowed the Israelites to manifest a matrix that hid the truth of the Godliness—the Matrix of Egel Masecha. Through the trick, two diverse levels of God consciousness were manifesting and rising in Adam's reality.

As Moses descended the mountain, passing through its many levels, he carried the portal of enlightenment. Now, Moses had arrived where his people were. There, at Sinai's lowest level, a dichotomy of consciousness faced the Israelites.

In truth, the Elohim was observing its many aspects of potential as Sinai reveled in the essence of the "Luchot" (the enlightenment and highest vibratory force), the "Elohim" (Jehovah), "Moses" (the Prophet), his brother, "Aaron" (the High Priest), the "Israelites" (mankind), and the Israelite's "false god" (the God of Egel Masecha). What is absolutely fascinating, each of these expressions reflected diverse facets of potential within the Elohim's Hashomayim coming to life through Adamic Consciousness. Adam was creating his reality.

As one would imagine, the God of Moses and the God of Egel Masecha were contradictory and incompatible. At the bottom of Sinai, the Israelites had made their choice and absorbed the God consciousness that most closely reflected their level of awareness, creativity, and vibratory energy consciousness.

Regardless of its validity, the "Egel Man" (the Israelites) had formed a new God/Man relationship with the God they believed to be real. Now, through their particular level of awareness, the Israelites would project their essence in their outer world and particular scenarios would manifest that reflected their inner Godliness.

Like the Israelites of long ago, this remains true for the man of today. Many levels of Godliness are manifesting in the human world. Through life, those who walk in a higher level of awareness realize creation shows us the level of creativity we manifest through; and that it is both God and man that experience this creation. A secret is revealed: *Consciousness drives man, and man drives reality.*

Enlightenment can never be forced.
Enlightenment is always chosen.

A portal had opened at Sinai through which new aspects of duality, information, and enlightenment would enter man's awareness. The portal offered a new beginning for mankind and the potential for an advanced human being to manifest in the Elohim's creation and become a new experience for God.

This advanced matrix of potential was deeply desired by the Godliness. Therefore, the potential for an advanced level of man, inspired by the possibility and energy of enlightenment, was projected through Sinai and the Luchot into the dimension of man within Adam's mountain of self.

Sinai was, and continues to be, a paradox within a paradox. Sinai is a "dimension of extremes"—it projects the highest vibratory force, the lowest vibratory force, and every vibratory force that is a potential within the two extremes. Both the Elohim and Moses knew that if balance could be attained within Adamic Consciousness' "extremes of potential," the "metaphysical level" (the highest level) could meld with the "physical level" (the lowest level and end destination), and extreme enlightenment would be experienced in Adam's dimension of matter.

Sinai was, and is, a transformative dimension within the Elohim. Through this magnificent portal in creation, Adamic Consciousness was coming to realize its essence and collective level of awareness. At Sinai, a battle of consciousness was projected into play between the "God of the Egel Man" (manifested at the mountain's base) and the "God of Moses" (realized at the top of the mountain).

Moses achieved the highest potential of Adamic Consciousness through his deep understanding of the Creator.

As we ponder over the events at Sinai, questions flood into our awareness. At Sinai, did the Elohim simultaneously manifest its powerful duality—the "Luchot" (a high-level matrix and portal of cosmic consciousness) and its opposite, the "Golden Calf" (the Matrix of Egel Masecha)? Is it mere coincidence that the Luchot was manifest through Moses, and the Matrix of Egel Masecha was manifest through Aaron, Moses' brother—another duality and paradox? Was the Matrix of Egel Masecha put in place to challenge human awareness and test man's ability to see through the mask that hid the truth of the Godliness? Did the Elohim manifest the scenario of the Luchot, knowing mankind would fail to absorb the Luchot's enlightenment? Was this event, together with its outcome, one piece of a larger puzzle—part of the grand story that would unfold over time?

While many questions surround Sinai, there is no doubt that Moses found himself standing in the midst of opposing realities. At the base of the mountain, contrasting matrixes of consciousness were battling to take hold in human consciousness and become the driving force in the Elohim's creation. The

Elohim had offered the highest level of spiritual enlightenment to mankind, and God's creation was in a dilemma. The Elohim's scenarios of possible realities were now unfolding through the illusion of time in the dimension of man.

The Rejection of the Luchot

Consciousness drives man. Consciousness drives events. Consciousness drives reality. Consciousness will always project its expression so that it can experience its potential. It is what it is in the moment—whether negative or positive. For the Israelites, and the future of mankind, their projection of self— the Godliness they believed to be real—would have profound implications within HaAdam. The story of man was unfolding in the Heavens and Earth.

 ### English Translation: Exodus 32:7-9

Then Jehovah said to Moses, "Go down, because your people, whom you brought up out of Egypt, have become corrupt. They have been quick to turn away from what I commanded them and have made themselves an idol cast in the shape of a calf. They have bowed down to it and sacrificed to it and have said, 'These are your gods, O Israel, who brought you up out of Egypt.'" "I have seen these people," Jehovah said to Moses, "and they are a stiff-necked people. Now leave *me alone so that my anger may burn against them and that I may destroy them. Then I will make you (Moses) into a great nation."*

At the highest level of Sinai, the Luchot had been activated by the Elohim in our world. Although Jehovah knew the Israelites had gone astray, Jehovah told Moses to take the Luchot—a portal of transformation—to the people. Moses understood the Egyptian Matrix, a powerful self-aware entity of consciousness, would not let the Israelites go without a fight.

Moses had left the dimension at the mountain's peak, only to find himself in a different dimension at the mountain's base. He had walked straight into a powerful paradox. Moses now faced his people and their God of Egel Masecha. The portal was open and vibrating with intensity, but it was now up to the Israelites to accept its energy and absorb its enlightenment.

History shows us it is extremely difficult for mankind to break away from established ideas and belief systems, and this was true for the Israelites as well. Although they had escaped the physical shackles of bondage, their minds and hearts were not completely free from the Egyptian Matrix.

For Moses, this was a moment of riveting realization. In the eyes of the Godliness, Moses knew the Israelites had taken a tremendous fall. There, as he faced his people, he realized he was alone amongst his fellow men—left with only himself and his inner Godliness. Sadly, Moses realized his people weren't ready for the Luchot's enlightenment, nor could they absorb the portal's vibratory force.

The Israelites' consciousness was no match for the Luchot's advanced enlightenment and vibratory force. This was a shattering blow for Moses, for he realized there would be serious consequences for his people whom he had shepherded out of Egypt. The Luchot's overwhelming energy force and power could, unintentionally, do great harm to—or even destroy—the very people it intended to enlighten and elevate.

What has never been realized, the Israelites weren't ready to absorb the Luchot's enlightenment. Understanding how consciousness operates, it becomes clear his people were unable to accept and absorb its energy. Unlike the Burning Bush, their bodies of physical matter would surely be consumed by the Luchot's fiery energy. Physically, and spiritually, the people had not advanced enough.

Moses had done as he was told to do. The portal had been opened. He had made it possible for great revelations to stream into man's reality. The Luchot had been brought down the mountain. It was now possible for an advanced level of human being to reach a higher level of God consciousness—a new level of man that would be perceived and experienced by the Elohim.

However, unlike Moses, the Israelites had not done as they were told to do. They created, worshipped, and believed in a false god. Choices had been made. Actions had been taken. Now Moses was forced to do the same. There was no doubt in Moses' mind, the Luchot's vibratory force could not pulsate amongst the Israelites. If it did, it would overtake their essence and destroy them. Moses knew the portal to God's greatest enlightenment had to be closed. To save his people, the Luchot would have to be hidden from the minds of mankind. Their hearts were not ready.

The Portal of Enlightenment Closes

 English Translation: Exodus 32:19

And it came to pass, as soon as he came near to the camp that he saw the calf, and the dancing; and Moses' anger burned hot; and he threw the tablets from his hands, and broke them beneath the mount.

The Egel Man was in play—idolizing their God of Egel Masecha. After rising to the highest level of self, Moses was forced to witness a devastating setback and undesirable reality in our world. At the base of Mount Sinai, the Israelites had created the path of their choosing—a path that led to a reality far different than what God desired to experience.

Then the realization hit. The Luchot, together with its enlightenment, would soon be a faded memory in the minds of man. Moses had to face an inescapable truth: *The Luchot's vibratory force far exceeded that of the Israelites, and Moses knew a melding of consciousness was impossible for this generation of man.*

With the overwhelming feeling of failure, Moses understood a deep and profound relationship with the Elohim was no longer possible for the Children of Israel. Overcome with anger, Moses threw the mystical tablets to the ground—breaking them into pieces. The Luchot was now broken, and so was the possibility of a high-level connection to the Godliness. And in this moment, in the dimension of man, the portal of Sinai closed to the Adam of yesterday.

In the Hashomayim of the Godliness, an advanced level of Adam would remain unrealized, and the Elohim was raging with anger against his people. Even though the "Elohim's spirit" (Aretz) had latched onto the most extraordinary potential within HaAdam's Adamic Consciousness and projected a new possibility into man's world, a new level of Adam would remain unrealized within the Elohim's Hashomayim.

The message for today's man follows: *We drive reality—not God.* The Israelites were unable to accept and comprehend the truth of the Godliness. It was a level of reality they could not absorb. This was a powerful setback to mankind's intellectual and emotional advancement, and the question is still being asked, "Will man be able to accept this level of reality 3,500 years later?"

The portal of enlightenment closed.
Adam was not ready.

As we scrutinize the breaking of the Luchot, we find there is much to know. For example, why does the Torah specifically state Moses threw the tablets and broke them at the "bottom" of the mountain? When the Torah specifies a descriptive detail such as this, one can be assured there is enlightenment to be discovered.

What then, does the "bottom" of the mountain reveal on a metaphysical level? The bottom of the mountain is where the Israelites were. The bottom reflects the lowest point—the starting point of a new beginning. The base of the mountain is where the people stood, where their power was, and what they reflected on a physical, metaphysical, conscious, and subconscious level. The vibration at the mountain's base matched the vibration of the people.

With the breaking of the Luchot, severe consequences would be felt in Adam's world. Mankind had closed the doors to the Godliness and, regardless of the number of apologies made to God by the people, the portal would remain closed to the consciousness of the Egel Man. Like the Israelites, the Elohim had also made a choice that would affect humanity's outcome. God would close the portal, and the enlightenment offered through the Luchot would soon fade away into the shadows of creation and become lost to human awareness.

*At the bottom of the mountain,
the Luchot was hidden
in the dimension of man—
where Adam's spirit moved.*

The Genesis Code's revelations into the Egel Man are quite phenomenal. The Egel Man would no longer have access to the Luchot's vast potential, for he was unable to absorb the Luchot's vibratory force. Therefore, the Egel Man's eyes would no longer witness the Luchot's letters and words floating into man's reality, nor would they be able to feel the essence of the Luchot's enlightenment permeate through their being. In the end, this aspect of Adam was unable to establish a deep connection with the Godliness or see creation through the eyes of the Divine.

The breaking of the Luchot was more than unfortunate. To the Elohim it was a devastating setback. Yet, we must also recognize something extraordinary did happen with the giving of the Luchot: *The Elohim's enlightenment did stream into Adam's level of existence.* Much like a waterfall that flowed into the valleys below, the vibration of the Luchot was brought down the mountain to where the people were. This, too, is a phenomenal revelation. Humanity doesn't thrive at the mountain's peak, but in the flat lands and valleys at the mountain's base.

Sadly, the Luchot can never be put back together again, and another astounding revelation is realized: *Even though the connection between the Luchot and Adam had been severed, the connection had been "seeded" in the dimension of man.* Although the Luchot was never absorbed by the Israelites, its potential was brought down to earth, and buried in the mountain of man where it would lay dormant—hidden from man's awareness.

This, in itself, becomes extremely important to the man of today. Even though the portal of Sinai had closed and the Luchot's connection to Sinai was severed, mankind is to know the potential for a deep and personal God/Man relationship is still possible. This time, however, will be different than before. In the time of Moses, God had opened the portal making it possible for the ancients to achieve extraordinary enlightenment in one quantum leap. Yet, this opportunity was lost as the portal shut to the man of our past.

It would be thousands of years before the Luchot's enlightenment would be gifted to a future level of Adam. Unlike the Adam of the past, mankind would need to evolve before he was given another opportunity to absorb and implement this understanding in our world.

Adam: An Extraordinary Creator

 ### Hebraic Text: Shemos 32:31-32

וַיָּשָׁב מֹשֶׁה אֶל יְהוָה וַיֹּאמַר אָנָּא חָטָא הָעָם הַזֶּה חֲטָאָה גְדֹלָה וַיַּעֲשׂוּ לָהֶם אֱלֹהֵי זָהָב: וְעַתָּה אִם תִּשָּׂא חַטָּאתָם וְאִם אַיִן מְחֵנִי נָא מִסִּפְרְךָ אֲשֶׁר כָּתָבְתָּ:

 ### English Translation: Exodus 32:31-32

So Moses went back to the Lord and said, "Oh what a great sin these people have committed? They have made themselves gods of gold. But now, please forgive their sin—but if not, then blot me out of the book you have written."

The Genesis Code: Exodus 32:31-32

And Moses said, "What a great sin these people have committed? They have made themselves gods of gold. But now, forgive them for their lack of awareness. And if you choose not to forgive my people, if you choose to destroy the Israelites and all of mankind, I no longer wish to exist in this dimension, nor any other dimension within the All. If destruction of the people is your choice, remove me from your mind and memory banks as if I never was.

Moses had offered all that he was to both God and man. He was the true shepherd, for he had led his people to the mountain of revelation. But the Israelites had failed to absorb the truth of what the Godliness is. Through the eyes of the Divine, Adam was a failed creation and severe consequences would be felt for what the people had done.

The Israelites had angered Jehovah so much so, God threatened to destroy the Israelites and replace them with Moses' offspring. This was a shattering blow to Moses, and he would never agree to God's angry terms. Moses stood up to Jehovah—putting himself in the breech and becoming the sacrificial lamb. If Jehovah destroyed his people, Moses asked to be taken out of creation—completely. If Jehovah destroyed the Israelites, Moses demanded there be no remnant of his existence.

This was a pivotal moment in the God/Man relationship, and Moses put his very reality—the truth of who he was and what he believed—on the line. He had to convince Jehovah there was hope for mankind. Moses knew another possibility and outcome was possible for a future generation—for a more advanced level of man. Moses knew he must somehow preserve the Luchot's enlightenment for a consciousness that had yet to be born.

If not for Moses, man's future would have been extinguished long ago. Due to his intercession and belief in Adam's potential, mankind was given another opportunity in the Elohim's creation. With a new chance, the Jehovah entrusted Moses to deliver his people to their unique land of enlightenment—a place that would vibrate in harmony with the Children of Israel. One day, when a future generation of Adam was ready, another path and portal would open in Adam's world.

*Maybe our consciousness was too young;
or possibly we just weren't ready to
absorb the highest level of Godliness
3,500 years ago.*

Through the eyes of the Elohim, mankind had chosen the wrong path. Moses understood this. He also knew the Luchot's enlightenment had failed to take hold within human consciousness. The potential for a high-level matrix had imploded with the breaking of the Luchot. Moses was faced with a dilemma. How would he preserve God's enlightenment for Adam's future generations? How would he keep the Luchot alive?

Moses Ascends Sinai Once Again

As Moses observed the Israelites bowing to the God of Egel Masecha, it was clear mankind needed more time before they could advance within creation. The Luchot had been broken, and both God and Moses knew another level of enlightenment was needed in man's world. Then, Jehovah called out to Moses and instructed him to climb Sinai's steep terrain and meet him on the mountaintop once again. There, Moses would stay for another forty days and forty nights waiting to receive another Torah from God.

What is interesting is that prior to his ascent up the mountain, Moses was instructed by Jehovah to create two new stone tablets and carry them up the mountain. Unlike the first Luchot that was both created and written by the Elohim, it was apparent this secondary set of tablets would be different from the first in every way. The second tablets would be created at the mountain's base—amongst the energy of the people—and brought up the mountain to where Jehovah was.

At the top of Sinai, Jehovah would give Moses a new Torah that emanated another level of enlightenment. Unlike the high-powered Luchot that vibrated the frequency of Sinai's highest point, the message carved within the second set of tablets would vibrate a lower frequency—a vibration aligned to those who were camped at Sinai's base.

Again, Moses would do as Jehovah had instructed him to do. Ten commandments had been given, and he would carry the ten statements carved in stone down the mountain and deliver them to his people. As one would expect, this second set of tablets contained a very different level of enlightenment than the first set of tablets.

It is true the Ten Commandments lacked a complex look into the Godliness; however, this enlightenment addressed man's needs at the time. While less complex than their predecessor, the Ten Commandments provided humanity with something they had never had before—basic and necessary truths, moral guidelines, and laws given to become the foundation for civilization and new societies.

There is much to learn from this story. First and foremost, the Ten Commandments were given to the Israelites to guide humanity on their life path. Also extremely important to understand, unlike the first Torah and Luchot, the second Torah and Ten Commandments was successfully integrated within the Egel Man's consciousness—the active consciousness of the times.

The Ten Commandments suited mankind's position at Sinai. Ten basic laws of wisdom were given to address the man at the base of the mountain—where Adam's journey into enlightenment would begin. Through their wisdom, human consciousness could begin its transformation into higher levels of awareness and begin the slow climb up the mountain of revelation.

Because these ten statements and moral laws were accepted, understood, and integrated throughout our world, we know, on a metaphysical level, the Ten Commandments projected a level of God consciousness that fused with the human mindset 3,500 years ago. As man accepted and absorbed this secondary level of enlightenment, this vibration became the "core relationship" between man and God.

Realize this particular relationship between God and man became the spiritual motivation for humanity. Powerful matrixes rose, spurred by religious ideology. These active levels of consciousness successfully projected doomful, fear-based realities in our world. Know the matrix of yesterday remains a powerful presence in today's world. This is so because the majority of mankind still empowers the age-old perception that God exists outside of man. The Matrix of the Egel Man, together with his idol gods, remains deeply embedded in human consciousness. Humanity is still struggling to grasp the God of our reality.

Wisdom from our past is vital. It is how we see and recognize where we began, together with how far we have travelled. No one denies the power or beauty within the Ten Commandments. Their laws and moral guidelines have become the cornerstone of the Western world's justice system. They are the measuring stick of morality that speaks to man's primal self.

However, it is imperative to address the vibratory force that emanates through their message. The guiding light of the Ten Commandments was intended to be a starting point for man, but certainly not a resting spot or final destination. From their words, we were meant to evolve and become more than we were before.

"My Face Is Your Face"

Nearly seventy percent of the world's population identifies with the translated Bible and deeply believes it is God's message to mankind. The words that flow from the pages of the Five Books of Moses are both beautiful and profound, yet we must remain aware of the Torah's secret: *Its words are riddled with a coded message of enlightenment that is the vibratory force of the Luchot.*

One cannot deny the following fact: *Man's belief systems have led us to where we are today.* Unfortunately, many have stopped searching for new understanding in the Bible. This is neither good nor bad. It is what it is.

The Genesis Code reveals a powerful revelation in God's second statement of the Ten Commandments: *Mankind must not embrace a mental image of God.* Yet, man has done so since the beginning. While this has been made clear by the Godliness, mankind continues to embrace and empower various images of God within his mind and heart.

Biblical Translation Exodus 20:3-5	The Genesis Code Exodus 20:3-5
The 2nd Commandment	**The 2nd Commandment**
"You shall have no other gods before me. You shall not make for yourself a carved image, or any likeness of anything that is in heaven above, or that is in the earth beneath, or that is in the water under the earth; you shall not bow down to them nor serve them."	"You should not have, for yourselves, any other gods upon my face. My face is your face. Do not motivate your aim of consciousness, in matter, to be anything other than what you set your face as. I am found in the 'now' through the face of man and man's perception of reality. If man creates a philosophy or image to motivate himself, man is putting a 'false' mask or 'face' on me, thus, hiding from the truth."

What is the Elohim telling us in this statement? When the Godliness states, "Do not have any other gods upon my face" it means, "My face is your face." But what is God's face that can be placed upon us? If God forbids an image, how can God have a face?

Know God's face can be seen in the dimension of "now." God is revealed in the present moment through human nature, and all that surrounds us. It is anything and everything that can enter one's consciousness. This is how the face of God appears to us, and reveals itself, in man's reality. The face of God is everything we see and all that we come across. The face of God is all that enters our personal universe. The face of God is everything and anything man can ever imagine, encounter, experience and know.

You, your awareness,
your joy and pain,
are truly me.
There are no other gods.
There is you and me.

Modern day man has mostly lost touch with nature, the depths of his vast soul, and what he is capable of. He has lost sight of the Godliness that is man. He doesn't believe in his powers of manifestation. He has become robotic in nature. Today's man knows this. Today's man knows we have put false faces on God. Today's man knows we have gone off course. Today's man knows it is time to change our path.

Humanity is searching for a doorway into a peaceful existence—a reality powered by love, compassion, and understanding—not greed, power, and wars that create unbearable suffering and pain. The portal exists. Man only needs to find it, allow it to open, and move through it. Man needs to recognize and empower the Godliness that is him and the Godliness that is all around him. The face of God is the face of man and man's perception of reality.

CHAPTER 10

The Metaphorical Mountain

The Torah explains the Children of Israel were forbidden to venture on Mount Sinai. They had been instructed to remain at the mountain's base and wait for Moses to return. Jehovah warned that death would be the fate of any man, woman, child, or animal that attempted to climb the mountain or set foot on the mountain's edge.

Also fascinating, the Torah clearly states any living thing—whether man or animal—that entered the dimension of Sinai after being instructed not to do so, must never be touched by anyone again—under any circumstances. Furthermore, the Godliness instructed the Israelites to kill those who entered the restricted Sinai by either stoning or bow and arrow. Interestingly, per God's orders, death by close combat was forbidden, and this detail offers further insight into the revelation of Sinai.

It becomes clear the Israelites were strictly forbidden to wander near the boundaries of the mountain or step foot on the mountain's soil. But why were the Israelites forbidden to go near the mountain? Furthermore, if they did set foot upon the mountain, why was no one allowed to touch them upon their return? Why must they be killed? There is much to be discovered within these scriptures, and the question rises, "Why did Jehovah command the Children of Israel, together with their animals and livestock, to stay away from Mount Sinai?"

English Translation: Exodus 19:10-13

And Jehovah said to Moses, "Go to the people and consecrate them today and tomorrow. Have them wash their clothes and be ready by the third day, because on that day the Lord will come down on Mount Sinai in the sight of all the people. Put limits for the people around the mountain and tell them, 'Be careful that you do not go up the mountain or touch the foot of it. Whoever touches the mountain shall surely be put to death. He shall surely be stoned or shot with arrows; not a hand is to be laid on him. Whether man or animal, he shall not be permitted to live.' Only when the ram's horn sounds a long blast may they go up to the mountain."

Mount Sinai is much more than current translations allude to. Sinai was an alternate dimension and a magnificent portal that opened long ago. Sinai is a point of connection that links the physical world to the metaphysical world. Through the metaphorical mountain, the Elohim is revealing to mankind how portals of enlightenment open and connect to earth consciousness.

Sinai is a portal that connects to the highest level in man's three-dimensional reality—the peak of the mountain. It also is a metaphor for the highest level in man's dimension of self. Through the portal of Sinai, enlightenment flows freely from an unrealized dimension of the Godliness into the dimension of man. From the top of the mountain to the valleys at its base, enlightenment streams freely—much like a waterfall cascading to the depths below where man drinks in its waters of consciousness.

Moses was the core of Hashomayim, meaning he was the highest level of Adamic Consciousness. Therefore, Moses was able to climb to the peak of his own mountain and meld with the consciousness and vibratory force of the portal's super-advanced enlightenment—a spiritual fire and energy that seared into Sinai's peak and vibrated within and throughout the mountain, itself.

Whereas Moses represented the core of Hashomayim's HaAdam, the Israelites represented HaAdam's many singularities of varying potential and the plight of Adamic Consciousness in this dimension. As experiences played themselves out at Sinai, it became clear to the Elohim that humanity required additional time to experience its essence and truth. Adam needed to evolve so that a future generation of man could resonate the enlightenment of Sinai.

There is another metaphor within this story. A man can only venture upon the mountain of revelation if he vibrates in harmony with the mountain's peak. If man does not resonate the enlightenment streaming through the portal, he cannot go near it, or come in contact with, the portal's energy field in any way, whatsoever.

Understand the entire mountain was trembling with the vibratory force of the Godliness. While many have interpreted this to mean God did not want the Children of Israel to enter the domain of Sinai, the true reason is they couldn't. If they did, they would die not a normal death, but a particular "type of death."

Even though it was possible for a man, woman, child, or animal to return from the vibrating mountain and re-enter the camp, their life force would, ultimately, be destroyed. The energy and vibratory force of Jehovah would overtake their spirit. In essence, both the physical and metaphysical aspect of the person or animal would have been overcome by tremendous energy and overtaken by a level of enlightenment ill-suited for their vibrational life force.

If this were to happen, God knew they would still be alive and breathing, but they would no longer be human as we understand "human" to be. For this very reason, no one could touch a person or animal that had absorbed Sinai's energy field. If they did, the overpowering energy of Sinai would transfer from one man or animal into another—much like a high-voltage electric shock that would short-circuit their life force.

Man cannot go too high too quickly. It can become extremely dangerous, even deadly. Because the Israelites were forbidden to go near Sinai, or journey up the mountain to reach its peak, we know they were physically and emotionally unable to absorb Sinai's energy and remain a living human being with an independent vibratory energy consciousness.

Now you know why the Torah clearly states any living thing that entered the dimension of Sinai, whether man or animal, must never be touched by another. Furthermore, you also understand why the Godliness ordered those who entered Sinai to be killed "from a distance" by stoning or bow and arrow. This warning was stated to protect the Children of Israel, and not an attempt to deny the people enlightenment. Until the ram's horn was blown from the top of Sinai—a signal that Jehovah's essence and vibratory power had lifted from the mountain—no man, woman, child, or animal would dare walk its path or enter its portal of transformation.

English Translation: Exodus 19:16-19

And it came to pass on the third day, when it was morning, that there was thunder and lightning and a thick cloud upon the mount, and the voice of a horn was exceedingly loud; and all the people that were in the camp trembled. And Moses brought forth the people out of the camp to meet the Elohim; and they stood at the foot of the mount. Now Mount Sinai was altogether on smoke, because Jehovah descended upon it in fire; and the smoke thereof ascended as the smoke of a furnace, and the whole mount quaked greatly. And when the voice of the horn waxed louder and louder, Moses spoke, and the Elohim answered him by a voice.

As they gazed towards the smoking peak of Sinai, the Israelites heard the Elohim speak to them from the mountaintop, through the roar and vibration of the thunder and lightning. Upon observing the happenings at Sinai, the Israelites ran in fear unable to take the Elohim's power and revelation.

It becomes obvious the Israelites were fearful of the Elohim. Since escaping Egypt, they had come closer to the Godliness than ever before. Also interesting, the place the Israelites stood—the base of the mountain—is a reflection of "where Adam's potential was" at that moment in time.

The Israelites had grown, were out of bondage, and were now at liberty to project their inner Godliness without interference. They could move at will and make choices on their own. In essence, the Israelites would embellish their own level of consciousness and climb the mountains that reflected their essence, internal vibration, and life force.

To fully understand the metaphorical mountain, we must delve into the dimension of Sinai—a vibratory realm that represents the portal connected to man's mountain of self. The top of the mountain reflects the highest level of enlightenment and the portal that leads to "the other side." At the "mountain's peak" (Sinai's point), the deepest connection to the Elohim is realized.

The Israelites were camped at Sinai's base. It is important to realize, while they weren't allowed to venture near the dimension of Sinai, they had successfully moved forward and progressed in many ways. They had moved out of Egypt and had survived their journey to the mountain of revelation—Mount Sinai. This was an amazing feat, for the Israelites had escaped bondage and made it to the mountain, itself. Even if they could not venture onto the mountain, but only stand at the mountain's base, they had made it. They had arrived at the mountain of transformation—the portal of the Godliness.

While one would imagine the top of the mountain is more important than the bottom, this is not so. The base of the mountain is just as important as the mountain's peak. The mountain exists to be climbed and experienced. Moreover, every climb must begin at the mountain's base, and through the climbing, we experience enlightenment.

Just as important, when one reaches the top and achieves enlightenment, the new vibration and energy consciousness is to be brought down to where the people's consciousness is active. Only then is it possible for new enlightenment to be accepted and absorbed by those at the mountain's base. This is what Moses did. He brought two different sets of tablets, offering different vibratory levels of enlightenment, to his people who were waiting in the valley below.

The metaphorical mountain represents levels within creation and levels within man. Throughout our life, we evolve and climb our mountain of self, reaching many plateaus and levels along the mountain's path. Sometimes we stop and rest, and other times we slip and fall along the way. Therefore, many of us end our journey where we find comfort—never reaching the top—a metaphor for our highest potential of self. This journey into the unknown is different for each of us.

We are creators of our own reality, and we each have our own unique mountains of spiritual revelation to experience. As we travel up the mountain, our vibration changes, as will our experiences and relationships. However, there is a secret: *Our journey will always begin at the opposite spectrum of what we desire.* Where we stand at the moment will always symbolize our lowest level of self and the potential for the new moment; and from the new moment, we will face our next mountain to climb.

The Revelation of the High Priest

Many believe the highest level of enlightenment can be found through lengthy meditations at the mountain's peak. Know this is not God's intention. God does not desire for man to be in a continuous state of meditative bliss, but be an active participant in life. We are intended to share our enlightenment and experiences with others as they move in and out of our personal universe.

The base of the mountain is where our journey into self begins. It is where we come from, where we live, and the place we will forever be connected to in this reality. The bottom of the mountain is vital within human consciousness, for it represents our earthiness, our humanness, and where our primal animal selves thrive.

One must remain aware of a hidden truth: *As we climb our mountains, the purpose in the climb is to reach the top, achieve enlightenment, then return to the mountain's base where our newfound enlightenment can be shared with our fellow man.* As revealed through "Aharon's" coded name, translated in English as "Aaron," we find that even the Godliness comes down the mountain to bring new aspects of enlightenment to man.

The Genesis Code reveals Aaron represented one of two diverse potentials of the Godliness expressing a probable future. Even though Aaron was a High Priest and Moses' brother, his role was significant in allowing the Golden Calf to become manifest.

Prior to ascending Sinai, Moses had left his brother in charge. Therefore, Aaron's input and approval of tribal matters definitely empowered the manifestation of the Matrix of Egel Masecha. Nothing could have been more detrimental for the Children of Israel.

Because of Aaron's agreement to the Israelites' demands, the possibility for a deep God/Man relationship was no longer possible for the Children of Israel. Through agreement, Aaron had empowered an idol God and humanity would pay a costly price. The potential for a high-level connection to the Elohim would be severed in man's world, forever changing the life path of Moses, the Israelites, and the future of mankind.

The Secret of AHARON (Aaron)

HEBREW	LETTERS AND CODE	VALUE	CODED MEANING
ALEPH א	ALEPH; LAMED; PHEY אלף	1	Prime Cause and Motivator; The Elohim.
HEY ה	HEY; YOD הי	5	Breath; Active seed.
RESH ר	RESH; YOD; SHIN ריש	200	Head; Beginning; Transformation.
"FINAL" NUN ן	NUN; VOV; FINAL NUN נון	50	Lowest level; Moving down.

As we unveil the hidden code within "Aharon's" name, we find this High Priest was the "apex of the Israelites' consciousness." (A)aron's name begins with the "Aleph" which represents "the Prime Cause and Motivator." The last letter of Aaro(n)'s name contains a "Final Nun" which represents "the Godliness moving down to the lower dimensions of man's consciousness." Therefore, "Aaron's" deeper meaning is: *The Godliness going down towards the people, with the High Priest being man's representative to God.*

The Godliness desired a more intimate and aware relationship with its creation. Yet, the people failed to integrate the highest level of enlightenment, and God was forced to relate to mankind through a lower vibratory consciousness. Therefore, the High Priest was reluctantly chosen to represent the spiritual aspect of humanity and plant seeds of potential in man's world. A revelation is given: *Within societies, man's spirit runs—from the lowest of levels to the highest of levels. Whatever man believes God to be—whether accurate or inaccurate—God is always present waiting for man to take a quantum leap into higher awareness.*

The Paradox:
Two brothers, one a High Priest and the other a Prophet, represented two diverse levels of God consciousness in this creation.

Aaron, the High Priest, represents an extreme—the Godliness being coerced to come down the mountain to integrate a lower level of God consciousness within mankind. Aaron allowed the

Israelites to create the God of Egel Masecha—a false god. This was a grave mistake for it manifested a matrix that hid the truth.

This chosen reality was absolutely unacceptable to the Elohim. However, because Moses boldly interceded and asked Jehovah to forgive the Israelites and Aaron, the Godliness ultimately agreed to come down the mountain and integrate with Aaron, the High Priest. What is important to realize, the Godliness came down the mountain to integrate a lower level of enlightenment because the people "were unable to go up."

Through Aaron's name, we are shown even a High Priest can lose sight of the highest level of enlightenment and unknowingly lead others into lower levels of God consciousness. In summary, because Aaron failed to deeply believe in himself and the God of Moses, he allowed the many to influence and disempower his own Godliness. His stance was weak, and he complied with those who walked in fear and needed a false God to worship and pray to.

Aaron represented the people of the times, and the particular level of God/Man relationship that was active in the lowest dimension of man. Unlike the meshing of energies between Moses and God, the Israelites' relationship with the Godliness was disconnected and hampered by illusions, doubt, and fear.

In fact, it is only because Moses intervened and pleaded with God that the Israelites weren't abandoned or destroyed by the Elohim. Even though they were misguided in their beliefs, Jehovah came down the mountain to be present in man's reality. The Godliness had reluctantly agreed to be active in the lowest level of man.

This is an unbelievable revelation. Because of Moses, the Godliness agreed to be present within all levels of human consciousness regardless of a singularity's status, race, culture, sex, or perception of God, reality, and creation. While the Godliness integrates with the enlightened man at the top of the mountain, the Godliness also integrates with man, at his lowest levels of self, at the mountain's base.

At the bottom of the mountain, Aaron, the High Priest, empowered the Matrix of Egel Masecha—an environment that hid the true reality of God.

Another subtle revelation surfaces through the two brothers, Moses and Aaron. Moses' name begins with the last letter of the Elohi(m), the "Mem," which reflects "matter" or "matter consciousness." (A)aron's name begins with the first letter of the (E)lohim, the "Aleph," which reflects "the Prime Cause expressing its essence in creation."

What is fascinating, Moses had to climb to the top of the mountain to reach the highest level of enlightenment. In other words, Moses represented man's consciousness going up the mountain to receive enlightenment from the "Prime Cause and Motivator" (the Elohim). Moses represented "man becoming" (be-come-to-me).

Paradoxically, the "Prime Cause and Motivator" (the Elohim), represented through the "Aleph" in "(A)aron's" name, went down the mountain—through the Luchot and Ten Commandments—to be with man at the lowest level. The secret code in Aaron's name reveals a phenomenal revelation: *Even through our mistakes, the Godliness is present.*

When we fall down and make terrible choices, God is always with us, even in our lowest and darkest moments. Man, regardless of his level of enlightenment, will forever define the Godliness of this dimension. God is always with us, waiting for us to take that quantum leap. Transformation is always possible, and God is with mankind in all scenarios, experiences, and outcomes.

Moses and Aaron were two diverse aspects of God consciousness. Furthermore, both were instrumental in bringing the Torah down to earth, from the top of the mountain to the bottom of the mountain, where humanity lives and projects realities.

Through The Genesis Code, we are shown that a lower level of consciousness can become a primary factor—and the very stepping stone—that allows new enlightenment to be implemented in the lower dimensions of man. From where we stand, even at our lowest point, we must awaken our potential before we can transcend our own mountain of enlightenment and realize the Godliness that is truly us.

The Last Mountain Moses would Climb

One more mountain awaited Moses—Mount Nebo. This would be the last mountain Moses would ever climb. There, Moses was shown the land God had promised his forefathers. As his eyes gazed upon the beauty of the land before him, he longed to enter, but it was not to be. He knew his life would soon be coming to a close.

As Moses reflected on his life and the quest of his people, he knew the Israelites had gained a greater understanding of the Godliness than ever before. He was proud of his people, for they had endured so much to arrive in this place of beauty. Through their forty years of wandering in the wilderness, Moses knew humanity had made a quantum leap and the Elohim's creation had experienced a major shift in consciousness.

As Moses embraced his people's journey, he was saddened in knowing the Israelites had never absorbed the enlightenment of the Luchot—for this was God's true gift to humanity. In some way, Moses must have felt as if he had failed his people.

English Translation: Deuteronomy 34:4

And the "Lord" (Jehovah) said unto Moses: "This is the land which I swore unto Abraham, unto Isaac, and unto Jacob, when I said, 'I will give it to your descendants.' I have let you see it with your eyes, but you will not cross over into it."

Moses had walked his own path and climbed many mountains with the Elohim. As he looked upon the hills and valleys of the Promised Land, Jehovah told Moses he was not allowed to enter into the land made for his people. The Elohim would deny Moses his heart's desire. Moses could only look upon the land of his people, but his feet could never touch its soil.

We can only imagine how he felt having gone through so much with the Israelites. He had wandered the deserts for forty years in an effort to deliver them to the land of their future. Now, however, he was not allowed to enter and would be with them no more.

There was a reason God denied Moses' entrance. The land of Canaan would take on and meld with the vibratory energy of its occupants. It is important to realize the Israelites differed greatly—both physically and spiritually—from Moses. They walked in a lower level of vibratory consciousness, and the land of Canaan had been created to vibrate in harmony with the Israelites' spiritual awareness.

What most have never understood, if Moses were to enter the land of Canaan, his people would not survive. He was a powerful energy being. In fact, his vibratory force was so bright and piercing his face was covered with a veil when he was amongst his people. Only when he was alone, or facing the Godliness, would the veil be removed.

What is absolutely fascinating, just as the Israelites could not venture into the vibratory force of Sinai, Moses could not enter the boundaries of the Promised Land. Just as the vibratory force of Sinai was ill-suited for the Israelites, the vibratory force of Canaan was ill-suited for Moses.

Because of Moses' overwhelming vibratory force, there would be severe consequences if Moses was to enter the land of his people. It is not that God wanted to be cruel to Moses—nothing could be further from the truth.

The land of Canaan was intended for the Israelites. If Moses were to enter his people's land, the land would actually transform, take on Moses' dominate and supreme vibratory energy, and no longer vibrate at the level of the Israelites. In other words, the land would spit his people out.

And so it was. Moses' feet would never touch the soil of Canaan, nor would he feel the breezes stir through its lush valleys. The land of Canaan was a matrix manifest for the collective consciousness of the Israelites—a reality specifically designed for the Israelites' vibratory force. This was a place Moses did not belong, for his reality had been distanced from theirs.

This phenomenal prophet—this Hebrew who would give humanity so much, the one chosen from the core of Hashomayim's HaAdam, the man who became the highest possible potential of Adamic Consciousness—would remain in the wilderness, stuck in a gap, between the metaphysical and physical worlds. There, outside of the Promised Land, Moses would be seeded in the earth and become the "Tree of Knowledge" for humanity.

No one knows where Moses was buried. What we do know is he died outside of the land of Canaan. There is a reason no one knows his final resting place. Like the Luchot, his burial place is hidden from mankind. Where he rests is a place man cannot go, for we cannot venture into a vibration that differs so greatly from ours.

The story of Moses is a beautiful story. Even though his people failed to make the vital quantum leap, their consciousness travelled far in this dimension. They had lived to hear and experience the Elohim, and their plight has given strength to many generations and cultures throughout the world. The passage of Moses and his people is one of humanity's greatest accomplishments, and their story has become our story.

Moses' life force is still amongst the people, moving and integrating where Adam's spirit runs. Though Moses no longer walks this earth, his essence, enlightenment, and legacy has reached billions of men and women around the world. Moses has not been forgotten and is alive as never before.

Everyone knows Moses' name, but few have known the truth of his metaphysical journey. That, however, has just changed. His coded revelations have risen to jolt man's reality. The mask has been lifted, and man's eyes have been opened to the prophet of yesterday—the one drawn forth from the core of HaAdam's raging waters of potential. We must realize, and deeply know, we are God's most magnificent creation and an extraordinary manifestation of consciousness.

Like the Children of Israel, we live in a matrix, on soil that vibrates in harmony with man's current level of consciousness. Like the man of yesterday, where we stand is where our power is. The environment and earth will always respond to our vibratory force. This, of course, can go either way—for better or for worse. The land's vibration will always reflect the consciousness of those who walk its "soil" (soul).

The Israelites would enter the Promised Land.
Moses would not.

Throughout his life, Moses overcame profound obstacles and transcended various levels of enlightenment. He was a man of many faces. He was born as a Hebrew slave, rose to be an Egyptian prince, exited Egypt to become a shepherd, and transformed into a phenomenal prophet. He left mankind with the Five Books of Moses and its extraordinary coded message of enlightenment.

Moses had proven to be the true Shepherd. He protected his flock and led them to their "land of promise." The Torah reveals as Moses drew in his last breath of air, he was kissed by the Godliness. His journey on this earth was over, and he would now ascend to the place of all potential—the Elohim's Hashomayim.

What is fascinating is that The Genesis Code reveals the Hebrew word, "Nebo," means: *That which is in him and will become.* Through the coded name of Mount Nebo, the Elohim has sent a powerful message, "The essence of Moses would one day become known in man's world." The enlightenment of the Luchot, the truth of Moses, together with his unbridled wisdom of creation, has risen through his coded writings to resonate within man's soul.

What is extraordinary is that long after Moses departed this dimension, he continues to lead us to the true Promised Land. From the waters of his consciousness, he will forever draw our potential forth. The secret of the Heavens and Moses has now been unveiled: *That which is in him will become through you.* Listen to his words, feel his soul, and may his enlightenment forever rain down on humanity and guide us to the Godliness that IS.

The Giving of "The Genesis Code"

The Luchot had made its journey into the dimension of Adam. It had been created by the Elohim, rejected by man, and broken by Moses. Buried in the dimension of mankind, the Luchot's enlightenment would lay dormant for thousands of years. The Luchot's vibratory force had been seeded in Adam's reality, but mankind failed to water its vibratory consciousness. With the rejection of the Luchot, Moses understood humanity had not yet arrived at its intended destination.

Void of the Luchot's enlightenment, Adam's spirit would wander the barren deserts—the winds of misunderstanding guiding him to his illusion of paradise. More time was needed for man to evolve. Following the gifting of the Luchot Haedot and the Ten Commandments, Moses would compile his life's work, the Five Books of Moses, leaving humanity a legacy that would change the world.

This is the point in human history when creation took a mysterious turn in God's phenomenal game. Both the Elohim and Moses understood the "portal of enlightenment" (the

Luchot's vibratory force) must somehow be preserved for a future level of Adam—an evolved male and female.

However, a tremendous challenge faced Moses. How would the vibratory essence and enlightenment of the Luchot be accessible for a future man? How would Moses preserve this enlightenment and ensure its revelations would survive the test of time? Moses knew a legacy was needed—a way to lead a future man to the revelation of the Luchot. How would Moses preserve the enlightenment of the Luchot for the Adam of tomorrow?

The Luchot had been broken—hidden in the earth's consciousness. Now, Moses would hide the essence of the Luchot in the words and letters of his five books of revelation. Much like a seed, the Elohim and Moses would plant the enlightenment within Moses' five extraordinary books and wait for man's consciousness to elevate and nourish this seed of transformation. The Genesis Code reveals an awe-inspiring revelation: *Embedded within the outer language of Moses' five books of revelation would be the enlightenment of another.*

Moses understood he would have to find a way to bestow humanity with the enlightenment of the Luchot.

What Moses believed to be possible, has become. One level of Torah—the enlightenment and vibratory force of the "second set of tablets" (the Ten Commandments)—has been widely accepted—its roots embedded deep in man's world. The Torah's stories have become Adam's legacy of creation. The Torah has been protected by the Jewish people and is a sacred doctrine handed down generation after generation. Yet, 3,500 years ago, only Moses and the Elohim knew what the Torah truly was and the secrets it held.

*The Torah is a mystery.
What we do know is "why" a
coded language was hidden
from man's awareness.*

Know the Luchot's energy never left; it was merely hidden from the Adam of long ago. This enlightenment has been waiting for another level of creativity to surface out of Hashomayim's HaAdam—a level of Adam who desires to implement the truth of his maker—a spiritual warrior who will challenge any matrix that opposes this transformative enlightenment.

The enlightenment of the Luchot's message would be impossible if not for the extraordinary passion and efforts of the Jewish people who have preserved the ancient Hebrew texts. Through this exact replica, we seek out the hidden code and find comfort knowing it is exactly the same today as it was when Moses documented his enlightenment.

The Genesis Code is a phenomenal program of enlightenment embedded in the Torah for man, through man, from the Godliness. The Torah is much more than metaphorical tales from the mind and imagination of man's past. It holds the enlightenment that will guide mankind into his next level of human consciousness. God offered his hand long ago, yet we were not ready.

A new moment is upon us. The Elohim's hand is extended, once again, to the man of today. Through his finger, he is projecting a potential new reality into this dimension. Now, it is up to us. Will we accept the Elohim's enlightenment? Will we allow ourselves to view God from a new perspective? Or are the revelations of The Genesis Code still too advanced for our collective whole? Are you ready to create a new matrix and reality? Are you prepared to become the next level of Adam?

The time for change is upon us.

We have lived at the mountain's base for over 2,000 years. Before we can begin our journey up the mountain—before we can enter the portal of cosmic transformation—we must first break free from misguided illusions that have slowed our ascent into higher awareness. The time has come to move away from the old and transcend into the new—into the higher dimension of the Godliness that is us.

The Luchot's presence in our world was brief, but its story is not over. The time has come for the energy of the Luchot to pierce human awareness once again. Know the vibratory force of the Luchot is humanity's guiding light that will lead humanity into our next level of experience.

Man's spirit longs for a new beginning and deeply desires to walk in a new level of awareness. This time, however, we must not be in fear, but accept the Luchot's enlightenment and vibratory force in our world. This will give rise to a new matrix that our creation has never experienced before.

Hashomayim has heard man's cry of today. The Luchot exists within you, the connection is within you, and you are the Adam for whom the Luchot has been waiting. You are one of the many mountains the Luchot was buried in. Because this book is in your hands, know you are one of the chosen singularities projected out of HaAdam to express your potential at this particular time. Your spirit is running through time, and your spirit has chosen this time.

You, being here on earth now, holding this book in your hand, is not a coincidence. You have been drawn out of Hashomayim because your consciousness has the potential to change our world. You have been selected because you can reach the mountain's peak. You are coming into your highest level of self, and the Luchot has come alive within your awareness. You are connecting to the Godliness that IS.

The Luchot is within you. The code was given for you. It has been given to change the minds and belief systems of man. The Elohim has directed his finger towards you. Absorb God's enlightenment and energy. Feel its fire burn within you. Feel its transformative force. Engage it. Implement it. Create through it. Become it.

The Power within Belief Systems

Revelations from the Godliness are streaming into the consciousness of modern-day man. History reveals new philosophies that challenge man's awareness will be opposed by the prevailing matrix. This is especially so when it pertains to God and creation.

We cannot deny or downplay the fact an age-old matrix has been more than successful in projecting a particular perception of God for over 2,000 years. This ancient matrix has become an integral part of human reality and its vibratory force is alive and active in man's psyche.

Man's perceptions of the Bible have survived the test of time. Since the beginning, interpretations of the Bible's stories have been taught within our churches, temples, and mosques. Today, millions of followers continue to accept the age-old ideas of God and creation. They worship and pray to the God of their imagination and live their lives through particular ceremonies, practices, and guidelines.

Whether a person's perceptions of God are accurate or inaccurate is a moot point. For them, their idea of God is very real. For them, their perception of truth has become a belief system that will project a particular reality in their world. For them, they will experience the Godliness they believe to be real.

How we perceive God is truly how we view ourselves. A person's projection of the Godliness is a mirror image of how they believe themselves to be. If a person is judgmental, be assured their God is judgmental. If a person is angry, know their God has a propensity to be an angry and jealous God. If a person is prejudiced, know their religion condones separation amongst men—one God being right over another God. If a person is compassionate and loving, so too, will be his God. Again, what we imagine and believe to be real becomes a potential reality in our personal universe. What you imagine as possible becomes possible. You manifest the God that you see yourself to be.

Where you are in the moment, is where your power is.

Whatever your belief—whether you define yourself as religious, non-religious, spiritual, or atheist—none of this is important. These are only labels we give to ourselves. What is important, and what must be brought to the forefront of your awareness, is the fact that your core beliefs project and transmit a vibratory force and powerful energy to the universe. The universe doesn't recognize labels, what the universe recognizes is your vibratory signal.

Your beliefs have a tremendous influence on your reality and the matrix they empower. Therefore, it is crucial you are continuously aware of the driving force hidden within the belief system you endow. At the core of any belief system—

whether a powerful religion, organization, business, or personal relationship—there is always a motive.

It is crucial to look behind the label and know the motivating force at the core of your belief system. For example, if you happen to describe yourself as religious, what motivated your religion to form? What actions were taken by the religious hierarchy to secure their position in history? If you are non-religious, what is it that motivates you to negate your inner Godliness and deny your power of creativity?

It is imperative you know the motivation within any group or organization you are part of—whether it has to do with religion, God, or otherwise. Every group and organization manifests its own matrix that influences man's reality. Know what it is you empower and support. Look behind the mask and know the energy that is projecting its force into reality.

It is time to address the belief systems that permeate man's world today. In truth, most lack higher understanding. While we have created much good, we have also empowered appalling scenarios projecting pain, anguish, and suffering upon humankind. Our creativity is out of balance because we have failed to understand the core energy and motivating force within the authoritative and dominate matrixes of today.

Our perceptions are fogged, and our reality is suffering due to our inability to see, or admit, the truth. Again, the outer world we experience is a reflection of our inner world's creative force powered through our beliefs. What we believe is possible, what our conscious and subconscious self projects as our truth, will ultimately manifest as an experience in our world.

Our internal energy is our vibratory force we project outwards, and know, it is also what we get back. We manifest the events and experiences in our life. Therefore, if our world is caught up in chaos, war, economic failure, and destruction, we can know our belief systems are misguided and distorted. Whatever is being projected into reality, whether we like it or not, is the mirror reflecting our inner self back to us. What we are on the inside becomes an experience for us to face on the outside.

Our belief systems have been formed by misinterpretations and misconceptions of the Godliness. Whether religious or otherwise, any belief system that fosters separation, hierarchy, and fear, will ultimately lead to destruction and disempowerment of the people in one way or another. Therefore, we shouldn't be surprised with the reality we are experiencing today. Our reality will always reflect our inner world and essence. If our reality is distorted and horrific, know our experience is the universe showing us who we are and what we have become. *We drive reality.*

God is all things, and hidden in all things.
God is faceless, yet the face of everything.

Your truth and your beliefs play an extraordinary role in not only your life, but the lives of others. From this moment on, know your creative power is driven through your beliefs, and know your beliefs manifest powerful matrixes of life. What you project, both consciously and subconsciously, creates realities. What you believe is truth manifests as life experiences. What you believe is possible, becomes possible. What you believe is impossible, will never be possible for you. What you believe in matters. Nothing is more important for you to understand.

The man of today has the power to choose the level of God he imagines and believes to be real. The Elohim is talking. *Are you listening?* God is not religion. God is not a church, mosque, or synagogue. God does not support one church, mosque, or synagogue over another—one belief system over another belief system. God IS.

DNA: The Program of You

While most of us don't see ourselves as a creative program, that is exactly what we are. You began as a seed—a phenomenal and intelligent program of genetic code. Your seed was implanted with infinite potential, and it conceptualized its essence into a powerful singularity of consciousness, "you."

We will now take a closer look at the word, "conception" which is "formation taking on a construct, idea, or perception" projecting its expression in matter. Life forms of consciousness begin as a seed planted into an aspect of darkness. Once nurtured, the seed evolves and rises out of the darkness into the light where its expression can be experienced.

Human beings begin as a concept—an idea and potential of energy. To make the concept a reality, your DNA was embedded with the "program of you." Through a duality of expression, your program takes on form in space through matter.

What is remarkable is that a single cell in the human body contains a complete copy of approximately three billion DNA base pairs, or letters, that make up the human genome—an organism's complete set of DNA. The DNA molecule is an intricate message system and the core of who we are. DNA can be compared to a unique computer program powered through a coded language. As the language communicates, it expresses "you."

As scientists work to unravel the complexity of DNA, they are finding vast amounts of embedded intelligence exist in all life and nature, itself. Furthermore, many in the scientific arena are moving toward the realization the program within DNA was embedded by a master designer. While this cannot be proven, the program, itself, is not an outcome of an evolutionary process. Therefore, a brilliant creative force had to create the program of life.

Life is an idea projecting its essence into matter.

Our universe is extraordinarily intelligent. For example, the DNA molecule for the single cell bacterium, *E. coli*, contains so much information it would fill every book in the world's largest library. According to research scientists, your body contains 50 to 75 trillion cells. The amount of code operating within the human body is truly mind-boggling.

Like software that operates a computer, your DNA is a genetic language of code that communicates information to the organic cell. Within the structure of DNA, complex sequences are played out much like words, sentences, and paragraphs that instruct the host cells.

So complex is your DNA, it not only contains the genetic code of your physical characteristics, attributes, traits, and features; it also contains the nature of your disposition, temperament, and emotional self. Through its expression, it greatly influences your nature of being.

Also fascinating is that your DNA processes your experiences, records the story of your life, and registers the history of your consciousness. As you live your life, your DNA will catalog your emotional experiences and store them as knowledge. This can be compared to a computer that captures and records your emotional experiences, understanding, intelligence, and insight.

Even more fascinating is that your DNA also contains the emotions and experiences of your parents and grandparents, going all the way back to your first and initial clan. Within your DNA are the memories of your genetic line—their hopes, failures, loves, losses, irrepressible beauty, and passionate desires. Every ecstatic experience, as well as the pain and suffering endured by, or inflicted on, your ancestral line is embedded deep within your DNA.

Know the vibratory energy consciousness of your genetic past is now part of your creative program and it greatly impacts your decisions and choices in life. In essence, your DNA is not only a powerful program of you, but the record keeper and storyteller of your genetic history. Because consciousness is an ever-evolving stream of creative energy, your DNA transfers its database to its next generation. Through the sexual experience, the DNA from the male facet is projected into the female egg—which also has its own spectacular DNA database.

Once the "male aspect" (the sperm) unites with the "female aspect" (the egg), this duality becomes a "singularity" (a single cell) which then multiplies as a duality to become a "complex singularity" (the child) and a new form of living self-aware consciousness. The sperm has successfully downloaded and transferred its data into the egg's existing database of information. Through this act, the next generation of evolving and transforming consciousness forms a new and evolved genetic line.

Also fascinating, the male's sperm is the "smallest living cell" in the human body. Paradoxically, the female's egg is the "largest living cell" in the human body. This is no coincidence, but another profound example of duality within the Adamic Universe. It has also been widely accepted that the first or strongest sperm to reach the egg, would be the sperm that won the race and pierced the egg.

Ironically, recent discoveries have found the female egg actually chooses the sperm she desires to unite with. It is not necessarily the fastest or fittest sperm, but the "chosen" sperm by the creativity that is the feminine energy. Therefore, one sperm out of the 600 million possibilities projected into her egg's sphere of awareness will be selected as her creative partner and allowed to merge with her consciousness. The female aspect always makes the choice of the creative consciousness she desires to meld and create through.

Also fascinating, the first act of creation and the consciousness that manifests life is death. The sperm's sole consciousness is to die unto the female egg. The moment the male characteristics unite with the female egg, they unite to become one. He dies to become her, and she absorbs him to come to life.

Life, and the master designer that has projected all life, is beyond fascinating. It is brilliant. It is genius in motion—from the subatomic world to the largest and most magnificent universe—it is a phenomenal creative program that retains every moment, from the beginning to the end, in time and out of time.

You are a projection of the sum total of your embedded past—your line of ancestors, their passions, desires, failures, dreams, and their most profound life experiences—merging together with your ever-evolving potential. You are your past, present, and future all at once. You are a highly intelligent and amazing creative program, projected by the Elohim—the Master Designer—being experienced through form and ever-flowing consciousness. You are God becoming.

CHAPTER 11

The Battle of Jacob and Esau

The Hebraic Bible sheds light on the lives of two fascinating brothers, Jacob and Esau. Their story signifies the duality within mankind—one man opposing another. It also reveals how man can transcend through enlightenment and influence human reality in a positive way. The coded message within this story opens our eyes to the particles of manifestation and their relationship to both man and God.

The Torah reveals twin brothers—Esau born first and Jacob on his heel—would begin their battle for ideology and dominance from within their mother's womb. They were brothers of equal power, and it was foretold that one brother would always prevail over the other. When one was down, the other was up, and vice versa. This is a story that delves into the ongoing battle within human consciousness and the secret of manifestation.

The Hebrew name, "Esau," means: *To get things done.* Esau was a man of power, rules, structure, and leadership. He was an earthly man, a man of the fields, a man who was practical and would rise to the occasion through battle. Esau was the ultimate warrior and would become the father of Roman ideology. He was the consciousness and commanding force that would propel the rise of future empires.

The Hebrew name, "Jacob," means: *Heel; Hold back.* Jacob was a spiritual man—a man who was aware of a higher calling and saw beyond the material world, the illusion of power, and the painful angst of war. However, Jacob was far from simple. He was an ideas man and contained immense understanding and awareness. Although extremely clever, Jacob would soon receive a transformative lesson from the Godliness.

As the story goes, Jacob and Esau were entangled in a life and death fight. Esau, and his army of 400 warriors had set out to kill Jacob and his family—Esau's motivation being envy towards his brother. Jacob feared for his life and the life of his family. If war were to ensue, the end result would be devastation. Furthermore, he could not escape the possibility of killing his brother to protect himself and his family—a thought that tormented him.

Jacob was at a crossroads and agonizing questions swirled within his mind, "Do I allow my brother to kill me? Should I flee? Should I surrender? Should I fight? What actions should I take to support my spirit? What can I sacrifice to avoid hurting, or destroying, that which opposes me—my brother and fellow man? Will I be forced to kill my brother in order to succeed in this world?"

Jacob and Esau's story is continuous, as it applies to each generation of humanity. While this story is rooted in our past, its message very much applies to the man of today. Colossal clashes occur when opposite philosophies meet and one level of consciousness wants to challenge, overtake, and even destroy another matrix of consciousness.

The metaphorical struggle between Jacob and Esau—the spiritual, compassionate, and humble man versus the man of power, control, and war—is a dichotomy that has always existed within human consciousness. Whether one is a spiritual seeker or capable warrior, both are diverse levels of consciousness that fight to protect their current matrix of operation.

Over the centuries, many spiritual men and women have been faced with the choice to kill another, or be killed themselves, to protect their way of life and belief systems. This scenario applies not only to individuals, but to every business, society, and government.

Important to realize, a man can be killed in many ways—not only by the sword. Through cunning acts and business deals filled with trickery and greed, one man can bring a type of death to another. There are those who employ slave labor to significantly improve their corporation's margins, caring not for the children they abuse both physically and emotionally. Then there is the dynamo in the workplace, the man or woman who will lie, cheat, and disempower his fellow man to climb his ladder of gold.

As you reflect on your own life, ask yourself the following questions, "Who is the warrior I face? Who am I as the warrior?" Each of us has a spiritual and compassionate side, yet we are naturally programmed through our genetic DNA to survive, overcome, and conquer perceived threats.

If you haven't already done so, you will come to face an internal struggle. Like Jacob, you will also ask, "Should I sacrifice my current power, wealth, and status to embrace a different type of wealth—the empowerment of the human spirit? Am I willing to fight for what I believe in? Am I willing to give something up to help my fellow man live a better life?"

While these questions were also Jacob's questions, they apply to each of us—whether the individual, business, or government. Therefore, what can you do for the sake of the human spirit? How can you influence others—whether an individual, company, or nation? What are you willing to sacrifice in order to succeed personally and professionally? Do you empower your fellow man, business, and nation? Everything begins with you.

While many view a spiritual man or woman as non-combative and weak, the true spiritual man and woman will use all of their power, both physically and metaphysically, to bring about transformation. The spiritual man and woman is also a warrior, but a warrior of a different kind.

There will be times when the true spiritual person is left with no other choice than to battle his opponent and fight for man's very spirit, for the betterment of humanity, and the pursuit of personal freedom on both a physical and metaphysical level.

As Jacob searched his soul for answers, he came to a powerful conclusion: *He would shower his enemy, his brother, with gifts.* Jacob had made a life-changing decision. In an attempt to avoid war, death, and suffering, he sent his servants, together with much of his material wealth, to Esau. Jacob would respectfully bow to his brother and placate that which opposed him hoping for a peaceful outcome.

 ### English Translation: Genesis 32:17-20

"When my brother Esau meets you and asks, 'To whom do you belong, and where are you going, and who owns all these animals in front of you?' then you are to say, 'They belong to your servant Jacob. They are a gift sent to my lord Esau, and he (Jacob) is coming behind us.'" He also instructed the second, the third and all the others who followed the herds, "You are to say the same thing to Esau when you meet him. And be sure to say, 'Your servant, Jacob, is coming behind us.'"

Jacob's plan was psychological. As Esau received Jacob's gifts, Jacob hoped that Esau would be swayed into believing Jacob was a man of wealth and power. In Esau's eyes, Jacob was sending a signal—he was now subservient to Esau as he conceded his wealth and power. Furthermore, Esau was told by Jacob's servants, Jacob would soon be arriving to meet Esau. This maneuver by Jacob discouraged Esau's advance, and Jacob was now coming to Esau.

By showering Esau with gifts, Jacob showed he came in peace. Jacob's giving of the gifts served another purpose as well. There was a time lapse between each caravan of gifts. The element of time would allow for Jacob to prepare for battle.

Jacob's scouts were perusing the land, looking for opportunities. Also true, with each new caravan, the offerings became more valuable in the eyes of Esau. He would receive one set of gifts at a time, rather than all at once. This was a psychological play and a tactic that allowed Esau's heated anger to cool.

Jacob's plan was working. Caravan after caravan arrived in Esau's camp. With each arrival, Jacob's servants informed Esau that Jacob was soon to follow. As Esau watched the caravan's pulling into his camp, his anticipation to see his brother continued to accelerate. Esau's emotional state was beginning to change. His anger and lust for death was diminishing, and there was now a possibility for Esau to accept Jacob and forego war against him.

Jacob had been wise, as well as humble. He had covered all possibilities, but Jacob, while hopeful, was still afraid of Esau and unsure of his intentions. He had done everything possible to prevent a needless war and utter destruction, but he had no idea what his future held.

A Dark Night of the Soul

 ### English Translation: Genesis 32:22-24

That night Jacob got up and took his two wives, his two maidservants, and his eleven sons and crossed the ford of the Jabbok. After he had sent them across the stream, he sent over all his possessions. So Jacob was left alone, and a man fought with him till daybreak.

Jacob knew the possibility of battle was looming, and he would either kill, or be killed by, his brother. He was emotionally distraught and consumed with intense fear. Jacob had remained behind and stayed in his camp that night. He knew if his plan failed, he would be forced into a life and death battle with his brother. Little did Jacob know, his battle within would soon be reflected in his outer world. For Jacob, this was to be a dark night of the soul.

Blackness surrounded Jacob in the camp that night, and he was left alone. The word, "alone," in Hebrew is "levado" which carries another meaning "dual heart." Because Jacob and Esau were twin brothers, their consciousness reflected a symbiotic relationship. Jacob's heart was now split in two, as signified by the hidden message of "dual heart." Regardless of which brother was to die, Jacob knew there was a strong possibility that death would soon face him in one way or another.

Alone in the darkness, Jacob's emotions stormed within him. Suddenly, a man appeared out of nowhere and began to wrestle with Jacob in the night. Jacob had yet to realize the man he faced was truly an apparition of the Godliness projected from Jacob's inner creative force. For Jacob, this would be a night of transformation as he faced and struggled with his own spirit. Jacob's battle with the "man" was truly a battle "with himself."

 ### The Man: the "Ish"

The Genesis Code reveals the "man" Jacob wrestled with was far more than a mortal man.

The description of "man" is derived from the Hebrew word, "Ish." Ironically, the word, "man," is nowhere to be found within the ancient Hebrew texts. Whenever the "Ish" is mentioned in the Torah, we know an aspect of "active and transformative" male consciousness is being referenced. In this story, the "Ish" reflects the "male aspect of the Elohim" which has been activated as a particular manifestation and scenario to face Jacob.

The Secret of ISH				
HEBREW	LETTERS AND CODE	VALUE	CODED MEANING
ALEPH א	ALEPH; LAMED; PHEY אלף	111	Prime Cause and Motivator.
YOD י	YOD; DALET יד	14	Active seed; Hand.
SHIN ש	SHIN; YOD; FINAL NUN שין	360	Transformation; Fire; Teeth.

The Genesis Code reveals the name, "Ish," contains the "Aleph" (the Prime Cause and Motivator). This is an important clue in this story that reveals: *The Ish contained the essence of the Elohim*. Through the apparition of a warrior that appeared to battle Jacob, God was revealing itself to Jacob, as Jacob's very reflection. Jacob was actually wrestling with an aspect of the Elohim that was truly a reflection of himself. This is an astounding revelation.

Also important to realize is that the apparition of the man reflected the energy embodiment of both brothers. Through the struggle, Jacob faced and came to know not only his own ideology, but his brother's. This new awareness allowed Jacob to objectively perceive reality through his own eyes, as well as the eyes of Esau.

Furthermore, because "I(s)h" contains the Hebrew letter, "Shin," we are being shown the apparition of the man appeared for the following reason: *To bring about transformation within Jacob.* We know this because The Genesis Code reveals "Ish" contains "fire and transformative energy" that is both destructive and creative. This coded message reveals this struggle within creation would profoundly affect both the Godliness and man.

The letter, "Shin," has a number of meanings "transformation," the "three fold fire" (ש), and "teeth." You may be asking, "How can 'teeth' have anything to do with transformation?" Humans and animals use their teeth as a means of "destruction" (the first fire ש). Following this, comes the act of transformation through "consumption" of energy consciousness (the second fire ש). Through death comes "new life" (the third fire ש).

The symbol (ש) for Shin clearly shows mankind the three fires necessary for transformation—destruction, consumption, and new life. Shin's fiery energy fuels life and death as it destroys one aspect of life and feeds another. Again, the code is revealing "Shin" is "an extraordinary energy force that carries the power of transformation." This is the energy Jacob faced through the apparition of the "Ish" (man).

Like Jacob, each of us will face our inner Godliness and internal struggles. This is when we ask ourselves, "Who am I? What should I do? What will I become?" Our battles are transformative, and as we emerge from our internal struggle, we are no longer the same person who entered the darkness of our soul. One part of us, the old self, has "died" (Shin), making way for our "new self" (Shin) that has risen out of the destruction. Like the Phoenix, man has the ability to rise out of his own "ashes" (dust) and fly to new heights. This is the transformative power of Shin—an energy embodiment that was the Ish.

 ## *The Struggle*

So Jacob was left alone, and a "man" (the Ish) fought with him till daybreak.

We will now explain the deeper meaning in Genesis 32:24, "So Jacob was left alone, and a man fought with him till daybreak." The Hebrew word, "vayabok," means: *Struggle; fight; and to kick up dust.* Within "vayabok" extreme enlightenment prevails. Unfortunately, its deeper insight and clues into manifestation have been overlooked and lost in translation. Due to misplaced insight, the more complex aspect of the story surrounding Jacob's struggle in the dirt with the man has never been revealed until now.

To unveil the mystery within "kicking up dust," we must first delve into the coded meaning within "Yakov" (Jacob) and "yavok" (dust). The differences between the Hebrew letters in "Jacob" and "dust" are slight, yet their coded meaning becomes vital as we seek to understand what the "dust in creation" stands for.

The Secret of JACOB (Yakov) and DUST (Yavok)	
HEBREW	CODED MEANING
YA (K) OV י ע ק ב	JACOB—Active heel; Eye; Mankind standing on the earth; Subjective consciousness; Man's stance through his unique consciousness; Controlling and causing the potential particles to manifest.
YA (V) OK י א ב ק	DUST—Active seed; Prime cause; Particles of potential that manifest into reality; Objective consciousness; Impartial nature; Potential that can be molded into anything when a given consciousness activates it—much like dust after water is added.

The Hidden Code of Jacob

Jacob's name means "heel." Because his name contains a "Yod" ('), Jacob's name transitions to "active heel."

The Torah reveals Jacob was given his name for a reason: *He was "holding the heel of Esau," his brother—the twin born first.* However, through The Genesis Code, you will learn the word, "heel," within Jacob's name contains another powerful revelation.

Interestingly, one's heel is an extremely important aspect of the human body. The heel touches the dust of the earth, yet this connection is something we rarely think about. One's heel allows man to walk upright, a feature that separates us from the animal kingdom. In the case of this story, The Genesis Code reveals: *As man's heel touches the dust of the earth, his energy consciousness is activated through the "dust he stands on" (earth consciousness).*

*The practical man's power is direct—
he plants the seed in the earth
and watches it grow.
The spiritual man's power is indirect—
he plants the idea and manifests change.*

As we continue to decode Jacob's name, the Hebrew word for "heel" is "ekev." Also true, the first Hebrew letter in "(e)kev" is "ayin" which means "eye." Interestingly, both brothers' names contain "ayin" which is another hidden code that reveals: *The outcome of one brother's perception versus another brother's perception was a primary factor in the lives of these two brothers.*

Each brother perceived the world through their own eyes—from opposing identities and subjective points of view. Jacob was an emotional being who represented the spiritual heart of mankind—the night, the metaphysical aspect of man, the unknown, and one's internal struggle to find revelation within the darkness of self. Esau, on the other hand, represented the man of the fields and the day—power, productivity, control, and the choices that are necessary in the morning's light.

Jacob thought deeply about situations prior to acting upon them. He was a man who was simple in some ways and complicated in others. While Esau was a prime mover, Jacob had mostly succumbed to secondary roles and was reactive in nature. This, however, was about to change.

The Hidden Code in Dust

Jacob's struggle continued throughout the night. He was fighting for his very existence in this world, "kicking up the dust" with the Ish.

The Genesis Code reveals "kicking up the dust" is much more than a metaphor revealing a battle between men. While most have interpreted this to mean Jacob and the man were "fighting in the dust," this message is far more complex than a fight in the dirt between men.

Jacob and the Ish were not "struggling with one another in the dust;" they were actually struggling over the "outcome of the dust" in this reality. The question becomes, "What was the 'dust' they were struggling over?" The hidden code reveals the following: *The "dust" is a metaphor for the "subatomic particles" that are the potential that "manifests human reality."* Through The Genesis Code, we are being told the subatomic particles play a powerful role in manifestation.

Initially, the particles of manifestation, referred to herein as "particles," are "impartial to any outcome" in man's reality. The particles are void of self-interest and have no point of view. The particles are a potential for anything and everything that is possible in man's world. They are pure potential and are activated only when human intent and emotional desires have come into focus.

Human consciousness is the power that activates the particles through intention, feelings, and action. The moment man projects his intention and creative force to the universe, the unmanifested and unbiased particles work to create an outcome in matter that matches man's intentions and emotions.

 ## The Battle over the Dust

Through this story, great emphasis is placed on the particles of the metaphorical dust, their significant role in creation, and the struggle that ensued to control the outcome of the particles, themselves.

As we walk an untraveled road, we are shown how the smallest particles in our universe manifest into particular realities through man's belief systems and consciousness. There was a purpose to this battle between the Ish and Jacob. The Genesis Code reveals the following: *The struggle between the Ish and Jacob would determine the actual outcome of the particles of the dust*. Jacob wanted to experience one particular reality, and Esau wanted to experience another. Obviously, both brothers desired a successful outcome.

Realize, even today, the particles that manifest realities are pure potential and, therefore, impartial to the outcome. The particles of the dust do not favor one brother over another, one man over another, one nation over another. The Genesis Code has placed great emphasis on a truth hidden from man's awareness: *Adam is a creative being that contains unfathomable power to manifest realities.*

However, The Genesis Code delves into another level of creativity within this story that sheds light on vital questions that rose within the Godliness, "Should the Creator interfere with the "outcomes" in man's world? Should God persuade and influence the particles to manifest one man's reality over another's? Why should God favor one brother over another if both are facets of the Godliness experiencing its essence in this reality?" In essence the Ish was saying to Jacob, "Why should I favor you, Jacob, over your brother, Esau? You are both facets of me."

Obviously, Jacob was trying to influence the Ish. He wanted the Ish to favor and support his successful outcome over his brother's. Moreover, he knew an agreement was needed to clarify the outcome. This is an extraordinary revelation that offers new insight into the struggle between Jacob and the Ish over the particles that manifest realities.

Manifestation is powered by mankind's various belief systems. Again, man drives reality. Many belief systems are active in our world today. Therefore, which belief system amongst men will ultimately be successful in human reality? This question applied not only to Jacob, but is also relevant to the male and female of today.

The All is All That IS. All is possible within the All, including the most horrific experiences man imagines and creates for himself to experience. Therefore, the pinnacle question surrounding the struggle over the particles was, "If everything is the All experiencing itself, why should the Elohim side with one man over another if both men are God, incarnate?" The Elohim's decision would affect all of mankind—then and now.

 ### Jacob Faces Himself in the Darkness

Jacob came to realize a phenomenal truth as he faced the "Ish" (man). The universe was manifesting Jacob's true reflection, showing him who he was and who he was not through the Ish. Jacob was truly facing himself and now struggled with his consciousness.

In all spiritual quests there is a time when it seems as if life is too much to take. When we can do nothing more than await an outcome, when we are faced with a choice to fight to the death, or accept and surrender to the relationships that surround us, each of us face a dark night of the soul.

However, there is always darkness before light. In times of despair, we are able to clearly see who we are, as well as who we are not. Before new light can enter our awareness, we must accept our true essence and nature. We must let go of preconceived notions and focus on who we want to become.

There will come a time when each of us faces our truth. To experience one's truth, we must admit to who we truly are. We must accept our true essence and nature before change is possible. If we accept our false face, if we believe in our own lie, we are only transforming one level of lie into another.

Once we accept ourselves for who we truly are, only then can we make a sincere choice to stay the same or die to ourselves. If we choose to die to ourselves—leaving our old self behind—a portal opens. As we surrender to the universe, our reality is altered from the inside out. When our inner world transforms, so do the particles that manifest the life we experience. This is how it happens.

In the darkness of the night, through his struggle, Jacob came to understand his outer world was merely a reflection of his inner creative force. Daybreak would soon crest, and he knew the outcome of this fight would be manifested in the light. Jacob's question was still unanswered, "Would the Divine favor him over his brother?"

 ## The Question of Divine Intervention

Within the Elohim's creation, a metaphysical battle was in play. Would God alter the laws of manifestation? The deeper message in this story reveals this was a battle far more serious than two men struggling in the night. This was a transformative event that would change the way the creative universe works.

In the story of Jacob and Esau, we delve into two opposing ideologies. Both men desired a particular outcome that favored their position and perception of reality. Through the eyes of the Godliness, the Ish knew Esau's ideology was equal to, and just as valid as, Jacob's. To reiterate, all men are a facet of the Godliness, and, through free will and independence, each man's intentions are a right of his own.

Now, however, the Ish was wrestling with the spiritual aspect of Adamic Consciousness. Should God favor one man over another? Jacob desperately wanted intervention from the Divine. If the Godliness were to influence the particles of manifestation, favoring one man over another, the rules in God's game would change radically. The outcome of the particles was of the highest importance, for they affected realities and God's experience.

This decision and choice by God was of the highest importance for it would transform Adam's reality. Would the Godliness side with Jacob's ideology and influence the particles of creativity to manifest a successful outcome for the spiritual man? Or, would the Ish side with the practical man who has a propensity to achieve power and prosperity through dominance, control, war, death, and suffering?

However, there was also another option. The Ish could forego support of both brothers and allow the laws of nature to govern mankind. This option would benefit those who are most fit to survive. Through the laws of nature, odds were the practical man—the man of the fields, the man of war, and the man of physical strength—would experience the successful outcome.

Because the laws of nature are impartial to an individual's spiritual side—the man of the spirit, the man who tends to the heart and emotional self, and the man of peace—may find himself at an extreme disadvantage overpowered by those who walk a more aggressive path.

"Let Me Go, it is Daybreak"

We will now explain the deeper meaning within the Ish's statement to Jacob, "Let me go, for it is daybreak." After Jacob's dark night of the soul, "daybreak" symbolized "a time for action." Interestingly, what was true for Jacob is true for the man of today.

The hour preceding dawn is the darkest moments of the night and a time of intense silence. When we are most fearful, the darkness and silence can stimulate feelings of utter despair. Submersed in blackness, our thoughts and emotions come together forcing us to seek out and find the light—a new realization. In our darkest moments, our true power and strength is realized, allowing a new door to open that leads to a new self.

With the light of a new day, the time for vacillation is over. At daybreak, our final choice must be made. This is when our newfound power rises within, and our internal darkness vanishes in our light. We will either take a quantum leap into a new orbit of self, or remain the same and continue to experience our current state of reality.

English Translation: Genesis 32:26

Then the man said, "Let me go, for it is daybreak." But Jacob replied, "I will not let you go unless you bless me." The man asked him, "What is your name?" "Jacob," he answered. Then the man said, "Your name will no longer be Jacob, but Israel, because you have struggled with God [the Elohim] and with men and have overcome." Jacob said, "Please tell me your name." But he replied, "Why do you ask my name?" Then he blessed him there. So Jacob called the place Peniel, saying, "It is because I saw God [the Elohim] face to face, and yet my life was spared."

 ### "Let Me Go for It Is Daybreak"

Then the "man" (Ish) said, "Let me go, for it is daybreak."

Jacob's battle within himself lasted all night. The darkness was fading, yet Jacob had failed to find his true power or convince the Ish to favor his desires over Esau's. But daybreak was on the horizon, and the Ish fervently called out to Jacob, "Let me go, for it is daybreak."

Just as the Ish called out to Jacob, this metaphor carries a profound revelation that calls out to mankind: *Daybreak is a call to awaken to a new level of awareness.* The Ish was saying to Jacob and to the spiritual aspect of mankind, "There is no time left. It is now or never. Make your choice. Your reality is now up to you. Let me go, for I am a manifestation of you." Jacob had run out of time. At daybreak, the apparition of the man—the Ish—would vanish.

Also profound, "daybreak" carries another message "until the end of time." Jacob had battled his own intentions, his brother's intentions, as well as the intentions of the Ish. Metaphorically, we are being shown that the spiritual man and the man of power and war will be locked into an endless battle unless humanity, as a whole, achieves enlightenment and forms a matrix of higher awareness.

 ## Jacob Asks the Ish for a Blessing

Jacob replied, "I will not let you go unless you bless me."

A profound revelation surfaces in this story. We learn of the Elohim's role and participation in the outcome of every man and woman's reality. Man lives in a universe filled with duality. Yet, when two equal and extremely powerful matrixes of consciousness desire to experience opposing realities, which matrix of reality will become an experience in God's creation? Which aspect of the All will prevail over another aspect of the All within its own creation?

The Hebrew word for "blessing" is "berach" which means "knee" or "bow to." The Genesis code reveals the following revelation: *The true blessing is realized when one bows to, surrenders to, and supports another in every way possible. The blessing is activated when one man gives both spiritual and practical energy to the talent of another.*

Through his many experiences, Jacob had shown his talent for giving. He was strong in many ways—mentally, emotionally, and physically. Why then did Jacob vehemently believe he needed a blessing from the Ish? Why did he even ask for one?

Through his struggle with the Ish, Jacob came to understand that being a spiritual man—one with intelligence, heart, compassion, understanding, and wisdom—does not necessarily guarantee a successful outcome in any battle, scenario, or situation.

Knowing this, Jacob asked the Ish for a blessing. When Jacob asked for the blessing, he was truly asking the universe—through the dust and the very particles that manifest man's desires—to grant him success.

Following his struggle with the Ish, Jacob deeply understood Esau through the Ish's reflection. Jacob realized that he and his brother were both equal and opposite. He also understood his brother was an ultimate warrior, would kill for power, get caught up in his own game, overstep his boundaries, and disempower mankind.

Jacob had seen a probable future. Esau would move forward and possibly enslave humanity and destroy the human spirit to gain wealth, power, and control. If this were to be the outcome, human freedom would be limited. To stop this oncoming war, the Ish had to be convinced to take Jacob's side and protect the spirit of man. Jacob needed divine intervention. Without it, there was no guarantee of success.

The Ish Asks Jacob His Name

The man (the Ish) asked Jacob, "What is your name?"

The Ish asked Jacob, "What is your name?" Within this question, there were underlying questions. The Ish was truly asking, "How do you, Jacob, define yourself? Do you know who you truly are? You want a blessing, but who is it that I should bless?" The Ish wanted Jacob to realize what he truly stood for. He needed Jacob to know his heart. He needed Jacob to know his spirit and who he truly was. And then Jacob answered the Ish, "My name is Jacob."

With Jacob's answer, the Ish knew that Jacob had found himself. Jacob was not the same man he was yesterday. He now understood true success was only possible through the empowerment of his fellow man and through the act of blessing others. Jacob had foreseen the potential within the act of blessing another. He came to realize his higher calling was to "bless and be blessed."

Jacob now realized that all men are different and operate from different points of view, but the true power of the Elohim shines when one man seeks to find and recognize another man's qualities. Jacob would now live to help others find their true talent and achieve their potential. Jacob would now empower the blessing that empowers the Godliness.

The Ish Changes Jacob's Name

Then the "man" (Ish) said, "Your name will no longer be Jacob, but 'Israel,' because you have struggled with God and with men and have overcome."

Jacob had faced the powerful metaphysical world of the Ish through the apparition of the man. Throughout the long night of battle, Jacob had shown the Ish his potential through his heart's struggle. Jacob had shown himself to be humble and wise.

Jacob had also dealt with man's opposing ideologies. He had overcome the challenges that faced him in reality. He had knelt down to his brother, Esau, when he embellished him with gifts and earthly possessions. Yet, Jacob had also shown incredible strength through his desire to fight for a peaceful outcome.

Jacob had struggled with both God and man. He had looked deep into creation and succeeded in his endeavor to find his true power and essence. He had come to realize the ultimate power in man's reality—the blessing that is one man's gift to another.

The Genesis Code reveals another extraordinary revelation: *From the moment the Ish appeared to Jacob, he had been present for one reason alone—to manifest the blessing Jacob desired to know. The blessing was the energy that flowed through his heart.*

The Genesis Code unveils a profound revelation given to Jacob by the Godliness: *"At the vibratory level of 'Jacob,' you will not succeed as Jacob, alone. This is so because the particles of manifestation will not side with you, as 'Jacob.' While you have proven yourself as capable, wise, and intelligent, the energy consciousness 'that is Jacob' lacks the power to overcome Esau's stance."*

At daybreak, the Ish projected a new level of understanding into Jacob's consciousness: *"To realize the blessing—to become the blessing—you will need a new name that reflects and empowers your newfound spirit."* In a moment, everything changed for Jacob. The Ish had changed his name to reflect his new energy field. He would no longer be known as Jacob, but "Israel."

As revealed through The Genesis Code: *Every man reflects the Godliness he believes to be real.* Jacob no longer saw himself as he did before. His Godliness had transformed and so, too, did his name. This is an exemplary metaphor for this revelation. He had transformed to reflect "the blessing" that was the essence of his inner Godliness. Jacob's heel, active and connected to the "particles of manifestation" (the dust), became the power of the blessing in the human world. Jacob was now Israel, and the blessing had been activated within the Elohim's Hashomayim.

The soul within the man no longer projected the energy of Jacob, but the energy of Israel.

In the end, Israel received the blessing from the Ish. As Israel, his energy embodiment represented the blessing—an energy consciousness realized at daybreak. Jacob had let go of his reflection and preconceived notions of self. As Israel, he now carried his brother's mantel.

Unlike before, he was now blessed with his brother's leadership skills, together with Esau's ability to fight. As Israel, he would no longer be in the shadow of his brother, but would face his brother knowing he had been blessed by the Godliness. Israel fully understood he had transformed into a supreme spiritual warrior.

This is the first time "Israel" is ever mentioned in the Torah. This was the moment a new energy field entered the Adamic world—projected out of HaAdam—reflected through the transformation of a man and his name. Every name reflects a particular consciousness and embedded code that reveals a deeper insight into the energy embodiment of the spirit that carries the name. Therefore, "Israel," reflected the essence of what Jacob had become metaphysically.

Through his relationships with both God and man, he had overcome. He had struggled with the Ish, his brother, and his own spirit. After Jacob's dark night of the soul, at daybreak "Israel" was projected into light. He had become the blessing and now projected the energy of Israel into the world.

 ## Jacob Asks the Man (Ish) for His Name

Jacob said, "Please tell me your name." But the "man" (Ish) replied, "Why do you ask my name?" Then he blessed him there.

A question rises, "At daybreak, why did Jacob ask the man his name, when he had already known the Ish through his struggle in the night?" When Jacob asked the man his name, the Ish answered Jacob's question with another question. The Ish asked, "Why do you ask my name?" Through this response, the Ish was making an underlying statement: *"There is no need to ask my name, for I am nameless. 'I am.' My name is your name, and my purpose is for you to realize the blessing. You, as 'Israel,' define me."*

Through this hidden message, another profound realization is brought to light: *Like Israel, those who bless are also defined in their blessing.* When you bless your brother by empowering him, something remarkable happens. Your blessing becomes his blessing, and his blessing becomes your blessing. You become blessed with the blessing that you have given to another. You become empowered through your blessing.

The moment the Ish changed Jacob's name to Israel, the Elohim altered the workings of HaAdam. A profound decision had been made—a decision that would change everything. The Genesis Code reveals the most extraordinary revelation: *An agreement was formed that would forever alter the particles of potential within Adamic Consciousness. Divine intervention would be granted to the man who exemplifies the energy of the blessing.*

Creation had transformed, and the spirit of Israel had become manifest in the Adamic Universe—realized in the dimension of Adam through the true spiritual man—the particular aspect of Adam that becomes the man of the "blessing" (Ish + Real = Israel).

The Secret Code within "Israel"

Most believe the Promised Land—the land of Israel—is a country confined by walls of stone and boundaries of state. However, The Genesis Code reveals Israel is much more than a land of milk and honey. Its power reaches far beyond this dimension or any lines drawn in the sand. The true state of Israel is much more than what you have been told.

The Genesis Code unveils "Israel" and exposes a level of energy that nourishes Adam's spiritual self through the "empowerment of the blessing." The reality of Israel has a tremendous effect on Adamic Consciousness and man's experience in his world. Those who engage the energy of Israel live through a heightened sense of awareness to creation. This is a level of knowingness mankind must reach, and do so quickly.

As previously mentioned, the first time Israel is mentioned in the Torah is when the Ish changed Jacob's name. This was the moment a new level of consciousness manifest within human reality. Once this name was given by the Godliness, its vibratory essence focused on the Hebrew tribe of long ago. Those who were once Hebrew slaves would no longer be referred to as "Hebrews," but the "Children of Israel." Interestingly, the Hebrew word, "Ivri," has been translated as "Hebrews;" however, there is another meaning within this name—the "one who is from the other side."

Not to be dismissed was the land of Canaan, the land promised to Abraham by the Elohim. This land would eventually be conquered by Joshua and the Children of Israel and would come to be known as the land of Israel—the land that would nourish the Israelites.

Also fascinating is that in 70 AD, the Children of Israel were exiled from their land; but in 1948, through unusual events and much human suffering, the Jewish people were able to return to the land promised to them by the God of Abraham. This event was extraordinary, as well as out of the ordinary. One might believe the Divine intervened and worked to influence the particles of manifestation.

While the name, Israel, is attributed to the Jewish people, know the coded message within Israel applies to all of humanity, and its vibratory essence is intended to be absorbed by every male and female in our world. Know, what happens to Israel will affect the four corners of the earth and all of humanity in one way or another. Israel cannot be ignored, both physically and metaphysically. The message within Israel, once deeply understood, will transform your perception of self, others, and the world that surrounds you.

The Secret of ISRAEL (לארשי)			
HEBREW	LETTERS AND CODE	VALUE	CODED MEANING
YOD י	YOD; DALED יד	10	Hand; Seed; Active potential.
SHIN ש	SHIN; YOD; NUN שין	300	Teeth; Devour; Transformation.
RESH ר	RESH; YOD; SHIN ריש	200	Head; Vibratory Duality; Transformative thought.
ALEPH א	ALEPH; LAMED; PHEY אלף	1	Prime Cause and Motivator.
LAMED ל	LAMED; MEM; DALET למד	30	Teach; Learn.
YESH יש	YOD;SHIN יש	310	Is; Exist; Brought to being.
YASHAR ישר	YOD;SHIN;RESH ישר	510	Straight; Honesty; Justice.
SHAR שר	SHIN;RESH שר	500	Sing; Praise; Head; Commander.
EL אל	ALEPH; LAMED אל	31	The highest level; The first two letters of Elohim.

 ## YOD = Hand, Seed, Active Potential

The beginning of realization comes from the seed of potential where new possibility can flower, in time, and reach its full bloom.

The "Yod," the first letter in the name "(I)srael," is the smallest letter in the Hebrew alphabet and denotes the seed. Each new generation begins with a seed planted by the previous generation. Every change within society starts with the seed of an idea that takes hold, flowers, and shines new light on the world. We are being shown human consciousness has been seeded, and the blessing is within the seed.

SHIN = Teeth, Devour, Transformation

The capability to defend, fight, and devour any opposition that threatens a given reality.

The Hebrew letter, "Shin," is the energy that contains the potential for "destruction." It is the fire that will devour and leave desolation in its wake. If a plant was ripped from the earth, the power of Shin would ensure no root would be left in its soil. Yet, through destruction, new creations rise. The power of the three-fold fire is not only to destroy life, but to re-create life.

However, there are two levels of Shin—one aspect is "aggressive" (Shin) and the other "reactive" (Sin). Within the word, "Israel," the "reactive aspect" (Sin) is present meaning: *The transformative fire within Israel is not aggressive, but reactive.* However, know the power to overcome any and all obstacles, even if reactive, is a power to be mindful of and to respect.

RESH = Head, Vibratory Duality

The head represents the "idea" worth fighting for within Adamic Consciousness.

The Hebrew letter, "Resh," represents the "head and motivation through choices." The head contains the infinite number of thought patterns that is implied in any given choice. Through the energy of Israel, the following will manifest: *The head will implement thoughts and emotions within mankind to empower and activate the blessing into reality.* Through the energy of Israel, the head activates its essence in the moment and asks, "What can I do in each and every circumstance to bring the blessing to others whether an individual, culture, or nation?" It is the striving thought pattern—to give the blessing through recognizing the potential in others—that is the true power that leads the way. When humanity endeavors to bless one another, the core of creation is empowered and the highest level of Godliness is implemented on earth.

ALEPH = Prime Cause and Motivator

When man implements the "blessing," the highest level of the God/Man relationship will be experienced in our reality. As the blessing is activated, humanity will come to experience a new beginning, and the most wondrous aspect of the Godliness will be realized on Earth.

Because the "Aleph" (the Prime Cause) is present within the name, "Israel," we are being shown "the Elohim desires a blessing for Adam." However, in order for the blessing to be activated, the Godliness understands a struggle will exist for man and this struggle amongst men will be timeless. Yet, if man's ultimate intention is to bless others, the Godliness has promised a successful outcome for the spiritual man and woman who honor the power of the blessing. Through the particles of manifestation an agreement has been made to those who bless: *Their blessing will become manifest.*

LAMED = Learn; Teach

The struggle exists so Adam can learn and evolve. It is continuous and will exist until the end of time.

Through our experiences we will learn and then teach others through our example. Our understanding will always be faced with challenges so man can face his fears, doubts, and insecurities. This is necessary in order for Adam to grow into the highest potential of self. Once mankind empowers the blessing, humanity will be on the road to profound enlightenment. When we rise to meet the occasion, the universe will abundantly manifest all realities through blessings.

YESH = Is; Existence

What has just happened, what has been brought into existence, is a new reality implemented in creation.

The universe has been seeded to give transformative power to the spiritual warrior. As man endeavors to actuate spiritual freedom and the blessing, the universe will respond and create new experiences that match the vibratory essence of higher consciousness. It is possible for the essence of Israel to be implemented in Adam's reality.

YASHAR = Straight; Honesty; Just

Power is given to the spiritual man who is honest, straight, and just. Power is never given for self-serving purposes.

The particles of manifestation will never be influenced by the Elohim to fulfill self-serving acts, greed, wealth, power, and control. We sometimes fool ourselves into believing we are something we are not, but we can never fool the universe. The Godliness knows our true motivation and hidden agendas. Our vibratory force is in constant connection with the universe. We can never hide from ourselves. God knows our truth, and our truth becomes our reality.

SHAR = Sing; Praise; Head; Commander

With the joy of praise, great power exists. Release the Godliness within and allow your inner light to shine on the world.

Voicing praise, acknowledging another's potential, and finding joy in all that surrounds us is the highest level of being. When mankind embraces this ideology, the Elohim's creation will manifest a creation of harmony, beauty, and spiritual enlightenment.

EL = Highest Level

The last two letters of Israel are the first two letters in the Creator's name, Elohim.

The relationship between these letters and the names "Elohim" and "Israel" is no coincidence. This is a revelation that Israel is the highest level of human operation and endeavor. Israel is the essence of the Elohim being realized on earth through mankind. Israel, the blessing, is the highest potential bestowed upon humanity.

The Blessing

We live in a complicated world, and the blessing is needed more than ever. The time has come for humanity to internalize the concept of the blessing. Humanity longs for empowerment, yet we have failed to understand a profound truth: *Empowerment is achieved through the act of empowering others.*

While there are those of us who understand this, the majority of mankind does not. If they did, we would not be experiencing the outcome of today's matrix. As a consciousness, we must project the energy of the blessing. There is nothing more important for us to achieve. If we fail to raise our awareness to the blessing, humanity cannot, and will not, reach the next level of human consciousness.

The "blessing of Israel" is very different than kind gestures mouthed through pleasant words. Again, the Hebrew word for "blessing" is "berach" which means "kneel" or "bow to." Many believe mankind must only bow down to the Godliness. However, this is a misconception.

When we bend our knee to another, we are showing a humble and subservient nature. When you truly bow to another human being, you are offering your active and emotional support for another's talent and internal power. This is how the true blessing takes hold in reality.

The Elohim wants mankind to recognize every person has a talent or power that is unique to their spirit. The Elohim never manifests two individuals to be the same, nor does HaAdam contain two aspects of potential that are exactly alike. Therefore, humanity must be accepting of one another and honor that which is unique and different from their particular consciousness.

Many times we need others to recognize our potential before we can recognize it ourselves. The blessing ignites a fire that has possibly lain dormant and never burned within our spirit or another's. When we bless another's potential, we possess the attributes of humility and a sense of vulnerability. The promise has been given: *Through the blessing, we not only find another's greatness, but our own.*

Mankind must deeply realize: *Through the blessing, we bless the Godliness that is everything.* The blessing is the highest possible level of spiritual existence in this dimension. It is one aspect of the Godliness recognizing another aspect of the Godliness and projecting, "I see your greatness. I recognize your potential. I empower your talents. In doing so, I am also aware of my own Godliness—my greatness, potential, and talents."

The Elohim desires for every male and female to bow down to each other, for one culture to bow to another culture, for one nation to bow to another nation. Through the activation of the blessing, one aspect of God will bow to another aspect of God and say, "I respect your essence. I acknowledge your purpose. I see your talent. I support you. I know we are part of the 'One' and that 'you are truly me.'"

Everything is God. Every man, woman, and child is a facet of the Creator. Every male, female, forest, ocean, insect, fish, and bird—it is all God experiencing this creation. Everything you will ever come in contact with—touch, see, feel, and know—it is all yet another aspect of the Godliness coming in contact with your energy field and personal awareness. Everything is God speaking to you.

The Genesis Code reveals another extraordinary revelation: *Those who bless, and those who have been blessed, will grow into their highest potential.* When one man genuinely empowers another, hidden potential is activated within the one being blessed and also within the one that is giving the blessing. This is the beauty of the blessing. The one giving the blessing and the one receiving the blessing—both reach a new state of awareness. When one man supports another, it changes both men's perceptions of themselves and their relationship evolves.

Every male and female is the vibratory "head" of the Godliness. We are the eyes, ears, and emotions of the Elohim.

With the giving of the blessing, an agreement was made between the Ish, the particles of manifestation, and Israel. The Godliness guaranteed divine intervention through the particles of manifestation, but only if the desire and foremost spirit of our motives, actions, and heart promotes the blessing and support of our fellow man, culture, and nation. When the spiritual man becomes a different type of warrior and fights for the blessing and spirit of man, the Godliness will intervene and support the spiritual ideology to ensure success. We have been given a promise.

As beautiful as the blessing may sound, this state of awareness is extremely difficult to absorb and live by. Much of mankind will be challenged to accept, respect, and empower those who look different, act different, talk different, and live a different lifestyle than they do. Yet, mankind has been warned: *If one's heart is void of the blessing, there is no guarantee of support from the Divine, nor will the particles of manifestation be influenced in his or her favor.*

*The time is now
to manifest a new matrix.*

It is time to rise up. Those of pure heart, those who are compassionate and kind, those who are willing to fight for the spiritual freedom of mankind—these are the spiritual warriors of today. The next level of human consciousness now faces us, and many of us will wear the mantle of Israel. Together, we will empower one another; we will prosper, and manifest the reality we desire through the blessing and beauty of the Godliness that is each of us.

God Has Spoken

God has spoken. Through this book, you have been gifted with the highest level of enlightenment in our world. We live in a time the prophets foresaw and the ancients documented with pen and parchment. The seed of man has fully flowered, and we must now take responsibility for that which we have created. A revelation has been given: *We are the generation of Adam that will choose to become a new level of Godliness.*

The Torah was given long ago—prior to any formal religion in our world. Yet, its translations have given birth to various aspects of God ideology, including the most extreme. There is no denying that religion, itself, has brought forth great travesty and injustice through a false face that portrays beauty, love, and compassion. A revelation has been given: *Religion's mask of trickery has been removed and the illusion is now exposed.*

We can no longer hide from who we are and what we have become. Adam's vibratory force and truth has been revealed. Adam's creative force is stirring, and the Godliness is struggling with mankind in the dirt—fighting for a desired outcome. The particles of dust are being kicked up, and our future is unfolding in Hashomayim. We have become wiser. We now understand the role of the dust, what it is, and how it manifests human reality. A revelation has been given: *Mankind can never hide from his truth, for God will always play Adam back to himself.*

We are the Adam of the moment, facing our highest mountain. We are where our consciousness has taken us, and we are keenly aware our future is at stake. We know we must climb our mountain, and climb it fast. A revelation has been given: *If we do not rise to meet our highest aspect of self, humanity will experience a tectonic shift that will jolt our world and the Elohim's creation.*

Are we ready to die to our old consciousness and make way for something new?

This is our most important battle. We are engaged with our fiercest opponent. We are battling ourselves. The outcome of this battle will determine humanity's course, for this struggle over who we are challenges our very existence. The end of one cycle is nearing, and the Elohim's vibration will soon be felt throughout our world. God's message to mankind will be heard and manifest in many ways. It will strike with sheer force, and man will awaken to the Godliness that IS, together with its wrath and beauty. A revelation has been given: *Mankind is facing the abyss of his own making. Our choices today will affect all of our tomorrows.*

Man is the ruler of his domain. Adamic Consciousness affects the earth that nourishes man and gives him life. Man has become unbalanced, and the earth is reflecting man's vibratory force. Humanity is experiencing a rise in natural disasters, famine, wars, flooding, drought, poverty, and disease. We must change, and we must do so now. We are running out of time. Mankind must take a quantum leap of consciousness. A revelation has been given: *The time for transformation is now, for our creation—the Elohim's creation—is at risk of destroying itself.*

The universe speaks to us in many ways. The signs are always given. God speaks to both nations and individuals through nature, events, metaphors, music, writings, strangers, friends, and even the perceived enemy. Mankind must open his eyes so he can see, know, and absorb the message being delivered. A revelation has been given: *The enlightenment of the Luchot will guide mankind.*

For two thousand years, Adam has been stuck in his own game—fooled by his own trickery. We have fought thousands of battles and shed vast rivers of blood. Sadly, we are still warring with one another. No longer are we innocent, nor are we uneducated. We know what we are capable of. We know we are powerful beings. It is time we face our truth and ask the question that requires an honest answer, "What have we become?" Will we continue on our current path through the Matrix of Egel Masecha, or will we break through and create a new matrix of a different kind—a matrix motivated by the blessing and helping one another? A revelation has been given: *Today's matrix will be broken. The time is now for the destruction and reconstruction of mankind's mind and soul.*

Regardless of how dominant and powerful, the age-old matrix is showing signs of stress. Today's matrix is cracking—bending under the duress of the many who are embracing new streams of consciousness. The people who breathe life into this matrix no longer identify with its reality. The masses have come to question its authority and have begun to challenge the system on a global scale. Humanity is revolting against the motivation that drives the matrix of today. A revelation has been given: *The many are changing direction, transcending, and crying out to Hashomayim. God has heard man's cry. The portal has opened.*

Modern-day Adam must face an agonizing truth—we are deadlier than ever before. We have advanced and no longer create bows and arrows, but nuclear bombs and biochemical weapons. Much time has passed, and mankind has experienced many levels within the game. Adam has faced himself time and time again. We have come to recognize both our darkness and our light. We have travelled far from the consciousness of our past, but our most difficult journey is before us. A revelation has been given: *There is no time left for contemplation.*

You are God becoming.

We must open our eyes to the Godliness that IS. We must no longer allow others to lead us into their den of illusions where grandiose idols of false gods exist. That is not God. That has created separation amongst men. That has led us where we are today. That will lead us into a future of great loss, pain, suffering, and sorrow. A revelation has been given: *The people must take their power back. The Godliness becomes through man—not a church, mosque, synagogue, or any other religious organization that supports an idol God.*

Through man, the Godliness experiences this reality. We are the eyes, ears, and emotions of the Elohim, with the ability to taste, see, smell, hear, feel, and absorb this reality. In essence, we are an energy consciousness becoming through matter consciousness which makes it possible to experience deeply felt emotions through the illusion of time. A revelation has been given: *Every male and female is the vibratory head of the Godliness observing and experiencing its truth and potential in a three-dimensional world.*

Extreme enlightenment dawns as man comes to understand the highest level of the God/Man relationship. The Godliness desires a deeper relationship with humanity—a path that has never before been travelled. A revelation has been given: *Through Adam, God comes to know passion, anger, love, hate, pain, despair, empathy, joy, and every other emotion that is possible in human reality.*

Each of us is a facet of the Godliness, and we create the reality we desire to experience. Adam manifests the Godliness he believes himself to be. The time has come to unveil the truth. The time has come to remove the mask that covers the truth. A revelation has been given: *Today's Adam will awaken to his inner Godliness and shatter the age-old matrix of yesterday.*

The fire deep within us, Shin's metaphysical fire of transformation, must burn strong. Each of us has a fire that desires to blaze to new heights—a spiritual fire that will destroy the old matrix and open the door to a new living consciousness. We must die to our old self before our new self can rise from the ashes. We must become spiritual warriors and fight for the betterment of mankind. The time has come to enter the portal that leads to the garden of the Godliness—where our inner Godliness lives and loves. A revelation has been given: *Each one of us is a highly advanced creative being with the power to change our reality and the world.*

Deep within, each and every person wants to love and be loved, to bless and be blessed. We have been given a gift, and it is now our choice to walk in the essence of Israel, to lead by example, and show others the way. As we meet our fellow man on the street, we must look to their Godliness—smile at them, open their inner doors, and let them know we see their essence, internal greatness, and potential. One by one, we will change someone's day, someone's reality, and someone's belief in themselves. Know by blessing another, the Elohim is empowered and so are you. A revelation has been given: *Become the enlightened one—use your power to bless the world.*

A promise of divine intervention has been made—an agreement between the Godliness and mankind. When the spiritual man and woman empower the best in others, knowing their efforts may cause them to face a dark night of the soul, the Elohim's blessing will overcome any and all obstacles. A revelation has been given: *Be. Become. Empower your blessing.*

The Godliness of yesterday has struggled in the darkness with the man of today. Like Jacob, we have stirred up the dust of tomorrow's reality. A new age is upon us that will give birth to a new level of human consciousness. This is the dawn of the true Israel that empowers the blessing. You chose this moment to shine. Become the blessing. There is no time left. Daybreak is upon us.

God has spoken.

About the Authors

Originating from London, England, Abraham Lopian is a new level of spiritual mastery. Born into traditional Orthodox Judaism, his family's lineage has produced leading rabbis and heads of Talmudic Academies throughout the world.

Surrounded by philosophers and scholars, it was only natural that Abraham would delve into the depths of creation's mysteries. As a young boy he studied with his rabbinical uncles and, years later, with his Grandfather, Reb Elia Lopian, a famous and well-respected spiritual man known for his remarkable insight into the "Torah" (the Hebraic Bible).

Abraham's decades of Talmudic study spans the oceans and includes several Talmudic Academies throughout the world. His enlightenment, however, would not be realized through scholastic studies alone, but through a metaphysical experience in 1988 that would forever change his perception of God and creation.

Years later, Abraham was led to Julie Snyder—the woman he calls his "enlightenment." Julie understood it was vital for The Genesis Code to be revealed to humanity and, nearly a decade later, their insight, passion, and creativity has given birth to The Genesis Code book series.

What most have not yet realized is the true "Adam" is both male and female. The Torah specifically states in Genesis 5:2, "Male and female, he created them; and God blessed them and called their name, Adam, on the day they were created."

The Genesis Code is a level of enlightenment that could only be activated through a joint perspective of *male/female* consciousness. Before this seed of enlightenment could flower in our world, it required the nourishment of a particular type of relationship—a union between a male and female that represents the "total" Adam on earth.

Abraham and Julie, through their diverse backgrounds, lifestyles, and experiences bring forth extraordinary revelations of enlightenment for the consciously evolved male and female of today. With passion and intelligence, the reader is taken into the rabbit hole of creation where a new and extraordinary perspective of God, man, nature, life, death, love, and reality emerges out of the shadows and into the light of human awareness.

Aaron	High Priest to the Israelites; Brother of Moses.
Adam	Mankind; Creation Imagined by the All.
Adamic Consciousness	The totality of all human experience.
Adamic Universe	The universe created for Adam, to be experienced by Adam.
All That IS	Source of the Godliness; All encompassing; Infinite; Eternal.
Aretz (Metaphysical)	The Elohim's (God's) spirit that runs.
Aretz (Physical)	Earth Consciousness; Adam's spirit that runs.
Awareness	Having knowledge of something through intense observation.
Belief System	A set of beliefs, especially religious or political, that form a unified system and form of consciousness; The power that forms and maintains a matrix of consciousness.
Burning Bush	Earthly matter that absorbed the fiery essence (energy) of the Elohim; the bush that did not burn and turn to ash.
Concept	Broad abstract idea or a guiding general principle.
Consciousness	Our conscious and subconscious self.
Core of the Elohim	Heart of the Godliness.
Dimensions	Various realities within the All.
Dualities	That which has two states or parts; where experience and emotions are possible.
Dust	Metaphor for subatomic particles that are the building blocks of manifestation.

Definitions

Egel Man	A level of human consciousness that idolizes wealth, power, status and material satisfaction through various forms of idol gods; low level of consciousness.
Egel Masecha	The Golden Calf; the mask that hides the truth; worship of false gods; idol worship.
Egyptian Consciousness	A dominant consciousness during the life of Moses; empowered master/slave ideology; narrow consciousness.
Egyptian Matrix	That which binds and supports narrow consciousness through various scenarios it manifests into reality.
Elohia	The aspect of the Elohim that transforms through a particular relationship with a unique aspect of human consciousness.
Elohim	Many creative energies; Creative program; God of the Adamic Universe; God of man; Plural in nature.
Energy Body	Supply or source of electrical, mechanical, or other form of power.
Facet of God	A part or aspect of the Godliness; Not the complete or total Godliness.
Finger of God	Metaphor reflecting the Elohim's focus on vibrating enlightenment to mankind.
Fire	Energy vibrating at immense speeds.
Five Books of Moses	Written by Moses during his lifetime after his meeting with God; also known as the Pentateuch.
Fluid Consciousness	Universal energy that flows within and through dimensions.
Formless Realms	The unseen world that exists, but is difficult to know; that which the mystics connect to and are aware of.
God	English translation for the All and Elohim; Generalization and man-given name that works to simplify the reality of the Creator.
God/Man Relationship	Man's realization and connection to the Divine that exists through and within each of us.

Godliness	An overall reference to the Creator's many aspects of self.
HaAdam	Dimension within Hashomayim containing all of the elements from which Adam's reality would manifest.
Hashomayim	The Elohim's place of all potential consciousness for any desired creation.
Heavens	English translation for Hashomayim; Place of infinite possibilities and potential consciousness; Where we "come from" (man's birth) and "go to" (upon man's perception of death).
Higher Self	Your totality in the higher realms of creation.
Illusion	That which deceives the senses or mind; distortion of senses.
Ish	The Godliness that appears as the male aspect of consciousness.
Ishah	The Godliness that appears as the female aspect of consciousness.
Israel	The energy of the blessing; To bless and be blessed; Highest level of spiritual being in man's dimension.
Israelites	The Hebrews Moses led out of Egyptian slavery; Children of Israel; People who would inhabit the land of Canaan.
Jehovah	The aspect of the Elohim that activates the moment of man's dimension; The now.
Jehovah Elohim	A facet of the Elohim that implements the idea of Adam (mankind) into reality; Aspect of the Elohim that breathes life into man.
Kabbalah	A body of Judaic teachings concerns with the mystical aspect of Rabbinic Judaism.
Knowingness	Knowing something without learning it through books; Mental and emotional knowledge one knows instinctively.
Land of Canaan	The land promised by the Elohim to Abraham; Conquered by the Israelites; Modern day Israel encompasses only a portion of Canaan.

Luchot	The first set of tablets Moses brought down the mountain; The highest level of enlightenment in man's dimension; Created and written by the Elohim.
Manifest	To bring out from the unmanifest and create into a reality.
Mass Consciousness	The many singular aspects of consciousness coming together forming one extremely powerful vibratory force; The collective consciousness of a group, society, or nation.
Master Designer	A creative force and higher intelligence that put forth the master plan and design for this universe and all it contains; That which has embedded the code and intelligence within all life.
Matrix	A surrounding substance from which something else originates, develops and/or is controlled; driven by man's consciousness; Self-aware entity that creates scenarios to uphold and maintain its existence.
Matter	Substance of which all physical objects consist; Defined by energy consciousness.
Matter Consciousness	Energy consciousness transforming into the space/time continuum.
Membrane	That which divides one aspect from another aspect and allows particular aspects of potential consciousness to filter through.
Moses	Prophet; the true shepherd; core of Hashomayim; Highest level of man.
Mount Nebo	The last mountain climbed by Moses; Metaphor reflecting that which will become through Moses' legacy.
Mount Sinai	Also known as Mount Chorebah in Hebrew; Portal of enlightenment; The place where the Luchot and Ten Commandments were given to Moses by God.
New Testament	The contents of the New Testament deal explicitly with first century Christianity.

No Man's Land	Metaphor reflecting the wilderness of the soul; One's state of transition between the self that has died and the self that is yet to become.
Objective Consciousness	Consciousness that sees reality as it truly is.
Observer	A singular aspect of consciousness that witnesses an act or intention.
Old Testament	The Old Testament or Hebrew Scriptures are the collection of books that is the revelation of creation written 1500 years prior to the Christian Bible.
Paradox	A moment of contradiction.
Perception	Using one's senses to acquire information about the surrounding environment or situation.
Pharaoh	A ruler and King of Egypt.
Philosophy	A particular system of belief, thought, or doctrine.
Projecting	The act of projecting something into something else; This act can be on a conscious or subconscious level.
Promised Land	Also called the land of Canaan promised by the Elohim (God) to the descendants of Abraham.
Quantum Leap	A sudden and dramatic change or advance; Transition of consciousness; Enlightenment.
Quantum Mechanics	Also known as quantum physics or quantum theory; A branch of physics providing a mathematical description of the dual particle-like and wave-like behavior and interaction of matter and energy.
Reality	That which we perceive to be real.
Reflection	The process or act of reflecting something—especially light, sound, heat, and consciousness.
Revelation	Information that is newly disclosed, especially surprising or valuable; The revealing of something previously hidden or secret
Singular Consciousness	An "individual's" energy consciousness.

Soul	An immeasurable abyss of potential and realization; the aspect of one's consciousness that contains the totality of a singularity's experience.
Source Creator	All That IS; The All; The I Am.
Space	A space or interval of time; The region that lies beyond the earth's atmosphere and all it contains.
Spirit	A formless energy consciousness that is self-aware and moves throughout creation's many dimensions.
Sub-atomic Particles	The level of existence hidden from our awareness.
Subconscious Self	Where one's suppressed emotions are hidden from one's awareness; Also termed Shadow Self.
Subjective Consciousness	Perceiving something from an internal point of view. The question, "Is it good for me?"
Talmud	The collection of ancient Jewish writings that forms the basis of Jewish law and philosophy.
Ten Commandments	The second set of tablets Moses brought down Mount Sinai containing ten laws and statements for mankind; Also known as the "ten statements."
The Genesis Code	The coded language secretly embedded within the Five Books of Moses; The highest level of enlightenment to stream into man's reality.
Time	A dimension that enables two identical events occurring at the same point in space to be distinguished, measured by the interval between the events.
Torah	A collective body of Judaic theology, laws, stories, and the interpretations of the prophets starting with the Five Books of Moses.
Total Consciousness	All that encompasses an individual; The totality of one's conscious mind and subconscious self.

Transformation	A complete change of consciousness; Usually a change into something with an improved appearance or increased awareness.
Transformative Knowledge	Knowledge that is so mind-shattering and shocking to man's emotional self it changes his reality.
Universal Mind	Thoughts and emotions of the Elohim (God).
Unmanifest	That which has the potential to manifest or become through Hashomayim.
Vibration	Continuous oscillation relative to a fixed reference point; a feeling communicated from one aspect of consciousness to another.
Vibratory Force	An energy feeling that acts upon something through realization.
Vibratory Self	The level of one's vibratory force; The vibration of one's total consciousness; That which is communicated to the Godliness.
Vibratory Signal	That which communicates one's vibratory self to the Elohim's (God's) Hashomayim.
Virtual Reality	A reality that is an illusion, but real to man's mind.
Water	Metaphor for flowing consciousness.
Witness	One who witnesses an act in creation.
Zohar	A thirteenth-century Jewish mystical text that is the primary text of Kabbalistic writings.

Made in the USA
San Bernardino, CA
30 October 2014